KU-296-274

The Splendour of Ethnic Jewelry

From the Colette and Jean-Pierre Ghysels Collection
Text by France Borel • Photographs by John Bigelow Taylor
Translated from the French by I. Mark Paris

THAMES AND HUDSON

EDITOR'S NOTE:
In all captions, the place of origin is expressed first and the name of the tribe or
ethnic group is in parentheses. Dimensions of objects are given in metric:
divide centimeters by 2.54 to convert to inches. Only one dimension is stated,
usually the largest dimension of the object. For linear objects that
are worn hanging down, such as necklaces and loincloths, the dimension given
is of one length of the loop, because the objects were measured hanging
from a fixed point. Unless they are round, the dimensions of pendants and
earrings are usually given as height since they hang vertically; width
is given for some unusually wide objects. Rings, unless they are simple
circles, are given as height because they frequently include vertical elements.

PAGE 1:
Pendants from Karnataka, India. Silver. Maximum width 14.7 cm.
These boxes in the form of an egg (right), a building, or a yoni figure representing
the female sex, are designed to hold sandalwood, stone, or rock crystal
"cosmic eggs," emblems of Siva the procreator.

PAGE 2:
Woman's dorsal pendant from Central Asia (Tekke Turkoman).
Partly fire-gilded silver and carnelian. Height 24.3 cm.
This is a fine example of an asyk, a heart-shaped ornament Tekke women wear
between their braids to help them hang straight down the back.
Resembling a spearhead, the design also suggests a defense against evil.

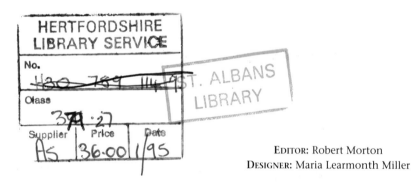
HERTFORDSHIRE
LIBRARY SERVICE
No.
H30 781 114
Class
379.27
Supplier | Price | Date
AS | 36.00 | 1/95
ST. ALBANS
LIBRARY

EDITOR: Robert Morton
DESIGNER: Maria Learmonth Miller

First published in Great Britain in 1994 by Thames and Hudson Ltd, London
First published in 1994 by Harry N. Abrams, Inc., New York

Photographs copyright © 1994 John Bigelow Taylor
Text copyright © 1994 France Borel
Captions copyright © 1994 Colette Ghysels
English translation copyright © 1994 Harry N. Abrams, Inc.

All Rights Reserved. No part of this publication may be reproduced or
transmitted in any form or by any means, electronic or mechanical, including
photocopy, recording or any other information storage and retrieval system,
without prior permission in writing from the publisher

British Library Cataloguing–in–Publication Data

A catalogue record for this book is available from the British Library

ISBN 0–500–01640–2

Printed and bound in Hong Kong

Contents

FOREWORD · 7

THE ART OF COLLECTING · 11

The Lure of the Unknown · 12

Cards of Identity · 20

Some Thoughts on Beauty · 21

A Major Art · 28

SPANNING THE CONTINENTS · 32

AFRICA · 35

THE EAST · 105

OCEANIA · 207

THE AMERICAS · 231

JOURNEY'S END · 245

NOTES · 247

BIBLIOGRAPHY · 248

INDEX · 252

FOREWORD

On Sunday December 27, 1959 Colette and I were married in Nepal. She arrived from Africa, I came in a 2-CV from Europe. At that time Kathmandu was still in the Middle Ages. In the markets the Tibetan refugees, arriving in groups, offered treasures of gold, silver, and bronze. The women wore caps of silk and fur; they unveiled ear-pendants set with coral and turquoise; and they allowed a glimpse of sumptuous reliquaries hung around their necks. The interest in adornment that Colette and I already shared was heightened further.

In Nepal our mutual passion for jewelry was confirmed. Without a doubt, it is curiosity, more than the desire to accumulate, that makes a collection. Interest provokes discovery. And in our case, the collecting passion was stimulated by our awareness of being the last generation whose eyes could glimpse these peoples whose culture is disappearing.

During thirty years of travel and research, we have scoured galleries, markets, and boutiques, stalls and small workshops. At home we have received travelers and merchants from all regions. We sought to learn, to distinguish, to assemble and to prune our collection. Constantly on the watch for quality, we have marveled at the variety of forms which have been exposed to us, revealing their beauty and the personalities of the generations that engendered them. We have been seduced by richness of imagination, creativity, material invention, and by techniques which, through tradition, expressed diversity. We followed our intuition and inspiration and together were carried away by our discoveries. With eyes always on the look-out, and with time on our side, we found our common passion shared by our children, who were always ready to follow us in our research, whether after school or during vacations. All these elements filled out our collection.

From Great Kabylia, northern Algeria (Beni Yenni).

Top: Fibula or forehead ornament. Silver, enamel, and coral. Height 27 cm.

Bottom: Necklace. Silver, enamel, and coral. Width 40 cm.

Kabyle women receive a set of jewelry, including an azrar (below), from their parents when they marry. A man gives his wife a tabzimt to wear on her forehead (above) on the birth of their first son.

It gives me pleasure here to thank all those who by their encouragement and efforts have contributed to the existence of this book, in particular:

My wife, who was there at the beginning. The choice of adornments reproduced and the writing of the captions are owed to her: she collaborated on the composition of the photographs.

Anne van Cutsem, for her documentary work, but also for making herself available and for her friendly involvement.

France Borel, who for many years showed a lively interest in the diverse forms of the collection and urged us to show it. Her authoritative text will introduce many to this subject.

John Bigelow Taylor and Dianne Dubler for their superb photographs and also for having shared their enthusiasm with Paul Gottlieb of Harry N. Abrams.

Robert Morton, not only for his editing with great expertise, but for his continual efforts to meet our wishes and solve any problem in the best possible way.

Maria Miller for her beautiful and creative design of the book.

Last, but not least, Paul Gottlieb for his confidence in the project and full support.

My wife and I would like equally to give recognition to the many travelers, dealers, collectors, museums and people of the country with whom for the most part we have woven ties of friendship. As numerous, varied, and passionate as were our excursions into this world, without these individuals we would never have had access to such a diversity of adornment. Unable to name them all, I prefer to let them remain anonymous. They will recognize themselves in the book because it is evidence of what each one has offered us.

To Marc, Eric, and David
This collection, which punctuated their adolescence, has grown with them.

Jean-Pierre Ghysels

Neck ring from Amun-Siwa Oasis, Egypt. Silver. Total length 32 cm.

A neck ring (aghraw) *and attached disc* (adrim) *are essential components of bridal jewelry in this region. B. Leopoldo reported that this type of ornament was first designed about 1920 for the wedding of a woman whose father was a smith by the name of Senoussi: "The women of Siwa gazed admiringly at its pure, beautiful form, and every one of them wanted an* aghraw *for her daughter." When the marriage ceremony is over, the bride keeps the* aghraw *and gives the* adrim *to her younger sister.*

THE ART OF COLLECTING

Collections have a way of sneaking up on you. Two objects look alike and pair off; they're joined by a third. You're caught up in a collection before you know it. Objects take over your life; they steal into every nook and cranny of your house. As more and more are added, they may mushroom into a collection truly deserving of the name.

Some people treasure little things like stamps or silly things such as bottle caps or key rings or, more recently, decorative pins that commemorate events like the Olympics. Others feel the need to build up something larger than life: The man called Facteur Cheval, a rural postman in France who constructed a fabulous backyard "palace" out of cement, stones, and sand, was a collector of sorts. Still other collectors seize upon a particular phase of art history and exhaust its possibilities. With an enthusiasm that comes from no identifiable source, they find themselves focusing on eighteenth-century French red-chalk drawings, or Persian miniatures.

The processes involved in beginning a collection are curiously analogous. But the way a collector goes about orchestrating a lifelong passion for objects is more than a process. It is an art. Some collections act as a tonic for the mind. We look at them and can hear them telling us about civilizations. We can peruse them as we would a book, only the story is about an entire culture. Some act more specifically on the senses, especially the visual. The nature of the objects and the way they are brought together can heighten our appreciation of their forms, the substances of which they are made, their textures and colors.

Pendant from Tibet. Gold, turquoise, lapis lazuli, and rubies. Height 13 cm.

Commonly referred to as a "mooneater," this magnificent ornament was worn by Tibetan officials and came with a matching counterweight. The name "mooneater" was inspired by the subject depicted on it because very little is known about its actual use. Such prestigious pieces of jewelry were rare to begin with, but the exodus of Tibetans from their homeland and efforts by the Chinese Communists to eradicate their culture has led to the destruction or disappearance of objects that might have shed a great deal of light on traditional Tibetan civilization.

Hip ornament from Nagaland, India (Konyak). Glass beads and dyed goat's hair. Height 39.5 cm.

The Naga made extensive use of multicolored glass beads, which were probably imported from China, Europe, and elsewhere.

It is easy to understand why collectors who donate their treasures to museums seek assurances that displaying them will not result in their dispersal. A lone object is often tight-lipped. But once a perceptive collector has provided it with neighbors and the prospect of a happy, richly textured partnership, it will break its silence and begin to converse. Real collections speak volumes. They tell us a great deal not only about the objects in them but about those who preside over their formation. They proclaim—not smugly— the uncompromising discernment of the individuals who have orchestrated them and made their innermost desires visible for all to see.

Collectors have existed for thousands of years, but the Italian Renaissance spawned a new breed of individual with a special flair for collecting. Giorgio Vasari, the painter and biographer, treasured drawings and engravings by his near contemporaries. Across Europe crowned heads of the period enlisted ambassadors to negotiate on their behalf for paintings or other objects that would enhance their surroundings and enrich their lives. Northern Europe witnessed a surge of interest in private curio collections, or *Wunderkammern*: hodgepodges of unfamiliar, unaccountable natural and manmade objects. In these repositories of the uncanny, anatomical oddities were displayed alongside mementos of perilous journeys to faraway places and inventions that modern scientists can only wonder at. Explorers and sailors brought back curiosities made of substances that defied identification. Among these astonishing objects were things that made Europeans question just how human the beings that made them could be, with their yellowish or dusky skin, incredible tattoos, and incomprehensible languages.

THE LURE OF THE UNKNOWN

When distant shores beckon travelers, collections happen. They bring remote places closer; exotic artifacts tell of worlds that operate according to unfamiliar criteria. There is something bewitching about that. But the knack for spotting treasures from distant lands calls for a sharp and sensitive eye. Marco Polo never lost his capacity to be wonderstruck at the things he saw. A merchant by

profession, the Venetian turned into an ethnologist before his time by being alert to the objects and customs of the lands through which he journeyed. Years later, as he dictated an account of his travels, he still described amber and musk, for example, with breathless admiration.

Back when the world was still largely unexplored, owners of vessels bound for parts unknown signed on physicians who doubled as scientific observers, experienced naturalists, and artists, who diligently reaped a harvest of visual impressions. At times, to be sure, these observers projected their own mindsets onto the sights that passed before them. But the value of these early firsthand impressions cannot be overestimated, for they tell of worlds that have since succumbed to the unforgiving centuries and the ruthless pursuit of progress. We now know that civilizations are fragile and mortal. As individuals die, entire cultures die with them, with nothing to testify to their existence save the things that outlive them. Such objects are their lifeline to timelessness.

Once objects have been cut loose from their contexts and packed off to new homes, they lose some of the collective memory stored within them. But their forms and textures endure. Those who are able and wish to do so are at liberty to read them, interpret them, draw them out in new and different ways, grant them a new lease on life. This, too, makes collecting an art: the process of renewal.

Collecting is an art in another, more literal sense. It is no accident that artists have always been, and still are, on the cutting edge of collecting. Serendipity involves a kind of sixth sense. Creative people have a knack for seeing beyond cultural differences and nosing out things that ring powerful and true half a world away. Collections of value are guided by intuition, by latent affinities that defy explanation and easy description. Some things are best left unaccounted for. The imagination can serve as a benchmark, too.

There is esthetic complicity between a painting by Paul Klee and a sculpture from New Mexico, a Giacometti and a clay-covered skull from New Ireland or a figure from Tanzania, a Gauguin and a relief carving from the Javanese Buddhist temple complex at Borobudur, a Zande throwing knife and a Matisse cutout, a Brancusi and a Baule mask, a Max Ernst and a Dan spoon. There are countless such examples. Creativity thrives on contact, interaction, and collision between conspicuously diverse cultures.[1]

A great deal—perhaps too much—has been said about the influence of African masks on Picasso's celebrated painting *Les Demoiselles d'Avignon*. The question of how direct, or subtle, that influence may have been need not concern us here. The crucial point is that one of the first revolutions in twentieth-century art, Cubism, began with someone whose voracious eyes were as intrigued by everyday things as they were by exotic artifacts. In his Paris studio at the Bateau-Lavoir and at his Cannes villa, La Californie, Picasso would throw together such things as a New Hebrides carving, old bottles, and folk ceramics, all in stimulating disarray.[2]

The years after World War II witnessed renewed, if limited, interest in bringing together exotic and modern art under one roof. Another emerging trend, notably among members of the CoBra group founded in the Netherlands, was to assemble specimens of, and infer close affinities between, folk or naive art, children's drawings, and the art of the insane. In 1949 Galerie Pierre Loeb in Paris exhibited Oceanic artifacts and modern artwork side by side—a Giacometti, a figure from the Sepik River region of Papua New Guinea, a photograph by Man Ray—to the mutual enrichment of them all. Another assemblage of this sort made news more recently at a show at the Fondation Cartier in Paris, where juxtaposing a Francis Bacon painting and an Eskimo mask brought out their common expressionistic power and intensity.[3]

The sights that Andre Malraux so eagerly took in as he traveled through Asia in the 1920s and 1930s sent prevailing attitudes toward art history reeling and shook up cut-and-dried classifications. He knew that a comparative study of a Khmer sculpture and a Gothic statue was liable to draw sharp criticism from hidebound art historians. But he also knew how mentally stimulating such encounters can be.

The Ghysels Collection is a model of stringent, uncompromising selectivity. The real force behind the collection is Colette Ghysels, who like some earth

TOP:
Woman's ornaments for neck, arms, and legs, from Burma (Padaung). Brass. Height 6 cm. to 18 cm.

Those who wear these rings seem to have elongated necks, but this is a purely visual impression. The purpose of the ornament is to protect the tribe, for the Padaung believe that the soul resides in the neck.

BOTTOM:
From Namibia (Bochimans).

Top: Pendant. Tortoiseshell, ostrich eggshell beads. Height 10.3 cm.

Bottom: Headband. Ostrich eggshell beads. Width 25.5 cm.

The nomadic Bochimans are among the last surviving hunter-gatherers in Namibia. The women wear decorative jewelry that they fashion from ostrich eggshell, a locally prized material also used in the making of long necklaces.

goddess, can breathe new life into objects by merely bringing them together. Through her are revealed the expert craftsmanship and myth-laden messages that only exemplary specimens of ethnic jewelry can convey. Through her enthusiasm, unflagging curiosity, and perseverance, Colette Ghysels shares in the kind of alchemy that only genuine collectors can generate, the ones with a certain feeling in the bones, the ones virtually obsessed with shunning well-trodden pathways, who depend instead on a sixth sense to bring a particular facet of civilization to the fore.

Another reason that the Ghysels Collection is such an eye-opener, a visual stimulant, is that it reflects sculptor Jean-Pierre Ghysels' familiarity with three-dimensional objects, his hands-on experience with materials. And as the Ghysels Collection ranges from Africa to the Pacific and from Asia to the Americas, it takes us on a journey to the very core of the esthetic experience. The criteria for selection are exacting technique and formal beauty. Lovers of contemporary art are bound to spot similarities.

Body decoration is a ubiquitous phenomenon that transcends time and space. There is not one civilization, however limited its available materials may be, that does not practice self-ornamentation. As long as our species has existed, the human body has been a focal point of adornment and a versatile medium for our every longing and fantasy. There is no part of the human anatomy that cannot be embellished with jewelry of one kind or another. At the very top of the body we find headdresses that may cost birds their finest feathers. Those convenient appendages we call the nose and ears may provide lodging for all manner of rings. The mouth, which contemporary Western cultures have seen fit merely to adorn with lipstick, can be decorated with far more permanent and sometimes spectacular artifice, including labrets that can stretch more than twenty centimeters across.

Few areas of the body receive as much attention as the neck, from which may be suspended decorations of every imaginable size, shape, and material: close-fitting neck rings (torcs), bouncing pectorals, impressively massed, yet supple strands of beads. The possibilities are limited only by the imagination. Some African necklaces weigh as much as six kilograms (more than thirteen

pounds); at forty centimeters across, some pectorals are wider than the wearer's body. The chests of both men and women may prominently display signs of fighting prowess and economic or social power for all to see.

Moving down to the waist, we find that belts abound, from humble bands of plaited plant fiber to sumptuous chains set with gems or enamelwork. Sometimes it is difficult to decide whether to call a waist ornament a belt or a loincloth. Not infrequently—and in ways that can bring a smile to the lips of European or American observers—the very thing designed to conceal hides very little indeed and can make parts considered far from private all the more noticeable.

At other key points of our anatomy, the joints—wrists, ankles, elbows, shoulders, and knees—bracelets and bangles emphasize, enhance, and thereby protect. Wealth is readily displayed at the very spots that enable us to move; yet, some anklets are so bulky and heavy they can make it painfully difficult to walk. When it comes to fingers, none is overlooked. The Western world may dote on what has come to be known, appropriately enough, as the ring finger, but ethnic societies leave no digit unadorned and do not confine themselves to the proximal phalange. On market days in Burkina Faso, old women wear a kind of ring that wraps around three fingers.

Tellingly, wearers of ethnic jewelry set absolutely no store by the practicality that dominates the thinking of efficiency-minded Westerners. How heavy or fragile or uncomfortable jewelry may be is of no immediate concern. Just the opposite: the more profuse the jewelry and the more difficult it is to wear, the wealthier the wearer is perceived to be. The peoples of the Eurasian steppe, for example, specialize in elegant, sophisticated jewelry that belies their inhospitable surroundings. Kazaks embellish the rings of their matchmakers with delicate granulation. Mongols deck out their womenfolk with incredibly elaborate and sumptuous headdresses. Heartless Genghis Khan knew what he was doing when he spared the goldsmiths among the groups he conquered.

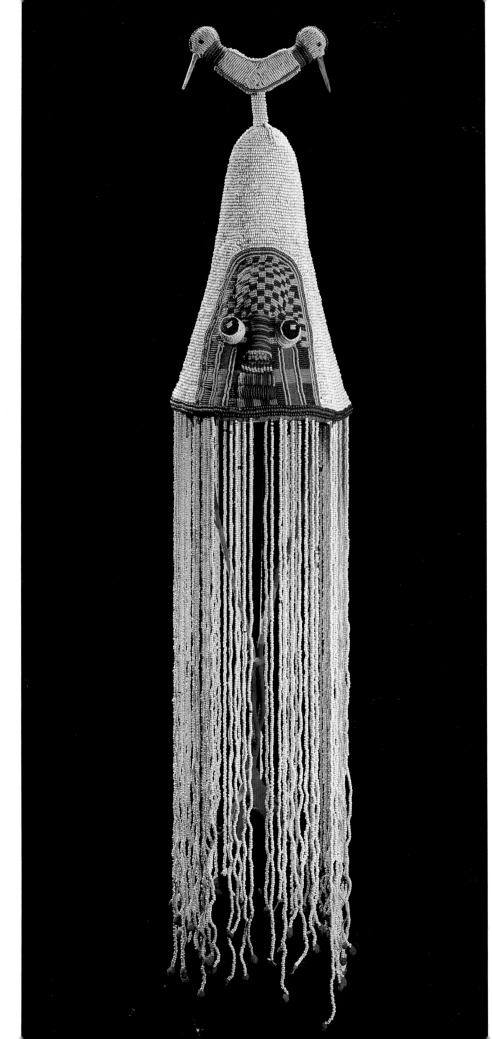

Headdress from Nigeria (Yoruba). Glass beads. Total height 95 cm.

Only the Oba, or Yoruba ruler, may wear an ade, *or ceremonial beaded crown. The images hark back to Oduduwa, the mythical first king of Ife who supposedly descended from the sky and presented an* ade *to each of his descendants as a symbol of authority. The birds are a reminder that the Oba is a holy person whose divine countenance must be covered by a veil of beads.*

CARDS OF IDENTITY

Body decoration is a timeless and ubiquitous social indicator. It summarizes the wearer's status and life history. It serves as a calling card, an instant ID. It indicates a person's tribal affiliation and chronicles the stages of his or her life. A certain kind of necklace might be worn only by little girls, another by marriageable females, and so on for wives, mothers, and widows. No one but hunters or warriors may be entitled to sport ear ornaments. Wearing a certain kind of belt might be the prerogative of sorcerers or healers or members of a secret society.

The complex of signals and prompts that are encoded in personal ornamentation constitutes a kind of visual language, the vocabulary of which, unfortunately, often can no longer be deciphered. Magnificent though it may be in its own right, such embellishment communicates many different kinds of information that ethnic groups—peoples, tribes, clans, what have you—rely upon for purposes of self-identification and mutual recognition.

There is nothing accidental or gratuitous about a people's passionate desire for self-ornamentation. For them, symbolism is not just intertwined with body adornment; symbolism is its very essence. The meaning of a visual vocabulary can be so obvious to its users that they take it for granted and end up forgetting its original significance. This presents no end of obstacles to ethnologists in the field as they attempt to rediscover the keys that might crack a code. Even the cautious ones may find it difficult, if not impossible, to come up with a definitive interpretation.

The language of adornment is richly textured, derived from the plant and animal worlds, from phenomena both terrestrial and celestial. It freely combines forms and themes; it dreams up monstrous hybrids that may be part man or woman, part bird or fish. It has no limits and easily rivals classical mythology, with its centaurs, sirens, and sphinxes.

As if this range of permutations was not enough, humankind has also devised a captivating array of geometric designs. Some arise from a particular technique of craftsmanship or perpetuate something remembered about it: for example, a pattern of plaited plant fiber might be translated into bronze or gold. Woven, wickerwork, and tattooed designs can be transposed into other mediums. At times these pathways are so muddled that one wonders if the shift from one medium to another is not working in the opposite direction.

Some designs are decorative by-products of the instinctive human need for pleasure and play. This need not preclude symbolic content; ethnic groups project their own identities onto the objects they design. Their creative freedom is virtually unlimited, and we cannot help but marvel at their ability to turn even simple materials into ornamentation of stunning splendor and sophistication.

This raises an important point. Body decoration, which the logically-minded might dismiss as superfluous, plays a decisive role in the lives of ethnic peoples and their craftsmen. They lavish time and patient effort on self-adornment. Their civilizations do not experience time with the sense of urgency that we do; they relive it over and over again, and their traditions are thereby passed on intact and unaltered from one generation to the next. A Maori artist may spend years polishing a single piece of jade with little more than Stone Age tools; women then rub it against their oiled thighs to give it the finishing touch. It may take an Indonesian artisan months to coil down some filigree or inlay niello. Using the lost-wax process, Africans can cast figures with a painstaking attention to detail that is the envy of Western goldsmiths. Using sharkskin as an abrasive, a Solomon Islander will take what seems forever to transform a chunk of giant clam shell (Tridacna gigas) into a bracelet. So pressed are Western jewelers for time that they sometimes find it difficult to duplicate the casting, chiseling, and filigree techniques of native craftspeople. There are some things our machines cannot do. They may save time, but they cannot take its place.

SOME THOUGHTS ON BEAUTY

Beauty is a relative, shifting, elusive concept; it varies from region to region, from tribe to tribe. It can be defined in purely anatomical terms or may also

involve clothing and jewelry. There is one invariable: no people on earth seem willing to leave the body naked, unadorned, a pure product of nature. No sooner does a child come into the world than its features are altered and adorned. In addition to tattoos, scarification, and other changes made directly to the body, clothing and jewelry are the principal means by which a culture asserts its value system.

No culture has failed to leave its imprint on the ways in which the human body may be altered. This is self-evident, and attests to the decisive, indeed, the vital importance of ornamentation. We take issue with the all too common belief that self-beautification is superfluous, and that the objects used to achieve it are mere accessories. Quite the contrary.

Adornment expresses the irreducibles of life. It underscores the stages of a person's life history; it marks such milestones as marriage, birth, and death. It is the force that drives seduction in the broadest sense of the word. And as a party both to seduction in the concrete and beauty in the abstract, personal embellishment is an active participant in the great cycle of human existence.

For thousands of years and in widely diverse cultures, self-adornment was equally prevalent among men and women. Not until the emergence of industrial society in late eighteenth-century Europe did men forgo their love of finery and enshroud themselves in dark, unrevealing suits; only then did the appanage of seduction devolve to the female of the species. Emerging trends suggest that this has been little more than a digression from the broader movement of history.

Ethnic cultures have always attached great importance to male adornment. There is an apparent reluctance to use ornaments interchangeably. Certain kinds of objects are worn only by men, others by women. Unisex adornment is little valued. In the objects themselves, the sexual distinctions may not be readily apparent: the subtle giveaway may be the slant of a pattern, or the use of one material instead of another. All of which suggests that, among its other purposes, self-decoration is designed to underscore or even flaunt differences between the sexes, to restate the anatomically obvious.

Neck crosses from Ethiopia. Silver. Height 3 cm. to 6 cm.

The neck pendants of Ethiopia, where Christian influence reaches back to the fourth century A.D., feature designs based upon the cross. There are countless variations on the theme: birds (representing peace), endless knots (symbolizing eternity), the Star of David (an example of Judeo-Christian syncretism), and the Maltese cross, a reminder of the Portuguese presence during the fifteenth century. Human faces are rarely depicted. Most of the crosses shown here date from the nineteenth century and are made of silver, but earlier versions were made of wood, bronze, or copper.

Ornament the body and it becomes theater; its wearers become performers in a show. When men and women transform themselves on festive occasions or when simply going about their daily lives, they turn to nature for inspiration and draw freely upon it for props. They stick feathers on their heads, drive pieces of ivory through their lips, suspend shells from their necks. There is no end to the combinations of shapes and textures that can be devised in the great theater of life.

Craftsmen often transpose natural forms into other mediums. Zulu chiefs wear necklaces with lion's claws carved from bone. The Dan people cast leopard's teeth in bronze. The Plains Indians of North America make bone replicas of bear claws. Naga headhunters carve little monkey skulls out of wood.

Bristles, bones, feathers, teeth, sea shells, hides, horn, and ivory are but a few of the raw materials available for use in self-adornment. At times, such embellishment can border on disguise; humans dress up as birds or tigers or crocodiles or jaguars.

The more ornamented a body, the more it stands out both physically and symbolically. The body resplendent commands attention while it is dancing, during ceremonies and initiations. In some regions, it may be adorned with precious metals or sparkling minerals, depending on local availability. But we must not underestimate the spectacular effects human ingenuity can achieve with even the simplest materials. Once the imagination joins forces with the patience of a creator, its potential is unlimited.

The world of animals not only provides artists and artisans with raw materials but inspires a large number of their themes and designs. Africans are unsurpassed when it comes to making animal images: a bronze anklet may turn out to be a procession of snakes; in Cameroon dignitaries wear necklaces festooned with decorative cattle heads. The Baule people of the Ivory Coast contrive hybrid creatures that appear to be part lizard, part frog. They might wrap stylized spiders around a bronze bracelet to mediate between gods and humans. The rings of Africa showcase a fabulous bestiary of camels, horses, chameleons, tick birds, and frogs, each more lifelike than the last. Ivory Coast

Man's ear ornaments from Peru (Aguaruna). Beetle-wing cases, toucan feathers, and seeds. Height 32 cm.

A superb example of body adornment that uses iridescent organic substances for effect.

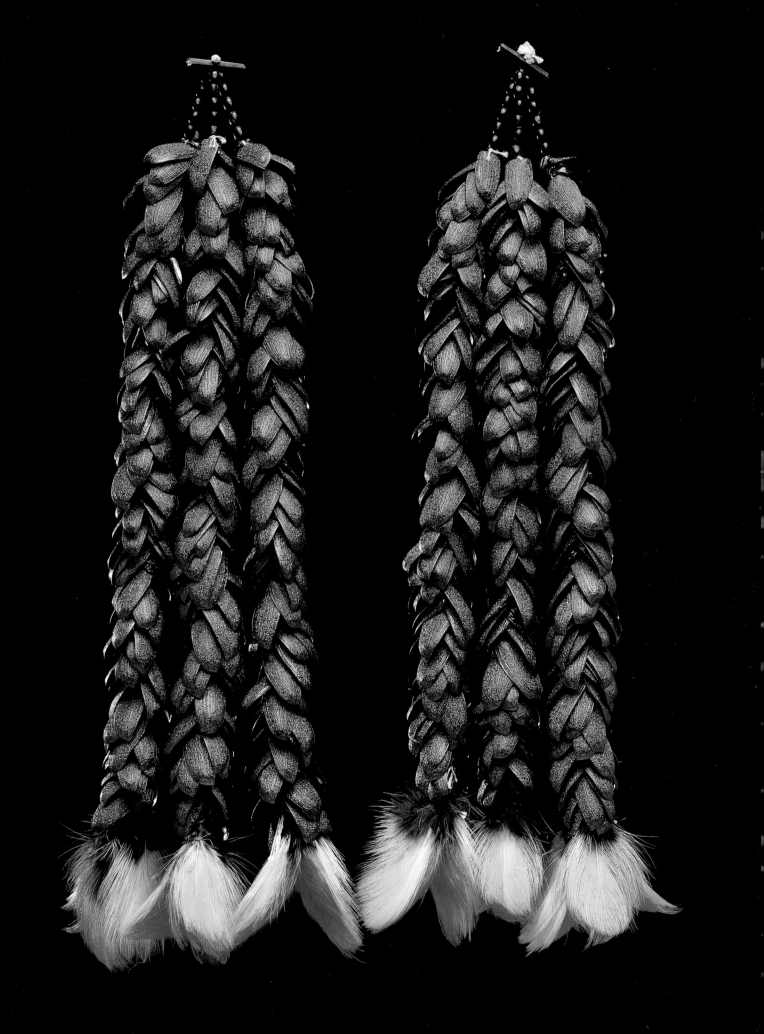

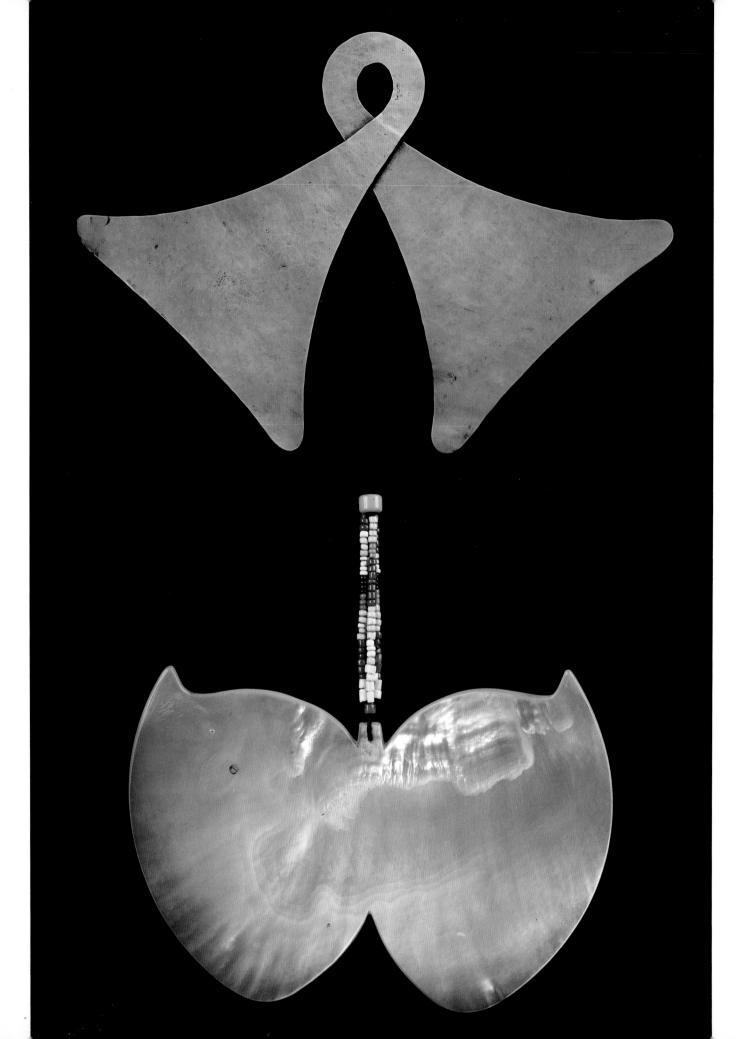

goldsmiths adorn their pendants with sawfish and swordfish, pythons and leopards, pangolins and roosters, water buffaloes and turtles. To make a bronze grasshopper more realistic, the casting may be made directly from an actual insect. A piece of ostrich eggshell can become a headband, and ivory can be fashioned into bracelets of every imaginable shape and style.

As a rule, the peoples of Oceania keep their animal imagery simple. Pendants from the Santa Cruz Islands in the Solomons bear a local interpretation of the frigate bird fishing for bonito: a virtually abstract play of lines that demonstrates a feeling for spare, severe design. Protean Asia leaves no visual language unexplored; animals, and their symbolic meanings, crop up in every conceivable guise. In India, a peacock on an amulet is thought to guarantee fertility. Some bracelets are decorated with Nandi, the bull mount of the Hindu god Shiva, patiently awaiting his lord and master; others assume the shape of hooded cobras. In some Asian cultures, for example, snake vertebrae can be turned into a headdress, and a pendant can be fashioned from some goat's hair.

Africa, Asia, and the Americas boast gold- and silversmiths renowned for their attention to detail and technical sophistication. Fortunately, the same virtues prevail even when they make use of less costly materials—unlike most contemporary Western jewelry, which cares only how showy an emerald or diamond can be made to look. Boldness, profusion of color, opulence—these things should dazzle us, too. Have we become as diffident as all that? Are we so out of touch with our sense of celebration that our concept of wealth amounts to a multi-carat stone stuck on the third finger of one hand?

In traditional societies, some ornaments are fragile things with brief life-spans. The fact that they are so short-lived does not diminish the importance that is attached to them on special occasions. An object's role in key ceremonies heightens its value far beyond its material worth. An initiation rite may call for three feathers lashed together with some coconut fiber and mounted on a piece of bamboo. A burial pageant may call for some clay and a few seeds. Personal adornment is an indispensable part of rituals; it intensifies their impact and expresses in visual terms a complex of symbols in ways that can be plainly understood by all the participants.

TOP:
Man's chest ornament from West Sumba, Indonesia. Beaten gold. Width 28.5 cm.

The laws, customs, and rituals traditionally observed in Indonesia are symbolized by a concept known as adat. *This ornament, a* marang-ga, *is part of the heirloom treasure that would be kept in the attic of* adat *houses for safekeeping. It embodies the essence of a family line and is worn only on important ritual occasions.*

BOTTOM:
Pendant from the Philippines (Isneg). Glass beads and mother-of-pearl. Width 19 cm.

Compare this unusually shaped pendant with the little mother-of-pearl ornaments seen on page 186.

A MAJOR ART

Personal adornment is a major art, a meeting point of social function and esthetic pleasure. In some cultures, it figures so prominently that it monopolizes the energy and expertise of leading artists. The artifacts they produce boast a physical sensuousness and formal inventiveness that infuse them with life even after they have been removed from their original contexts and have been made part of a collection.

Everything that can be done, should be done to preserve objects as they were. Patinas must not be tampered with; original configurations of complex objects, if known, must be scrupulously respected. That in itself would add immeasurably to what we know about them. Masks provide a telling case in point. Uprooted, stripped of their original complements of attendant accessories and fiber raiment and hung in museum showcases, they cease to exist as functioning objects; they lose much of their meaning. In their esthetic impact, however, masks hold up remarkably well; their power of suggestion is undiminished.

Ethnological information about body adornment can be surprisingly hard to come by. Spurred by a sense of urgency, field workers have focused on orally transmitted traditions which they feared might otherwise die out forever. But conventional esthetic parlance has proved difficult to use: coined in the West and evolved through that particular artistic tradition, it does not readily lend itself to non-Western, much less tribal, cultures. There are any number of sources, however, that remain to be tapped, at least wherever traditions endure and potential informants still remember them.

Ethnic jewelry conjures up entire worlds that have ceased to exist or are vanishing before our very eyes. Craftsmen have let time-honored techniques fall into disuse; entire codes of symbolic meaning have been lost. Although some forms are being replicated even as their significance is fading from memory, they are turning into arbitrary decorative designs—a play of lines, not unattractive at times, but barren of meaning. Geographic distinctions are becoming less pronounced, standardization is setting in, and more often than not what does survive is geared to turning a profit. While acculturation does not necessarily preclude freshness, cloning traditional designs for the tourist trade can force a craft to degenerate into a woefully sterile business.

What's done is done. There's no turning back the clock. Civilizations, too, must die. Knowing that can only deepen our appreciation of what the Ghysels Collection has to impart. There is much to learn from looking at objects like these. And since the clues that might unlock their meanings are often missing, we have to look at them long and hard. We must strain our eyes to fully fathom their enigmatic presence, the way the artists at the turn of the century did when they began to collect artifacts from faraway places.

Some esthetic criteria and standards of workmanship transcend time and space. As we roam the continents, it will become apparent that what we call originality is inexhaustible and wide ranging. Individual artists and craftsmen bring their interpretive skills to bear on value systems that allow them more or less freedom and latitude. More often than not, they are expected to comply with the dictates of tradition and adapt their work accordingly. However, they can still make their presence felt with a singular detail or technical idiosyncrasy.

That was more or less the modus operandi of Byzantine art. An icon maker was expected scrupulously to adhere to a model that was purportedly divine in origin, a model not wrought by human hands. Everything was predetermined—canons of proportion, prescribed colors for particular subjects—and the tolerated range of individual interpretation was tightly circumscribed. Yet, that did not prevent Andrei Rublev, for example, from rising above a field of obliging, submissive fellow-painters.

Therein lies another facet of the art of collecting: the ability to pick out objects that convey, not just a symbolic message, but that indefinable quality only talent can impart. The names of most ethnic artisans have never been known or have faded from memory. Unlike European artists, some of whom have been put on pedestals and venerated as geniuses ever since the Renaissance, these artists and smiths fulfill social and cultural functions. They have been singled out for inclusion because of their proficiency and most of all for their acknowledged ability to translate a cultural vocabulary and convey its symbolic impact.

Among ethnic peoples personal adornment is motivated not just by the obvious desire for beautification, but by the instinctive need for self-protection. Things cannot be left as they are; measures must be taken to safeguard life and limb. Baneful forces are constantly lurking. Clothing and jewelry act as a physical and psychological shield. Among Nepalese, for example, every item strung on a "health necklace" has a particular healing property. The peoples of North Africa feel compelled to ward off the evil eye with a variety of amulets and charms. Certain substances are invested with symbolic power; suspending them from the neck or waist is bound to protect the wearer. The veneration of religious relics in the West stemmed from just such inclinations.

Many pieces of jewelry make no secret of their original purposes: bracelets bristling with spikes can be found the world over. The Nuba of Kau are known to have wielded razor-sharp bracelets when they engaged in organized hand-to-hand combat. Some bronze bracelets in Cameroon feature a deadly protuberance which can be camouflaged with a tuft of feathers and thus be made to look like nothing more than an ornament.[4]

Forms associated with warfare and aggression can often reappear in a decorative context. Functions change and practices shift with time. Although the process is difficult to trace, it is fairly safe to assume that some forms originally designed for protection or some other purpose eventually drifted into women's jewelry and became tools of feminine provocation.

The same phenomenon has surfaced in the West, affecting male and female clothing and adornment. Work clothes and sportswear are trending away from the purposes for which they were originally intended and increasingly are turning into insignia of other meanings. Closets are filled with dungarees, studded leather motorcycle jackets, athletic sweatshirts, and similar outfits that are undergoing just such a transition. Bomber jackets have landed on city streets, basketball sneakers are in the subways. Fishermen's sweaters and ski pants have become part of the urban landscape. Fashion designers

Paco Rabanne and Courrèges have taken cues from one-piece astronaut suits.

Similar trends affect so-called accessories, which are subject to occasionally swift and unexpected shifts. In the 1930s women took to wearing dog collars around their necks. Diver's watches began turning up in offices seldom dampened by seaspray. Non-dancers walked around in ballet slippers. Wellingtons and duck boots protected the feet of people who never went hunting or fishing. The backs that knapsacks are slung over nowadays are apt to belong to city-dwellers, not campers. Some jewelry designs have been inspired by sailing gear and ship's tackle. The list goes on and on.

Whenever a form undergoes this kind of shift, it may, for a while at least, symbolically retain something of its original purpose, at times to a fetishistic degree. Then even that association fades and the object becomes purely decorative. It will go on being repeated, unchanged, for quite some time and completely lose touch with its long-forgotten source. Certain elements of dress can even switch gender in the course of their lifespans. Blue jeans still came equipped with a fly even after women started wearing them. Aggressively spiked men's bracelets clatter on the forearms of African women. How many battle-axes and tomahawks in primitive societies have turned into the purely ceremonial regalia of power? By the same token, adornments reserved for specific festive occasions and restricted to a particular social stratum can trickle down to ordinary folk. That can work the other way, too. Certain kinds of commonly worn traditional jewelry can become so scarce they turn into prized possessions displayed only on special occasions.

This tangle of trends and counter-trends demonstrates the vitality of body ornamentation and its significant role as an illuminating cultural barometer.

OVERLEAF:
Woman's forehead ornament from Bukhara, Uzbekistan. Gold, semi-precious stones, and seed pearls. Width 31 cm.

This tilla bargak *is an example of the jewelry produced in the khanate of Bukhara, which was also famous for its magnificent textiles.*

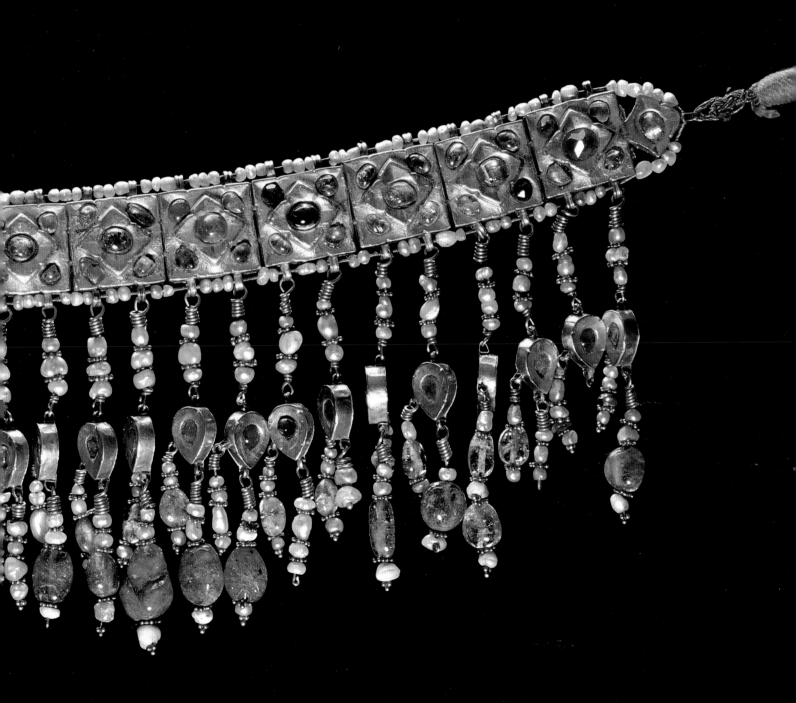

On the continent of Africa, the human imagination holds sway and can turn anything into adornment. Organic and mineral substances of every description end up on the bodies of its peoples, who have perfected the art of assembling and massing an astonishing variety of body decorations. This tendency surfaces in jewelry and sculpture alike; in fact, some ornaments are so bulky they more or less straddle the boundary between the two. Feathers, teeth, horns, and the little rodent-skulls used for gris-gris and fetishes that the poet Guillaume Apollinaire found so fascinating, crop up time and again in all areas of African art.[5]

Tribal Africa is fascinating and unsettling. Its masked dancers leap out at us from a weird bestiary, not unlike the grotesque figures and gargoyles that adorned church façades during the Middle Ages. Artists, writers, and collectors alike have found themselves falling under the spell that captivated the earliest explorers.

For all its tribal diversity and stylistic variety, there is one thing about Africa that clearly never changes: individuals there devote as much energy to adorning themselves as they do to feeding themselves.[6] Another important point: often it's the menfolk who sport the most spectacular embellishment. During the periodic Geerewol festival in Niger, young Wodaabe men deck themselves out in all their finery and dance as part of a male beauty contest; the girls then choose the ones they consider the handsomest.[7] The Somba hunters of Dahomey may be unclothed, but their bodies have been worked over like pieces of sculpture: partially shaven heads, finger rings, a porcupine quill through the nose, wooden ear plugs, leather bracelets and cowrie-shell wristlets, shell-festooned loincloths. Peoples who may seem to be naked are, in fact, lavishly adorned.

Body ornaments can underscore differences between the sexes (as nature does in the animal kingdom) and highlight anatomical features. The woven buttock shields that Mangbetu women wear are embellished with geometric patterns calculated to catch the male eye. Mongo women sport a conspicuous and highly provocative raffia pompon on their buttocks. The forged-iron loincloths worn by the Kirdi women of Cameroon draw attention to the pubic region. (This fine line between self-adornment and self-display is reflected in the similarity between *parare* and *parere* in Latin and in their French derivations, *parure* and *paraître*.) Whatever form a labret may take—a slender stalk of millet or a wooden, ivory, or terracotta plate—it draws attention to the sensitive, strategically located conduit of human speech: the mouth.[8] The symbolic significance of the body area that lip plugs are designed to protect is obvious. Lobi women drive a thorn through their children's lips when they are about four years old. Three days later the thorn is replaced by a piece of straw. Stalks of increasingly thicker grass are inserted over time, gradually dilating the hole until it is big enough to accommodate a plug of wood or stone.[9] In Ethiopia, women fashion their own lip plates from ocher-colored clay and charcoal, and the size of the labret a young, unmarried woman wears signals how many head of cattle her family will require for her dowry.

Woman's necklace from Tiznit, Morocco (Berber). Silver, amber, and shell. Length 43 cm.

Symbol of eternity, the spiral motif has been found the world over from earliest times to the present day.

35

In addition to the ornaments they insert directly into, under, or through their skin, the peoples of Africa use beads liberally in their headdresses, necklaces, and bracelets. They have long prized the pieces of ancient stone or glass known as aggrey beads.[10] The passion for these beads in Dahomey and the Ivory Coast impressed Portuguese explorers as far back as the late fifteenth century. In the 1600s, Benin craftsmen are known to have sent them as far away as the Gold Coast, and for centuries natives continued to comb abandoned village sites and graves for ancient beads.

Quartz, its varieties chalcedony and carnelian, and other hard stones also proved to be popular jewelry-making materials. Their provenance and source are often difficult to trace. Quartz is found throughout the continent. Egyptian craftsmen worked with carnelian as far back as predynastic times. India long enjoyed a virtual monopoly on carnelian and distributed beads to distant lands.

Africans have always had a particular weakness for glass beads, which were imported into the continent before the Christian era. Eye beads from Ptolemaic Egypt dating from about 300 B.C. have been recovered from sites at Djenne, in Mali. However, the techniques needed to make them appear to remain largely unknown. Beads were traded by merchants from India, the Middle East, and Europe; shipments of beads were routinely unloaded along the coast of Africa starting in the fourth century A.D. The oldest indigenous glass beads are thought to have been made in South Africa.[11] During the ninth century, more than one hundred and sixty-five thousand beads, most of them produced in India, were used in the ceremonial decoration of scepters and sculptures in southern Nigeria.

Gradually, the supply lines shifted. Beads were exported far and wide by Murano glassmakers who literally guarded trade secrets with their lives: spies and turncoats attempting to leave the island and set up shop elsewhere risked the death penalty. These drastic measures notwithstanding, independent beadmaking traditions developed in other lands. Bohemia and Moravia flooded Africa with glass beads. Craftsmen in Mauritania, Nigeria, and elsewhere learned how to work bits of glass into cylinders, cubes, spheres, cones, ellipsoids, and prisms. So overpowering was Africa's passion for beads that incense, tortoiseshell, rhinoceros horn, palm oil, ingot iron or gold—even slaves—were traded for them.

Beads are used in both clothing and jewelry; they are worn by men and women alike. Information is built into them; each and every bead has an assigned meaning and communicates a specific message. The rules governing their use vary from one ethnic group to another, but invariably they act as a visual component of seduction. Even the sounds that eclectic assemblages of beads produce are calculated to catch the ear as well as the eye.

Another material found repeatedly in African adornment is the cowrie shell. These little mollusks shaped like female genitalia have circled the globe. Their voyage is thought to have begun along the shores of the Maldive Islands, in the Indian Ocean, and they were long distributed through Bengal. (The word "cowrie" comes from the Hindi *kauri*.) It is difficult to say exactly when they started to spread through black Africa. They have been found in Egyptian tombs dating back to the time of the pharaohs. By the Middle Ages, they were being carried by caravan from North Africa into the Sudan. Cowries were found in the cargo of a caravan that was abandoned in the western Sahara in the eleventh or twelfth century. The Berber traveler Ibn Battutah reported their use while visiting Mali in the fourteenth century. The shells were prized and often traded for gold. For centuries, European ships laden with cowries emptied their holds along the west coast of Africa, and natives incorporated them into their jewelry. Used as a medium of exchange and circulated as money, they filtered even into remote regions of the Congo and were often traded for ivory and slaves. European vessels brought cowries back on their return trips from India, the Philippines, and Indonesia. The Maldive and Laccadive Islands of the Indian Ocean supplied most cowrie shells used as a form of money in world trade until the eighteenth century.

Whereas cowrie shells served as currency, by and large gold was used for personal adornment. Mined and worked primarily in sub-Saharan West Africa, gold was relatively easy to extract from the ground and spawned a sophisticated crafts tradition. The lustrous metal that shone like the sun dazzled travelers wherever they encountered it. Medieval Arab geographers reported a trade in small twisted gold rings said to come from Wangara, "the land of gold." They also noted that gold could be as frightening as it was alluring. This gleaming, non-corrodible metal, some believed, had a life of its own; the maleficent gold spirit had the power to kill or drive the finder insane. It was thought that gold could grow and move in the earth as though it were a plant. Merchants from Portugal and Holland long ago marveled at the profusion of gilded and solid gold ornaments and furnishings owned by African kings.

The amazingly inventive goldsmiths of sub-Saharan Africa absorbed North African and European influences and thoroughly mingled them with local traditions.[12] The Portuguese began selling wrought gold objects to the Wolof people of Senegal in the sixteenth century; three hundred years later, Senegalese goldsmiths were still turning out countless variations on European rings and bracelets.

So important was gold that it was often melted down and recast, making it difficult to precisely date individual pieces. In 1817 a royal decree issued in Ghana ordered that all gold ornaments be melted down and recast into new objects to celebrate the annual Yam Festival. Despite this practice, however, we have good reason to believe that certain forms endured.

Few objects are as spectacular as the earrings worn by Peul women in southern Mali. These inordinately large four-lobed ornaments of beaten and twisted gold sheeting can weigh as much as three hundred grams each. Explorer Mungo Park, who reported seeing them during his travels in 1797 and 1798, described them as "massive and ill-suited," further commenting that "they were often so heavy that they stretched and tore the earlobe, and to avoid that they were attached to a red leather thong that ran across the top of the head from one ear to the other."[13]

To complement their sumptuous earrings, Peul women wear a necklace featuring a huge, filigree biconical bead with profuse granulation. Nose ornaments and a headdress of large amber beads round out this already lavish ensemble. It is the ultimate in ostentation. Women wear most of the gold jewelry in this region nowadays, but the record shows that at one time men positively reveled in it. The kings of the Sahel fairly blazed with gold, which also embellished the weapons of their attendants. The spread of Islam in the nineteenth century discouraged this practice.

The Asante of Ghana have been renowned practitioners of the goldsmith's art since the fifteenth century. After the Portuguese landed at the fishing village of Shama and found that gold nuggets and jewelry were obtainable, the prosperous region came to be known as the Gold Coast. The Akan ethnic community at the time consisted of a host of small states racked by frequent warfare. In 1482, a Portuguese expedition that landed at Elmina to set up a trading post was greeted by the staggering sight of an Akan chief whose arms, legs, and neck were "covered with chains and trinkets of gold in many styles, and countless bells and large beads of gold were hanging from the hair of his beard and his hair." [14]

The arrival of the Portuguese, the English and, in time, the Dutch, might reasonably have been expected to play havoc with Akan goldwork. Oddly enough, local smiths were encouraged to step up production and met demand by adulterating the precious commodity with brass and silver obtained from the Europeans themselves. The caravans from North Africa also brought Jewish goldsmiths whose techniques survive to this day in the jewelry of the Songhai people. Gold remains so important that in some regions women who cannot afford gold jewelry wear imitation objects made of beeswax and straw that has been soaked in a henna or saffron bath to simulate the color of the precious metal.

In the past as well as today, personal ornaments are displayed on special occasions such as marriages and official ceremonies. Captain John Lock, an English merchant, reported that the women wore "certain foresleeves made of plates of beaten gold, and on their fingers, rings made of golden wires, with a knot or wreath."[15] English envoy Thomas Bowdich witnessed one Yam Festival at which he saw the king covered with gold, adding that his attendants "made for an equally splendid sight." In 1817, Mrs. Bowdich reported visiting a bride at Cape Coast with jewelry in her hair and brooches on her shirt, "manillas encircling her arms halfway up to the elbow," chains across her shoulders, and beautiful girdles. To this day, Asante kings and queen mothers adorn their wrists and forearms with huge hollow-cast gold bracelets, some of which bear a knobbed angular design inspired by a shrub with sharply angled branches. Used in local house building, the bush spreads so quickly that it has come to symbolize fertility.[16]

In Africa gold is worn in many places on the body. Gold rings, ostentatiously displayed on every finger and toe, flaunt an individual's wealth. But the birds, fish, insects, fruit, and seeds depicted on them also illustrate proverbs and adages that convey moral messages about the individual's place in society. Pectorals, often called soul disks or soul washer's badges, were the insignia of officials responsible for purifying or washing the chief's soul. They were also the emblems of royal messengers or young attendants. Their use varies somewhat from tribe to tribe.

The exquisite flat, disk- and rectangular-shaped gold beads cast by the Baule people of the Ivory Coast defy duplication by modern goldsmithing techniques. Chiefly worn by women and children, but also used to adorn so-called spirit spouse figures, these beads go by such evocative names as "pool of water," "setting sun," "the slave's toe," "fish tail," "corn stalk," "taro root," and "back of the tortoise." The Baule also attach golden head pendants to their hair or suspend them from the neck, but these scarified faces with short beards are associated with ancestor worship; they are not portraits in the Western sense of the word. All these treasures are publicly displayed during an exhibition of gold, a status-enhancing ceremony during which influential men parade their accumulated gold objects in order to advance their status in the community, rising to the rank of elders.

Bronzesmithing was also highly developed in West Africa, where lost-wax casting techniques allowed craftsmen tremendous latitude in the creation of designs. The process calls for purifying beeswax in very hot water, sculpting it into a desired shape, and applying successive coats of clay to the wax model. When the clay hardens, the entire mold is fired, the wax melts, drains out (is "lost"), and the resulting cast is then filled with molten metal. (Strictly speaking bronze is an alloy of copper and tin, but the word is often used to describe objects of brass, which is composed of copper and zinc.)

Lost-wax casting is a versatile technique that encourages creativity. For generations, resourceful bronzesmiths have risen to the occasion with fanciful jewelry designed to offer protection and enhance status. A bronze snake with ornamental spirals can be fastened around the calf of a person's leg to avert snake bites. Some ancestor figures are lined up as a way of obtaining forgiveness and protection. Suspending an oblong ancestor figure from a neck ring is thought to ward off malevolent sorcerers and unseen perils. Members of a healers' society wear a finger ring bearing a figure of the long-horned bush cow to give them knowledge of medicinal herbs and to use during the healing process. It is known as the "ring of silence" because members hold it between their lips at the funeral of a fellow-member.

West African metalsmiths also availed themselves of forging techniques. They would melt metal down into molds, then alternately hot-hammer and quench the slender ingots, repeating the process until they took on the desired shape. In Zaire, Gabon, and other regions where the lost-wax method was hardly used, open-mold casting was practiced in hollows scooped right out of the ground; a mallet was then used to beat the objects into shape. Young nomad women in Niger wear heavy bronze anklets that Hausa smiths forge from metal ingots and incise with Islamic designs. These shackle-like rings, which also serve as currency, make it difficult for the women to walk, but a cumbersome gait is considered highly attractive.

Among the Dan people of the Ivory Coast, certain bronze bracelets weigh as much as nine kilograms (nearly twenty pounds). These are probably ritual objects for use in divination. At one time they were believed to provide a way of communicating with spirits and therefore considered sacred. Other bracelets are meant to be worn: they may be festooned with bells, the number and size of which indicate the owner's wealth and status. In addition to their role as status symbols and dowry items, the heavy bronze anklets favored by the Kru people of Liberia are thought to protect against evil spirits in the ground.

In Cameroon, where the buffalo is held in high regard for its strength and cunning—attributes supposedly shared by the king and other officials—high-ranking men used to sit on buffalo skulls at gatherings. Dignitaries were entitled to wear necklaces adorned with bronze buffalo heads; but as their original significance gradually faded from memory, women also took to wearing necklaces with bovine-shaped heads.

The Tiv people of central Nigeria offer pinches of snuff to notables and high-ranking guests on a specially designed ring with a tall, flat-topped extension. A Dogon man's finger ring depicting a warrior on horseback is presented to war lords to wear during ritual prayers. Elsewhere, chameleons, frogs, birds, and scarabs cling to finger rings and other objects, attesting to the inexhaustible imagination of African bronzesmiths.

A GORGEOUS PROFUSION

A burst of color swept across North Africa with the spread of enameled precious metalwork. Jewish smiths fleeing the Spanish Inquisition in the late fifteenth century settled in North Africa and introduced cloisonné and niello techniques. A wealth of symbols have emblazoned enameled fibulas and diadems ever since.

Jewelry in North Africa has often taken the form of amulets, worn to protect directly or indirectly against disease, and talismans. (The word talisman, comes from a Hebrew word, *tsedem*, and means image.) Amulets often contain holy materials, such as religious verses or sacred inscriptions, and are still produced and worn to avert misfortune. Among other things worn for protective purposes are stones, glass, metal, and pieces of boar's tusk.

Perhaps the most powerful image in North African iconography is the hand, worn to ward off the evil eye, which particularly imperils the very young and women in childbirth. The hand is the focal point of all forces. Hands are kissed and clasped; they seal alliances; they are raised imploringly to heaven in prayer. The right hand is used to bless, the left to curse. The most commonly worn amulet in North Africa—the hand of Fatima, daughter of the prophet Mohammed—is believed to deflect evil spells.

The jewelry of nomadic Berbers abounds in symbols inspired by local flora and fauna. The ram is thought to have supernatural powers. The jackal's paw drives away evil spirits. The cat, whose flesh is eaten to chase away impending misfortune, symbolizes fertility. Fish ensure longevity. The salamander helps protect against fire. The snake, widely feared because of its reputedly poisonous eyes, magically safeguards the wearer.

The plant kingdom is also amply represented: roses, carnations, jasmine. The pomegranate is associated with fertility because of its many seeds. Almonds symbolize immortality. Trees bridge the gap between the worlds above and below, thereby connecting all three levels of the cosmos. And because Islamic artists are forbidden to depict the human form, they replace it with luxuriant geometric patterns associated with symbols, numbers, and natural phenomena. Spirals symbolize eternity.

The raw materials employed in North African adornment are themselves full of meaning. Silver, the metal favored in rural areas, symbolizes honesty and purity. Yellow amber is thought to attract sunlight and deflect darkness. Wool is a propitious substance. Wondrous red coral, the "tree of the deep," partakes also of the animal and mineral kingdoms and is associated with life-sustaining blood because of its color. Color symbolism is part and parcel of this vocabulary: yellow stands for the sun, green for the vital force, white for light and nourishing milk, blue and black for protection against the evil eye.

Sensuality and seduction guide not only professional artisans, but also the women who produce some of their own jewelry. No one but young brides may wear necklaces strung with fragrant beads prepared with ambergris, musk, aloe wood, rose petals, nutmeg, and sandalwood. Ancient formulas recommended blending in some dove's blood, turtledove's blood, and sparrow's brain with the ambergris (a reputed aphrodisiac that was reported long ago by the Moorish traveler Leo Africanus).[17]

The womenfolk craft their own headdresses as well as ornamental and protective temple pendants, which hook into the hair, frame the face, and partially cover the upper torso. These supple creations follow every movement of their bodies, yet discretely cover them. Designed to hold their draped garments in place are a varied array of weighty fibulas, which local craftsmen hammer, cast, and chase in metal. They turn practicality into a pretext for sumptuous display.

RIGHT:

From Tiznit, Morocco. Enameled and nielloed silver, coral, amber, and glass stones.

Top: Pair of woman's headdress pendants. Height 22.5 cm.

Bottom: Pair of woman's hair ornaments. Height 6.7 cm.

The ring-shaped hair ornaments hold aromatic herbs or scented wool.

OPPOSITE TOP LEFT:

Woman's headdress from Morocco (Berber). Silver, coral, and goat's hair. Height 37 cm.

This type of ceremonial wedding headdress from the late eighteenth century is very rare.

OPPOSITE TOP RIGHT:

Woman's necklace from the Anti-Atlas, Morocco (Berber). Coral, enameled silver, and glass beads. Length 42 cm.

Jewish smiths traditionally played a dominant role in jewelry-making not only in the Maghreb but throughout the Near East. Some of the Jews expelled from Spain in the fifteenth century settled as far south as the Anti-Atlas region. The techniques these refugees brought with them from Andalusia included cloisonne enameling, niello decoration, and gemstone setting.

OPPOSITE BOTTOM:

Woman's neck ornament from southern Morocco (Berber). Amber, coral, amazonite, other materials. Total length: 222 cm.

The Berbers prized coral for its healing properties. Amber was believed to offer protection against the evil eye. Shells, brought in by caravan from East Africa, symbolized fertility.

TOP:

From Tiznit, Morocco.

Top: Anklet. Enameled silver, coral, and glass stones. Diameter 11.5 cm.

Bottom: Earrings. Enameled silver, coral, and glass. Height of the hoops 12.6 cm.

This blue-and-yellow-enameled redif *(above) is believed to be older than anklets with green and yellow enamels. The hoops of the earrings (below) are in the shape of snakes. When they are worn, the heavy earrings are supported by a hook in the hair.*

BOTTOM:

Women's pendants from Morocco (Palmeraies du Bani). Silver. Width 4.5 to 7.9 cm.

Herz *(literally, amulets) which Jewish women of the Anti-Atlas sometimes string on their necklaces contain sacred substances believed to work on the wearer's behalf.*

OPPOSITE:

Fibulas from Tiznit, Morocco. Silver, enamel, and glass stones. Height 60 cm.

Known in Morocco as tizerzai, *fibulas are essential components of female adornment and are worn in pairs as cloak fasteners. Their size, weight, and workmanship reflect the wearer's social status. The inverted triangle represents the female form, and the central egg-shaped bead (tagemout) symbolizes fertility.*

44

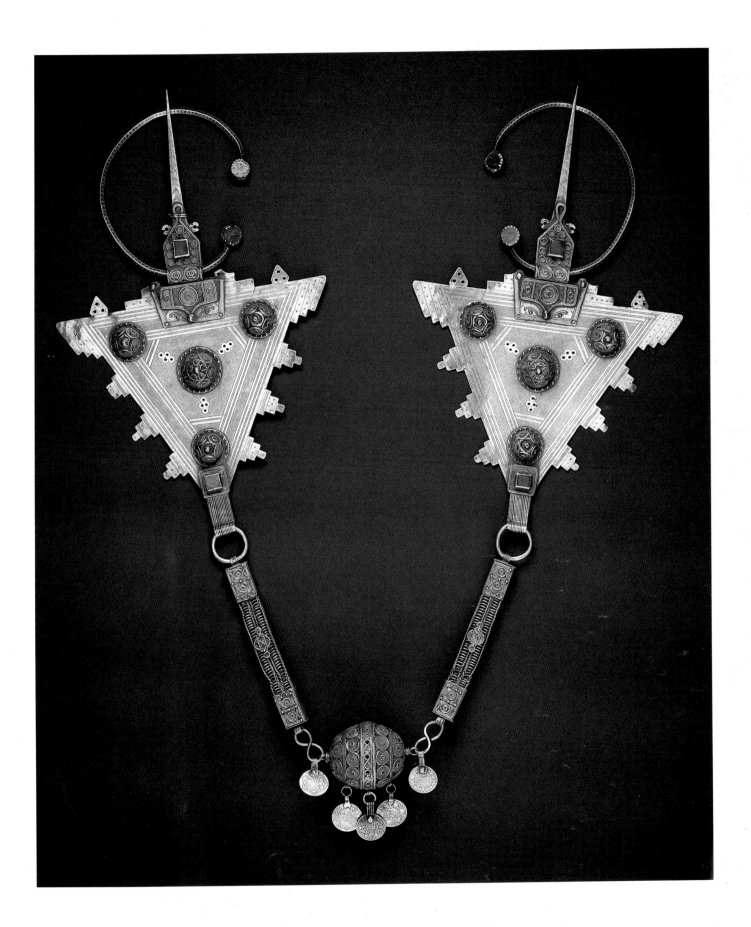

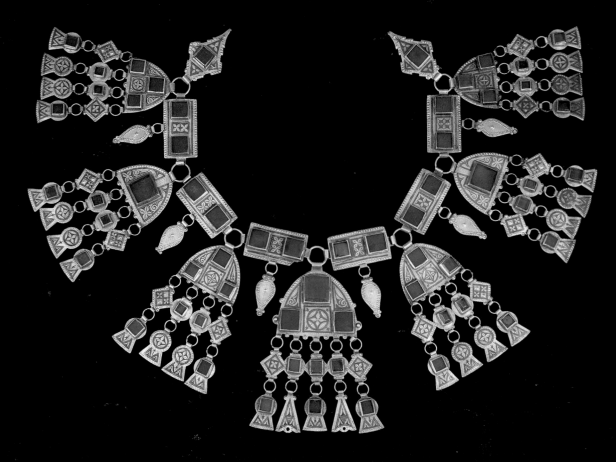

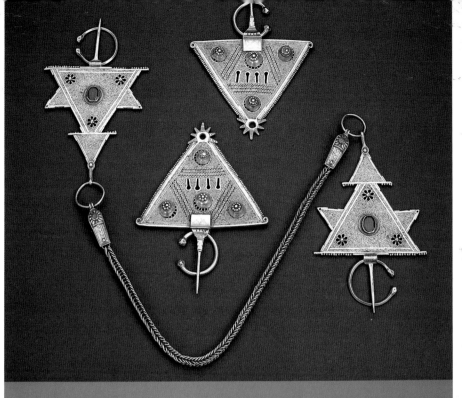

OPPOSITE TOP:

Pair of woman's fibulas from Rif, Morocco. Silver. Height 37 cm.

Chains link these tizerzai *to a central element representing a turtle, which in North Africa is believed to be a beneficial and protective creature. Elsewhere, the turtle symbolizes knowledge and longevity.*

OPPOSITE BOTTOM:

Necklace from Morocco (Ida Ounadif). Silver with niello decoration and glass stones. Total length 60 cm.

This magnificent necklace is sometimes worn as a head ornament at important celebrations.

TOP:

Fibulas from the Anti-Atlas, Morocco. Silver, 18th century. Height 18.5 cm. (center) and 19.5 cm. (far left and right).

These fibulas consist of tiny tubular elements that have been soldered together within a triangular frame. This age-old technique, which has since died out, gave rise to many variations on the inverted triangle, a female symbol. They are worn only by wealthy women.

MIDDLE:

Bracelets from Morocco (Fez to the Southern Atlas). Enameled and nielloed silver, and gold. Diameter 5.7 cm. to 10.2 cm.

The shams u kmar bracelets from Fez (far left) feature gold and silver, symbolizing the sun and moon. Yellow and green enamel work is a hallmark of the Tiznit region.

BOTTOM:

Group of women's bracelets. Silver.

Top row, left to right: Morocco, Morocco, Ethiopia, Sudan; bottom row, left to right: Ethiopia, Morocco, Ethiopia, Ethiopia, Libya. Largest diameter 12.5 cm.

Spiked bracelets once designed for self-protection have since become purely ornamental. The bracelet at top right is worn by Rashaida women in Sudan, but a similar type can be found in the Egyptian part of the Nubian Desert.

47

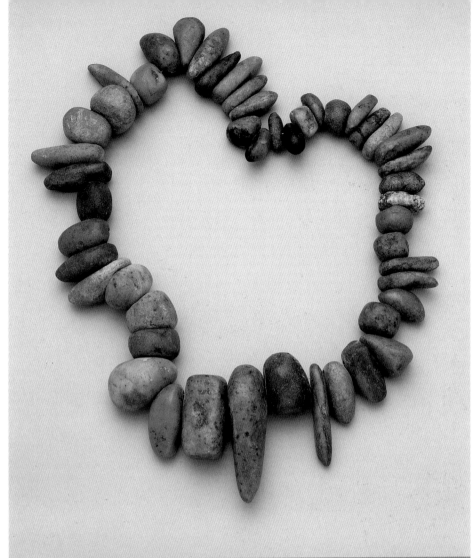

OPPOSITE TOP:

Woman's anklets from Mauritania. Aluminum and gilded brass. Diameter 13.2 cm.

This pair of khelkhal *provide a striking example of how the Tuareg recycle old saucepans, airplane parts, and other salvageable materials.*

OPPOSITE BOTTOM:

Ornaments from the Sahara. Silver. Diameter 6 cm. to 11 cm.

Far left: Pair of bracelets from Niger (Tuareg).

Top left: Anklet from Mauritania (Moors).

Top right: Pair of anklets from Mauritania (Moors).

Far right: Pair of earrings from Niger (Tuareg).

The character of Tuareg people is reflected in the clean, geometric lines of their jewelry. They prefer silver, a symbol of purity, to gold, which is believed to bring bad luck.

TOP:

Necklace from Niger. Amazonite. Length 39 cm.

Amazonite was highly prized in Morocco, Mauritania, and Niger. Necklaces like the one shown here, strung with beads of Niger amazonite, date from ancient times.

BOTTOM:

Pendants from Niger (Tuareg). Shell or silver mounted in leather. Height 6.3 cm. to 8 cm.

The khomissar *represents the stylized hand of Mohammed's daughter, Fatima, and is worn to protect the wearer. When made of shell it is said to promote fertility and is handed down from mother to daughter. In Algeria, silver is sometimes substituted for shell.*

ABOVE:
Pendants from Niger (Tuareg).
Silver. Height 7.5 cm. to 9 cm.

The Tuareg prefer silver, the metal
of the Prophet, to gold, which is
considered impure.

OPPOSITE LEFT:
Chest ornament from Niger
(Tuareg). Silver. Height 27.5 cm.

Tuareg women of high standing
used to let their teraout *hang down*
the back.

OPPOSITE RIGHT:
Counterweight from Niger
(Tuareg). Copper, brass, and iron.
Height 28 cm.

Tuareg women fasten an assrou n'
swoul *(literally, "key that is slung*
over the shoulder") to a corner of
their headcloths and let it hang
down the back as a counterweight.
It symbolizes wealth and prestige.

50

TOP:
From Great Kabylia, northern Algeria (Beni Yenni).

Left: Pair of anklets. Silver, enamel, and coral. Height 10.3 cm.

Right: Bracelet. Silver, enamel, and coral. Diameter 7.9 cm.

Kabyle women always wear their ihelhalen *(left) and* amesluh *(right) in pairs. On festive occasions they wear several bracelets on each arm.*

BOTTOM:
Woman's necklace from Great Kabylia, northern Algeria (Beni Yenni). Silver, enamel, and coral. Length 40 cm.

Like most Kabyle jewelry, this tazlagt emm elherz *features plaques with enamelwork on front and back. Cloisonne enameling is a hallmark of Maghreb jewelry.*

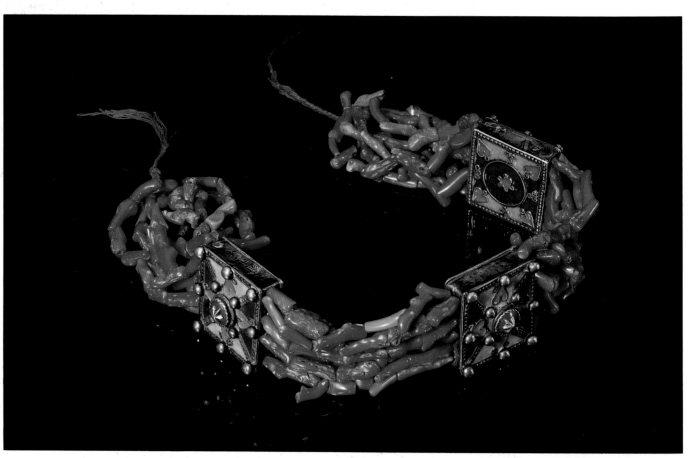

TOP:
Fibulas from Great Kabylia, Algeria (Beni Yenni). Silver, enamel, and coral. Height 40 cm.

Women in Morocco and Algeria wear fibulas in pairs. When chains are added to support an amulet case, they form a valuable ornamental ensemble.

BOTTOM:
Pair of fibulas (ibzimen) from Kabylia, Algeria. Silver and Bakelite. Height 25.5 cm.

In the late nineteenth century Bakelite, the first successful plastic, was imported from France and Germany to alleviate the shortage of far costlier coral.

TOP:

From Tunisia (Berber). Silver.

Top: Belt ornament. Diameter 10.5 cm.

Right and left: Headdress pendants. Height 21 cm.

Middle: Earrings. Height 8.1 cm.

Tunisian women receive some of their jewelry from their mothers; the rest is given to them by their prospective husbands in the form of a dowry (mlak).

MIDDLE:

From Tunisia.

Left: Pair of anklets. Silver. Width 11 cm.

Right: Pair of bracelets. Silver. Height 7.5 cm.

Center: Bracelet. Silver. Width 2.8 cm.

These khelkhal *(left) and* swar *(right) are the work of Mouschi Ennamni, a Tunisian smith. Although the seal of Solomon means different things to Jews and Muslims, it has been a motif in Tunisian art since ancient times. The* deblej *seen here (center) happens to come from Djerba, but the same type of bracelet can be found in Libya.*

BOTTOM:

Pair of fibulas from Tunisia (Bedouin). Silver. Diameter 17.6 cm.

These crescent-shaped hillal *were made by Mouschi Ennamni. Among Tunisian symbols that date from the Punic or Christian eras and derive from Jewish or Islamic tradition, doves stand for love and fish symbolize fertility.*

OPPOSITE:

Woman's necklace from Moknine, Tunisia. Silver and aromatic beads. Length 67.5 cm.

This eighteenth-century wedding necklace consists of a talisman case (qannouta) and heart-shaped aromatic beads (shab) made from a mixture of musk, ambergris, aloeswood, rose petals, and other rare substances.

TOP:

Anklets from Chad. Bronze. Width 11.2 and 13.1 cm.

These anklets are striking examples of beautifully integrated form and surface decoration.

BOTTOM:

Pair of armlets from Chad (Kenga). Bronze. Height 14.8 cm., weight 2 kg.

These armlets are shaped to look like cattle horns.

OPPOSITE LEFT:

Man's finger ring from Sudan (Dinka). Ivory. Height 16.5 cm.

The unusual size of this ring suggests that it probably belonged to a man of high status.

OPPOSITE TOP RIGHT:

Armlets from Sudan (Shilluk, Nuer, Dinka). Ivory. Width 8.5 to 19 cm.

Ivory ornaments increase prestige and are therefore much sought after by the peoples who live along the upper Nile. Unusual shape is the hallmark of the armlets produced by the Shilluk (top left, top right, and bottom) and their Nuer neighbors (far right). The cattle-herding Dinka (center, far left) are also very fond of body adornment. The segmented afiok bracelet (center) is worn by Dinka girls eligible for marriage.

OPPOSITE BOTTTOM RIGHT:

Pair of bracelets from Sudan (Fur). Ivory. Diameter 10 cm.

Both the Rashaida of Sudan and the Azande of Zaire wear this type of bracelet, which shows the influence of Islamic design.

OPPOSITE TOP:

Bracelets from Sudan (Shilluk). Copper wire and bronze. Front: Width 10.5 cm. Rear: Width 9.1 cm.

These bracelets, with zoomorphic heads were designed for use in combat.

OPPOSITE BOTTOM:

Earrings from Sudan (Nubian Desert). Gold. Diameter 5.8 cm.

Resembling Byzantine earrings, these ornaments, are worn by herders' wives. As in other pastoral societies, wealth in livestock is a source of prestige. A smaller version of a similar earring type can be found in the Egyptian sector of the Nubian Desert.

ABOVE:

Pendant from Sudan (Toposa). Bone and leather. Width 31 cm.

The lives of Toposa herders revolve around their cattle. On ceremonial occasions they bedeck their livestock with ornaments, such as this pendant for a young calf.

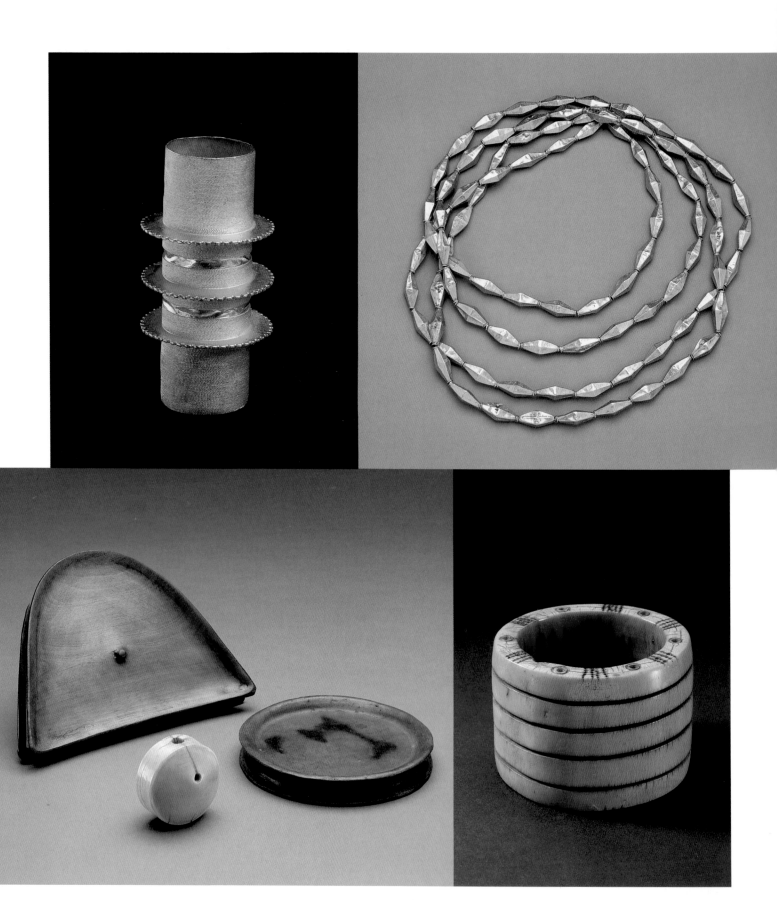

OPPOSITE TOP LEFT:
Forehead ornament from Egypt. Gold. Height 5.6 cm.

Islamic women used this ornament to secure the veil or face covering they were obliged to wear in the presence of men who were not members of their immediate family.

OPPOSITE TOP RIGHT:
Woman's necklace from the Sinai, Egypt (Bedouin). Gold. Length 91 cm.

This necklace (also worn in Palestine) is strung with a type of bead that goes back to the days of the pharaohs.

OPPOSITE BOTTOM LEFT:
Group of lip plugs.

Left: Sudan (Kichepo). Wood. Width 16.8 cm.

Only older women still wear lip plates like this one in the presence of outsiders.

Right: Ethiopia (Sorma). Terracotta. Diameter 12 cm.

Made and worn by women prior to marriage. The diameter of the disk indicates how many head of cattle are required as a dowry.

Bottom: Kenya (Turkana). Ivory. Diameter 5 cm.

Elders wear an ekalaitom *to indicate their standing among men in the community.*

OPPOSITE BOTTOM RIGHT:
Bracelet from Ethiopia. Ivory. Diameter 11 cm.

The grooves carved into this bracelet probably imitate a type of Ethiopian bracelet that consists of separate loops connected by leather lashing.

ABOVE:
Pendants from Ethiopia (Sidamo). Bronze and copper. Height 3.7 cm. to 9.2 cm.

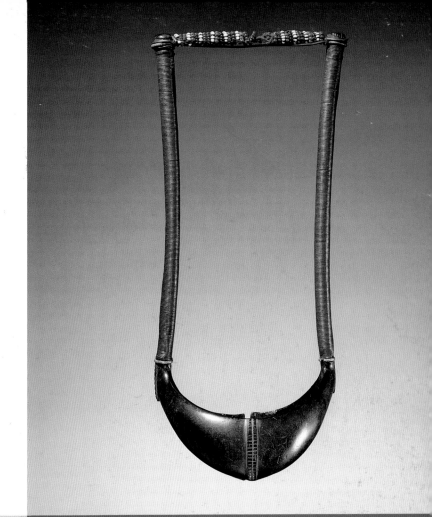

OPPOSITE:

Necklace from Somalia. Amber, silver, and silk. Length 60 cm.

This necklace of amber represents a significant part of a Somali woman's dowry. Other necklaces substitute beads of copal, a semi-fossilized resin up to 300,000 years old that is not believed to have the prophylactic properties of genuine amber.

TOP RIGHT:

Man's arm ornament from Kenya (Maasai). Horn, copper wire, and glass beads. Length 26 cm.

Only warriors who have killed a man in battle may wear an errap above the elbow.

BOTTOM LEFT:

Man's skullcap from Kenya (Karamayong). Human hair, clay, and ostrich feathers. Height 30 cm.

A ceremonial siliop becomes more elaborate as a man's standing in the community increases.

BOTTOM RIGHT:

Man's shield and armlet from Kenya (Kikuyu). Height 58.7 cm.

Initiated youths carry an ndome on the left arm above the elbow. The inner surface is decorated with chevron patterns; the designs on the other side vary with the owner's rank by age and territory.

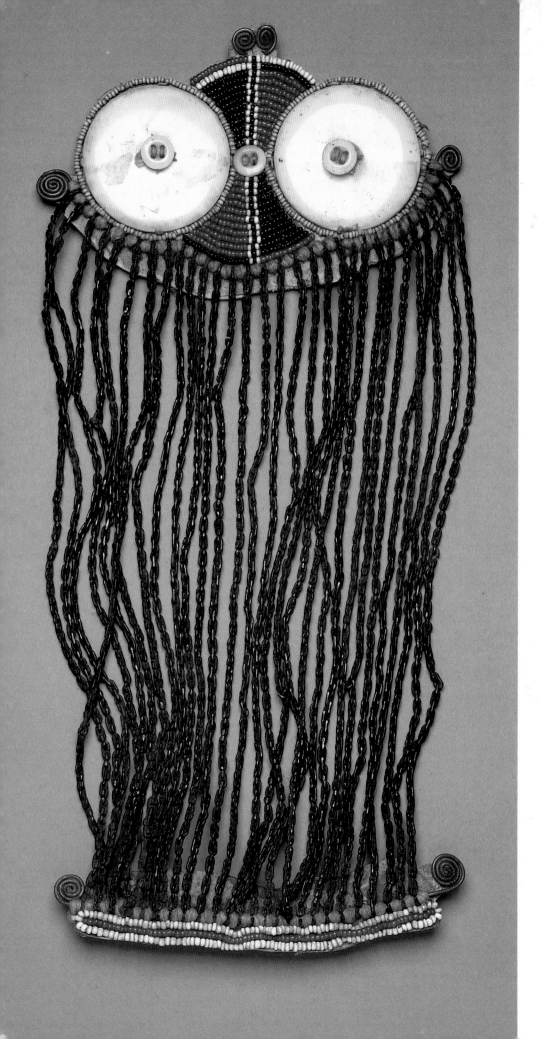

LEFT:
Chest ornament from Kenya (Maasai). Porcelain, glass beads, and iron. Height 29.5 cm.

Some examples of this very old type of pectoral incorporate cone shell disks, but this one features Czech-made porcelain imitations that became a popular substitute for cone shell late in the nineteenth century.

OPPOSITE TOP LEFT:
Woman's necklace from Kenya (Turkana). Plant material and horn. Diameter 34 cm.

OPPOSITE TOP RIGHT:
Bracelets from Uganda. Ivory. Diameter 6 cm. to 8.5 cm.

OPPOSITE BOTTOM LEFT:
Group of ornaments. Ivory and lizard skin.

Top right: Bracelet from Kenya (Giryama). Diameter 13.3 cm.

Top left: Comb from Zaire (Lega). Height 14.4 cm.

Bottom right: Bracelet from Zaire (Shi). Diameter 11.2 cm.

Bottom left: Bracelet from Zaire (Lega). Diameter 11.4 cm.

Some Africans cover their bodies with palm oil and red earth powder, which impart a golden patina to their jewelry. Occasionally ivory ornaments are dipped in a mixture of oil and pigments to prevent them from cracking.

OPPOSITE BOTTOM RIGHT:
Necklace element from Tanzania (Sukuma). Ivory. Height 12 cm.

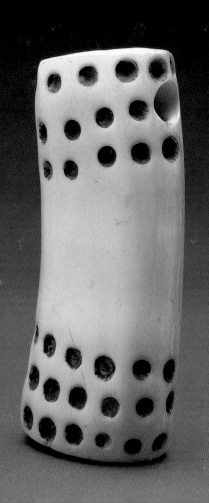

TOP:

Bracelet from Zaire. Wood, iron, and brass. Diameter 17 cm.

This bracelet features an unusual decorative design of small metal plaques. Wooden bracelets are seldom found in Zaire.

BOTTOM:

Left: Man's bracelet from Burundi (Tutsi). Wood with copper inlay. Width 20.7 cm.

This igitembe, *or archer's bracelet, is worn by Tutsi noblemen.*

Right: Neck ring from Zaire (Ngbaka). Copper. Width 25 cm.

This prestige-enhancing wrought copper ornament boasts a level of technical expertise that would put many a contemporary metalsmith to shame.

OPPOSITE:

Top: Pendant from Rwanda (Tutsi). Shell. Width 11.5 cm.

Worn by both sexes, the igihete *can be worth as much as several cows. Tutsi men wear one, but women of high rank may wear up to seven. Another type of shell pendant, the* ibirezi, *is of less value.*

Middle: Pendant from Zaire (Ndengese). Copper, brass, and aluminum. Width 20.2 cm.

Bottom: Pendant from Burkina Faso (Bwa). Bronze. Width 10.2 cm.

Often ascribed to the Bobo people, this pendant protects the wearer from evil spirits.

Pendants from Zaire (Pende).

Left: Bone. Height 7.5 cm. Right: Ivory. Height 5 cm.

Only men are entitled to wear ikhoko *of bone or ivory; women and children may wear ones made of wood or some other substance. They afford males protection during initiation and later serve as reminders of the laws they are taught at that time. Mask pendants crowned with three points may be worn only by chiefs.*

Hairpins from Zaire, all Mangbetu except second from left (Kuba),third from left and third from right (Azande). Ivory except for two iron pins at far left. Length 23.5 cm. to 38 cm.

Some women wore hairstyles so elaborate they had to be held in place by rigid frames. The length and number of decorative hairpins indicated the wearer's status.

Pendants from Zaire. Ivory and bone.

Top left: Kuba. Height 7.3 cm.
Top right: Lulua. Height 4.1 cm.
Bottom: Kongo. Height 5.7 cm.

Leg ornament from Zaire (Mongo). Bronze. Height 29.5 cm.

Women wear kongas *in pairs; this one alone weighs six kilograms.*

Neck ring from Zaire (N'gombe). Brass. Diameter 19 cm., weight 5 kg.

Only in the name of prestige would a woman wear a torc as heavy and uncomfortable as this one, embellished with delicately incised animal designs.

Anklet from Zaire (Mbole). Copper. Diameter 26.5 cm.

In Africa women's anklets are always worn in pairs. This one weighs two kilograms.

Man's belt from Zaire (N'gombe). Lion's mane and plant fiber. Length 2 meters.

The mane of this hunter's belt (kamba na njala) is probably calculated to give the wearer the strength of a lion.

Buttock shield from Zaire (Mongo). Plant fiber. Length 90 cm. Pompon diameter 14.6 cm.

This bakonga, which features a conspicuous decorative rear pompon, is worn by women about the hips.

TOP:

From Zaire and Angola (Tshokwe).

Top: Pendant. Cone shell. Height 8.6 cm.

Bottom: Necklace. Porcelain and plant fiber. Length 36 cm.

The central pendant of a cimba, or chief's necklace, was traditionally made from a cone shell to symbolize the moon. Porcelain imitations, like the one shown here (bottom), have been produced since the nineteenth century. In 1854 the British explorer, Dr. David Livingstone reported that a slave could be purchased for two ornamental cone-shell disks (mpande, top).

BOTTOM LEFT:

Left: Man's ear ornament from northern Zaire (Nzakara?). Ivory and brass. Diameter 5.6 cm.

Right: Pendant from Zaire (Shi). Ivory. Width 15.3 cm.

Center: Man's ear ornament from northern Zaire (Nzakara?). Ivory. Diameter 6 cm.

One of the earrings (left) is decorated with nails and a cartridge case, acculturated elements that add to the wearer's prestige.

BOTTOM RIGHT:

Necklace from Zaire (Tabwa). Glass beads. Length 17 cm.

In our view, the sense of poetry expressed by this beadwork object bespeaks an individualism seldom encountered in Africa.

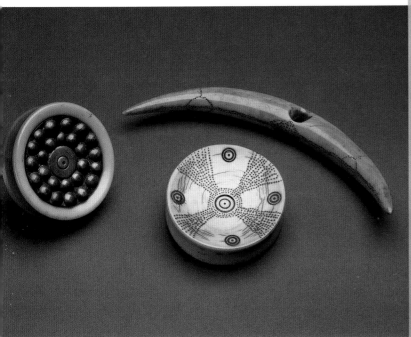

Opposite:
Neck ring from Zaire (Teke). Bronze. Diameter 32.5 cm.

The more notches in a chief's onlua, *the greater his prestige. They denote not only his rank but also the number of villages under his jurisdiction.*

Top:
Anklet from Gabon (Kota, often attributed to the Fang people). Bronze. Height 17.5 cm., weight 5 kg.

Reminiscent of crested hairstyles, djokelebale *were used as a form of currency during marriage transactions.*

Bottom:
Armlet from Gabon (Fang). Bronze. Height 11.5 cm.

This akal-e-ngo *is also worn in Cameroon. Jewelry styles often, of course, cross modern and arbitrary political boundaries.*

OPPOSITE TOP LEFT:
*Bracelet from Cameroon (Tikar).
Diameter 11.5 cm.*

*Stylized spiders form a decorative
pattern around this brass bracelet
of the Tikar, who believe that the
spider mediates between God and
humans.*

OPPOSITE TOP RIGHT:
*Necklace from Cameroon. Bronze.
Length 34 cm.*

OPPOSITE BOTTOM:
*Necklace from Cameroon
(Bamileke). Pearls, cowrie shells,
and leather. Diameter 18.8 cm.*

*Cowrie shells (Cypraea moneta)
from the Indian Ocean once figured
prominently in African exchange
systems.*

TOP:
*Necklace from Cameroon (Bamum).
Bronze and iron. Diameter 32 cm.*

*The mbangba, an element of Fon
regalia, identified high-ranking
individuals at tribal meetings.*

BOTTOM:
*Belt from Cameroon. Glass beads.
Length 98 cm.*

*Glass beads have long been
popular in Africa, where they have
been extensively used in jewelry,
on clothing, and in the making of
prestige-enhancing objects.*

LEFT:

Bracelet from Cameroon (Bamum). Ivory. Height 10.7 cm.

Worn by the wives of high-ranking dignitaries, this bracelet has a massive simplicity reminiscent of modern sculpture.

OPPOSITE LEFT:

Bracelet from Cameroon (Bana). Bronze and feathers. Height 29 cm.

Intended as a weapon, this ushira *can be transformed into an ornament by blunting its spikes or, as we see here, camouflaging them with feathers.*

OPPOSITE TOP RIGHT:

Woman's loincloth from Cameroon (Kirdi). Iron. Length including the belt 44 cm.

A complete cache-sexe—*like the one pictured here, worn by married women—is seldom found intact.*

OPPOSITE BOTTOM RIGHT:

From Nigeria.

Protective neck ring and armlet. Iron. Width of torc 31 cm. Height of armlet 24.2 cm.

This warrior's gear includes a neck ring of a type rarely seen.

Finger rings from Nigeria (Tiv). Bronze. Height 13.3 cm.

Snuff was placed on this ring and offered to distinguished visitors.

Buttock-shield from Nigeria (Jaba). Plant fiber and glass beads. Diameter 19 cm.

This woman's ornament is believed to protect the wearer from evil spirits—and calculated to attract the male eye.

Pair of anklets from Nigeria (Ibo). Brass. Diameter 21.5 cm.

Smiths hammered ogba into shape and attached them to the ankles of women who were married to high-ranking Ibo men. They were not removed unless the wearer had to be fitted for even bigger ones (30 to 35 centimeters in diameter). It is unusual to find ogba as small as the pair shown here, because small ones are melted down to make larger ones.

Leg ornament from Cross River, Nigeria. Bronze. Height 24 cm.

Similar to ornaments from the twentieth century, this ancient artifact is thought to have been fastened lengthwise to the leg to afford the wearer protection from snake bites.

OPPOSITE:

Amulet from Nigeria (Margi or Fali). Bronze. Height 25 cm.

The ifa is a large amulet designed to protect the wearer from sorcerers.

TOP:

Bracelets and anklets from Nigeria (Ibo and Idoma). Ivory. Diameter 7 cm. to 19.2 cm.

The Ibo made large bracelets and anklets for their wives. The weight of these ornaments alone was a sign of a woman's high standing in the community.

MIDDLE:

Top left: Pendant from Togo (Moba). Bronze. Diameter 9.2 cm.

The balogal symbolizes the sun.

Top right and bottom: Pendants from Mali (Dogon). Bronze. Diameter 6.4 and 6.8 cm.

These pendants, though called "Dogon suns," do not appear to be sun symbols.

BOTTOM:

Group of excavated ornaments from Cross River, Nigeria. Bronze. Width 9.5 cm. to 24.5 cm.

ABOVE:

Necklaces from the Ivory Coast.

Top: (Dan). Bronze, glass beads, and tooth. Length 24 cm.

Bottom: (Kuba). Bronze, glass beads, and teeth. Length 45 cm.

Chevron beads are highly valued in Africa, especially in Cameroon and by the Kuba of Zaire. Beads are less popular among the Dan, who find bronzework more appealing.

OPPOSITE TOP:

Top: Anklet from the Ivory Coast (Dan). Bronze. Width 17.2 cm.

A Dan woman's status can be determined by the size and number of bells on her anklets.

Bottom: Belt from Cameroon (Bana). Bronze. Length 39 cm.

Young women wear this bell-festooned belt in dances.

OPPOSITE BOTTOM LEFT:

Pendant from the Ivory Coast (Baule). Horn, lizard skin, and leather. Width 13 cm.

This pendant represents a cat-fish, which appears in local lore as a water spirit that brings good luck and offspring.

OPPOSITE BOTTOM RIGHT:

Bracelet from the Ivory Coast (Dan). Bronze. Width 14.3 cm.

Note the differences between Dan and Akan (Baule and Ashanti) bronzework. Though both use the lost-wax method, the Akan produce objects of exquisite delicacy; Dan ornaments are bold and massive.

TOP:

Bracelet from the Ivory Coast (Baule). Plant fiber, leather, and cowrie shells. Width 13.9 cm.

Shells everywhere are associated with wealth and fertility; cowrie shells in particular recall the shape of the female genitals and, thus, symbolize women.

BOTTOM:

Anklet from the Ivory Coast (Dan). Bronze. Length 24.5 cm.

It is hard to believe that anyone could have worn one of these heavy nine-kilogram anklets, much less a pair of them. Since jewelry and weapons were often used as mediums of exchange in Africa, this ornament may have been used for that purpose.

OPPOSITE:

From the Ivory Coast (Baule).

Necklace. Gold. Length 41 cm.

Pendants. Gold. Width 5.8 cm. (above), 8.5 cm. (below).

Europeans in search of precious materials first made landfall along the coast of West Africa in the fifteenth century. They discovered such an abundance of gold in what is now Ghana that the area came to be known as the Gold Coast. This striking group of ornaments attests to the consumate skills with which Akan craftsmen practiced lost-wax casting.

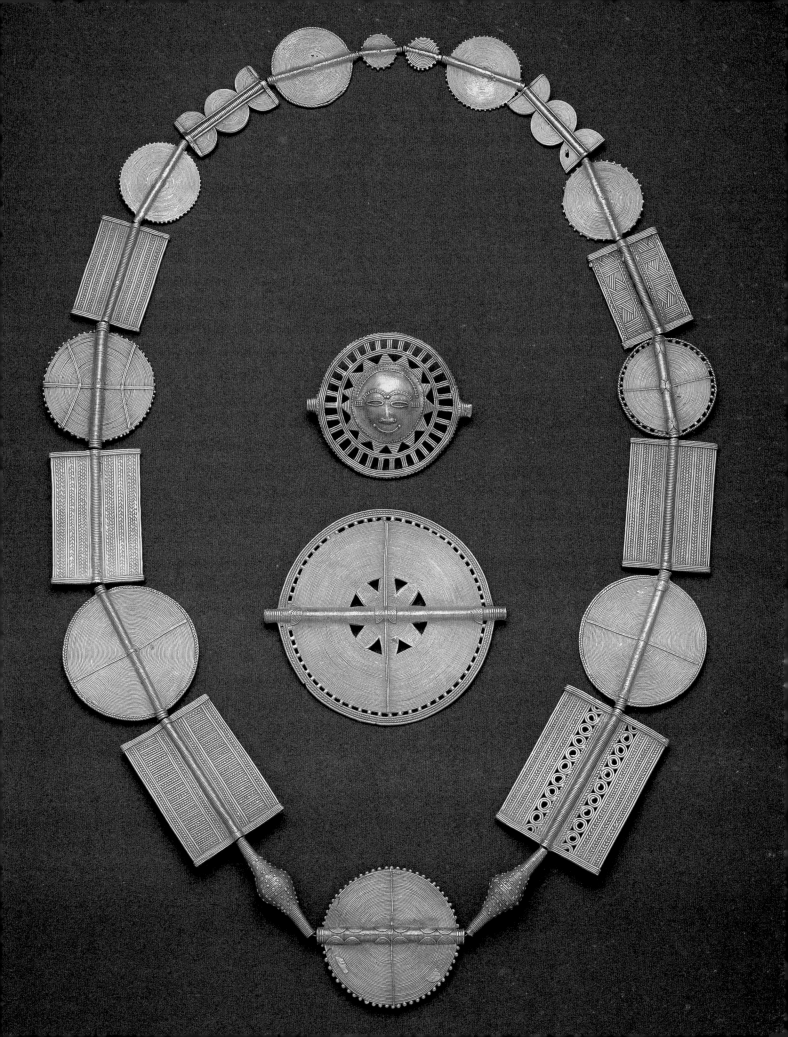

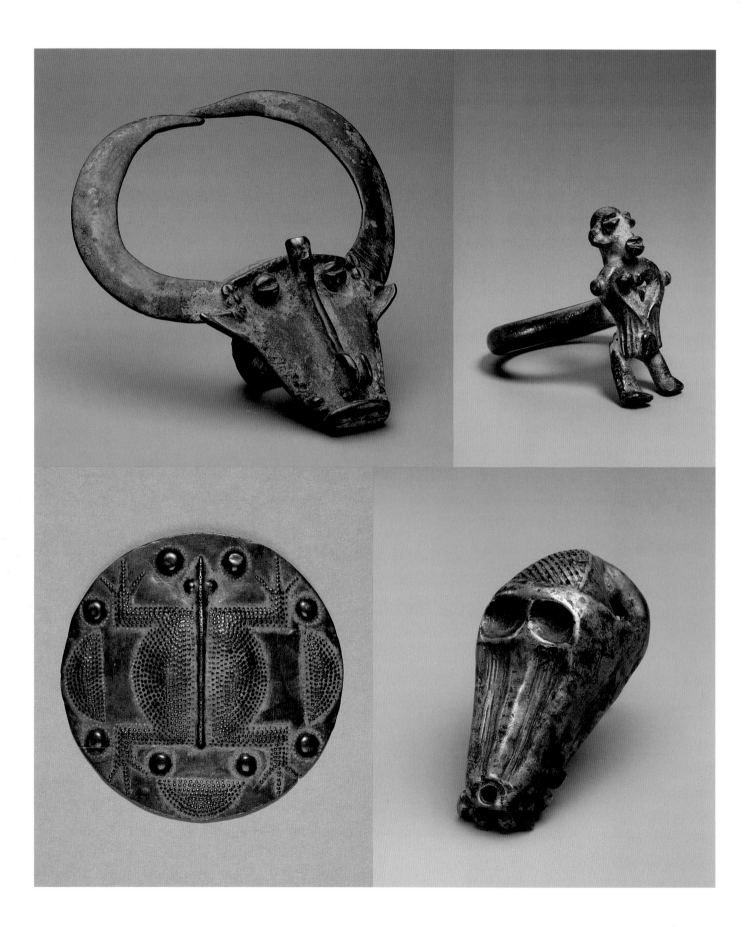

Opposite top left:

Ring from the Ivory Coast (Senufo). Bronze. Height 10.4 cm.

Called a nyi-kar-yi, or "ring of silence," because it is held between the teeth during funerals.

Opposite top right:

Man's finger ring from the Ivory Coast (Senufo). Bronze. Height 3.3 cm.

Opposite bottom left:

Ornamental plaque from the Ivory Coast (Baule). Brass. Diameter 8 cm.

Although plaques like this were usually attached to ceremonial chairs, it is included here because similar ornaments may have been sewn onto clothing. Its creativity and symbolism make it doubly intriguing.

Opposite bottom right:

Pendant from the Ivory Coast (Baule). Bronze. Height 7.9 cm.

This monkey skull is an exceptionally fine example of skillful bronzecasting.

Top:

Bracelets. Bronze. Height 7 cm. to 10.5 cm.

Far left, bottom, far right: Ivory Coast (Baule).

Top left: Cameroon (Kirdi).

Top right: Burkina Faso (Gurunsi).

Center: Djenne, Mali.

This group of ornaments, all cast by the lost-wax process, attests not only to the variety of bracelet types but to their fine workmanship.

Bottom:

Anklet from Liberia (Kru). Bronze. Height 25.5 cm., weight 8.5 kg.

Only chief's wives and wealthy women could afford anklets like these.

ABOVE:

Woman's anklets from Burkina Faso (Gurunsi). Bronze. Height 21 cm.

Anklets of this type commanded a high price—perhaps as much as several sheep or even a cow—because they were made from European metal that had to be brought in by caravan from the southwest coast of Africa.

OPPOSITE TOP LEFT:

Man's pendant from Burkina Faso (Lobi). Ivory. Height 19 cm.

P. Meyer points out in his book on the Lobi that this pendant's name, thungbubiel, literally means "elephant flute." This prized ornament is worn by high-ranking men.

OPPOSITE TOP RIGHT:

Ear ornaments from Burkina Faso (Lobi). Ivory. Width 6 cm. to 8 cm.

Only a few ear ornaments of this type are known to exist.

OPPOSITE BOTTOM:

Armlets from Burkina Faso (Gurunsi). Ivory. Width 27 cm. (left) and 24.8 cm. (right).

Also worn by Kasena women in Ghana, gungulu are a sign of wealth and believed to ward off evil spirits.

TOP:
Pendants. Bronze.

Top row: From Burkina Faso (Bobo). Width 12.5 cm. (left) and 7.2 cm. (right).

Middle row: From the Ivory Coast (Senufo). Width 6.2 cm. (left) and 8.3 cm. (right).

Bottom row, left and right: From Burkina Faso (Lobi). Width 10.5 cm. and 10 cm.

Bottom row, center: From the Ivory Coast (Baule). Width 5.3 cm.

BOTTOM:
Pendant from Burkina Faso (Lobi). Bronze. Width 10.5 cm.

This bateba (with added loop), was probably worn at the behest of a wathil, or protective supernatural being, to safeguard against sorcerers and other unseen dangers.

OPPOSITE TOP LEFT:
Pendant from Burkina Faso (Tusyan). Bronze. Height 7.1 cm.

A nyambele is worn to obtain the protection of ancestors. A specimen with four figures is rare.

OPPOSITE TOP RIGHT:
Bracelet from Burkina Faso (Bobo). Bronze. Width 13.5 cm.

According to Professor Bruyninckx, this object is believed to protect the wearer because it embodies the spirit of the animal represented at its center.

OPPOSITE BOTTOM:
Pendant from Burkina Faso (Lobi). Bronze. Width 13.5 cm.

Although the snake motif is commonly found in Lobi bronzework, this particular pendant, worn to protect the wearer, depicts a seldom seen double-headed variation on the theme.

OPPOSITE TOP LEFT:

Man's finger ring from Mali (Dogon). Bronze. Height 7.1 cm.

Ceremonial ring given by the Hogon (spiritual leader) to the military leader. The mounted warrior is probably an ancestor figure.

OPPOSITE TOP RIGHT:

Finger ring from Mali (Lere). Bronze. Height 6.3 cm.

This ancient ring shows a camel, seldom depicted in African art.

OPPOSITE BOTTOM:

Group of ancient body ornaments. Bronze.

Top left: Neck ring from Burkina Faso. Width 17.5 cm.

Top right: Anklet from Djenne, Mali. Height 11.5 cm.

Middle row, left to right: Bracelet from Cross River, Nigeria. Width 18.5 cm. Pair of bracelets from Cross River, Nigeria. Diameter 10 cm. Bracelet from Djenne, Mali. Width 12.4 cm. Armlet from Cross River, Nigeria. Length 22 cm.

Bottom row, left to right: Finger rings from Djenne, Mali. Height 9 cm. and 6.6 cm. Bracelet and necklace from Djenne, Mali. Diameter 12 cm. and length 36 cm.

TOP:

Group of finger rings. Bronze. Tallest 6 cm., widest 7.6 cm.

Center: Mali (Dogon). Clockwise from top: Ivory Coast (Senufo), Ghana (Akan), Ivory Coast (Senufo), Ghana (Ashanti), Burkina Faso (Bobo), Burkina Faso (Lobi).

In sub-Saharan Africa, bronze rings are generally worn by men to indicate rank.

BOTTOM:

Finger rings from Burkina Faso (Bobo). Bronze.

Diameters: 5.4 cm. to 8.9 cm. Top: Width 12 cm.

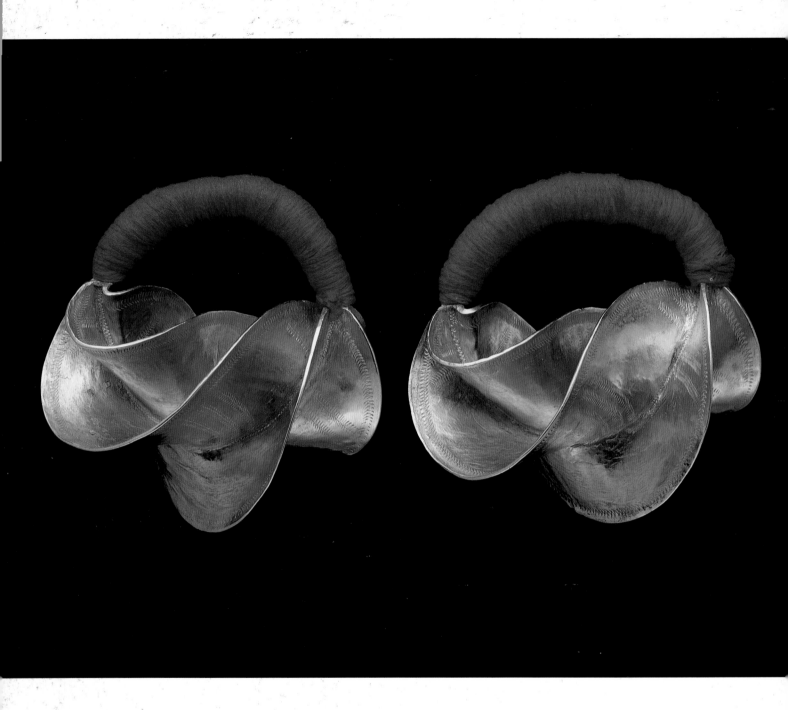

ABOVE:
Earrings from Mali (Peul). Gold.
Width 9 cm.

Prized kwoteneye kange *earrings,*
fashioned from twisted blades of
beaten sheet gold, have long been
traditional in the Sahel.

OPPOSITE:
Woman's necklace from Mali and
Senegal (Peul and Tukulor). Gold.
Length 41 cm.

The techniques exemplified by
this magnificent kuruwel *were*
introduced by Moroccan Jewish
goldsmiths.

TOP:

*Headdress ornaments. Silver, carnelian, shell, and other materials.
Far left: Mali (Tuareg). Height 8 cm.*

Second from left and top right: Bani Oasis, Morocco (Haratine). Height 29 cm. and 4.8 cm.

Ornaments like these are sometimes worn in nearby Mauritania.

Middle right: Nigeria (Fulani). Height 6 cm.

Center: Niger (Tuareg). Height 6.1 cm.

Bottom right: Algeria (Tuareg). Height 17.5 cm.

Headdresses are a focal point of adornment. Some are decorated with beads of amber or carnelian, which are believed to have beneficial properties; others, like the prized amerouan of the Tuareg people, are enhanced with glass beads or shells.

BOTTOM:

From Mali (Sarakole).

Top left: Bracelet. Silver. Diameter 7.3 cm.

All others: Finger rings. Silver. Diameter 2 cm. to 3 cm.

Some of this jewelry was probably influenced by European playing cards. Most are made with copper inlay.

From Mali (Dogon).

Center: Necklace. Iron and stone. Length 58 cm.

Top right: Finger ring. Iron. Height 7.6 cm.

Bottom right: Finger ring. Iron. Height 2 cm.

Bottom left: Bracelet. Iron and stone. Diameter 9.3 cm.

Top left: Bracelet from Burkina Faso (Lobi). Iron. Diameter 9.4 cm.

Ironwork was produced in sub-Saharan Africa before the advent of bronzecasting. The stones (douge) encased in the necklace, which is sacred to the Dogon, represent the bones of their first spiritual leader. The number and pattern of stones symbolize the structure of Dogon society.

BOTTOM:

Group of finger rings. Silver. Height 2 cm. to 5.6 cm.

Top row, left to right: Mali, Mali, Nigeria, Mali.

Middle row, left to right: Mali, Cameroon, Ethiopia, Niger.

Bottom row, left to right: Niger, Cameroon, Niger, Niger, Mali. Africa's silver finger rings are every bit as remarkable as their bronze counterparts, which are famous for their fabulous array of animal designs.

Silver rings in Islamic Africa are often massive and plain and feature abstract shapes because of religious proscriptions against figurative depictions.

TOP:

Necklace from Mali (Koutiala). Bronze. Length 35 cm.

Each of the tiny elements that make up this necklace was individually cast by the lost-wax method.

Center: Pendant from Mali (Dogon). Bronze. Height 6.6 cm.

The central stone of this pendant, believed to protect the wearer from lightning, is encased in bronze overlay—a technical tour de force.

BOTTOM:

Necklace from Léré, Mali. Quartz. Length 34 cm.

Trade between Africa and India flourished as far back as the dawn of the Christian era. Ships brought gold and ivory from Africa, agate and glass from the subcontinent.

OPPOSITE:

Bracelet and necklace from Mali (Dogon). Stone and terracotta.

Top: Diameter 14.2 cm.

Bottom: Length 26 cm.

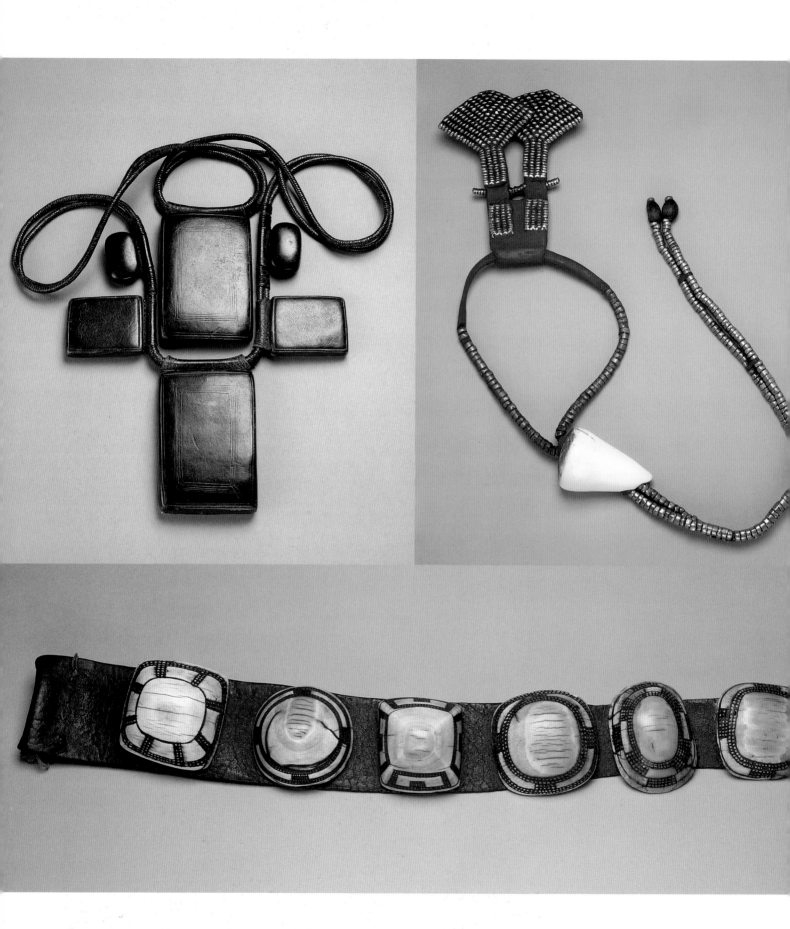

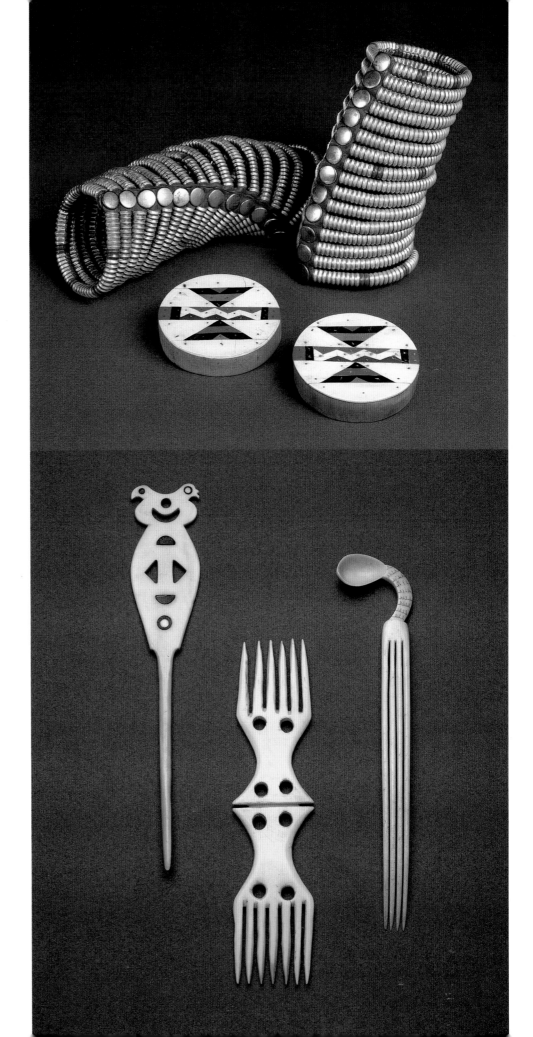

OPPOSITE TOP LEFT:

Necklace from Mali. (Tuareg). Leather. Total length 76.5 cm.; largest amulet holder 11 cm.

In Mali, wearing large ettouben *amulet boxes around the neck appears to be the prerogative of men. This type of ornament is also popular among sub-Saharan peoples such as the Malinke and the Peul, who have adopted Islam.*

OPPOSITE TOP RIGHT:

Woman's necklace from Namibia (Himba). Iron, shell, other materials. Total height 1 meter, counterweights 18 cm.

This necklace with twin dorsal counterweights is worn by married women; nothing comparable can be found in any other part of Africa. Himba women coat their bodies with a mixture of animal fat and ocher to protect themselves from the sun—a practice which imparts a characteristic look and odor to all of their jewelry.

OPPOSITE BOTTOM:

Belt pendant from Namibia (Cuanhama) and Angola. Leather and ivory. Length 59 cm.

On their wedding day, a husband presents his wife with one or more ornamental belt pendants depending on how much livestock he owns.

TOP:

From South Africa (Zulu).

Top: Bracelets. Aluminum, leather, and copper. Height 14.5 cm.

Bottom: Earrings. Wood and bakelite. Diameter 6.9 cm.

BOTTOM:

Hairpins from South Africa. Ivory. Longest 17.5 cm.

The Zulu intshegula *right, with its spoon-shaped extension for taking snuff, was usually made of bone.*

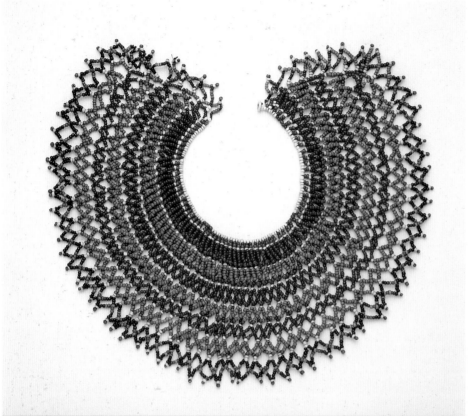

OPPOSITE TOP:

Necklaces from South Africa (Xhosa). Buttons and glass beads. Length 36.5 cm. (center) and 19 cm.

Most jewelry worn by the Bantu of South Africa takes the form of beadwork. Every color in these patterned bead tabs known as "love letters" (ubala abuyisse) has a particular meaning and conveys part of an encoded message. Human or animal figures are rarely depicted.

OPPOSITE BOTTOM LEFT:

From South Africa (Zulu).

Top: Pair of leggings. Glass beads. Width 25 cm.

Bottom: Apron. Glass beads. Width 28 cm.

These ornaments of imported European beads are noteworthy for their understated patterns and meticulous craftsmanship.

OPPOSITE BOTTOM RIGHT:

Pectoral from South Africa. Glass beads. Height 47 cm.

TOP:

Necklace from South Africa (Xhosa). Glass beads. Diameter when closed 36 cm.

This necklace, worn by married women, compares with ancient Egyptian counterparts though they come from opposite ends of the continent.

BOTTOM:

Man's necklace from South Africa (Zulu). Glass beads and bone. Diameter 19.5 cm.

This chief's necklace is a sign of the wearer's power and prestige. The carved bone elements imitate a lion's claws.

Enameled and coral-studded belt buckles, or headdresses fashioned from gold, pearls, and turquoise—the tinkling jewelry of the Near East—evokes the atmosphere of *Tales of the Arabian Nights*. There are times when profuse granulation and mounds of slender chains take body ornamentation to unimagined heights of baroque extravagance.

Further east, the Turkoman groups of central Asia prize blood-red carnelians and set the semiprecious stones into their magnificent jewelry. (Carnelian is believed to protect against miscarriage and prevent horses from misstepping.) A Turkoman woman on her wedding day—the day she presents herself to the world in all her glory—may be weighed down with as much as seventeen kilograms of silver and gold. Her lavish ensemble remains in place for an entire year, until the birth of her first child. She then gradually lightens her complement of everyday jewelry but continues to display objects of value on festive occasions. Once past childbearing age, she removes silver ornaments.

These pastoral peoples, constantly on the move with their herds of camels and sheep, define wealth primarily in terms of jewelry because it is portable and can readily be converted into currency. For spiritual reasons, a pectoral can be turned into an amulet by slipping inside it a verse from the Koran.

Local variations in adornment persist among Turkoman groups. Tekke boys wear pendants in the shape of a bow with an arrow at the ready to symbolize the fighting spirit and hunting prowess expected of the wearer. Sharp, spearlike forms are believed to help keep evil forces at bay. The Ersari festoon their distinctive embroidered caps with flat, thin silver plaques, while a ram's horn motif graces the rectangular plaque hanging down the young men's backs. A number of tribes, including the Yomud, are partial to earrings with stylized animal designs, bracelets notched with teeth-like "snake's heads," flexible neck circlets hung from wide engraved plaques, and heart-shaped ornaments designed to keep long braids hanging straight down the back. As if this array of jewelry were not enough, women also spangle their cloaks with embossed silver disks, shoulder ornaments, and clasps. The menfolk wear little jewelry, but they do sport wrought belts and daggers and see to it that their horses are decked out as lavishly as their women.

INDIA
A PASSION FOR SELF-ADORNMENT

Perhaps no land on earth clings as stubbornly to time-honored ways as India. The wife of a New Delhi shopkeeper might be seen wearing the same kind of jewelry depicted on a statuette from Mohenjo-Daro, where the Indus Valley civilization flourished two thousand years before Christ. Unbroken threads reach from the body ornaments shown in the Ajanta cave paintings and Khajuraho relief carvings to the women of modern Rajasthan. There is little difference between the belts hugging the waists of the divinities at Sanchi and those worn by female dancers in modern-day India.

From Tamil Nadu, India.

Top: Bracelet. Silver and colored glass. Width 10.3 cm.

Bottom: Belt. Silver and colored glass. Total length 41 cm.

The makara *heads on both the bracelet and the female dancer's belt symbolize intellect and intuition. Everything in India is laden with meaning, symbolism, and religious overtones.*

The importance of jewelry in Indian culture has underpinnings in religious literature. The Rig Veda describes jewels as having divine attributes. Moreover, precious stones are revered by the gods themselves: Vishnu worships sapphires; Indra, rubies; and Agni, diamonds. Until diamonds were discovered in Brazil in 1732, the gem that fueled strife between kings and emperors came from nowhere but India.

Because cremation is traditional on the Indian subcontinent, few pieces of ancient jewelry survive. Yet, the old forms endure, even when the materials and techniques have gone into decline. The variety of body ornaments in India is astonishing, and the people's delight in decorative combinations is unending. Jewelry transforms its women into goddesses, sets off their graceful movements, and continually underscores their link to nature with a host of religious and mythological connotations. A woman's personal jewelry is the only property she may legally possess; she carries it wherever she goes.

In India, life is leavened with sensuality in ultra-sophisticated ways. A Moghul comb redolent of musk mingles the allure of jewelry and cosmetics. A sandalwood necklace suffuses the wearer with fragrance. To promote fertility, women carry a silver box containing the cosmic egg, a smooth, ovoid, rock crystal lingam that symbolizes Shiva's virile power. Anklets and toe-rings, while calculated to attract the male eye, are worn as part of everyday attire and confer a regal bearing on even the humblest women, who can afford nothing but glass and white-metal ornaments. Jewelry transfigures the landscape of daily life.

Indian jewelry frequently turns to nature for inspiration. Many designs derive from flowers, seeds, and fruit, which can be strung and worn as such or copied in metal. Symbol of the Sun and the river Ganges, gold has purported prophylactic properties and is conducive to physical well-being. Silver, associated with the Moon and the river Jamna, is worked north, south, east, and west; each region adapts age-old forms to suit its particular tastes.

Indians everywhere wear torcs, the ubiquitous neck rings that reach back to prehistoric times and appear among peoples as far-flung as the Scythians, Vikings, Gauls, Chinese, and Greeks. Tubular, flat, smooth, twisted, engraved, embellished with semi-precious stones—there seem to be as many variations on the theme as there are localities. The neck rings worn by the Swat people hint at Greek influences dating back to the invasion of Alexander the Great. The women of Kutch coil single pieces of silver wire into heavy, bulky torcs that are their pride and joy.

In addition to large sculptural ornaments, Indian craftsmen contrive ultra-delicate precious metalwork designed both to set off gemstones and bring out their astrological and prophylactic properties. The nine planets of the Indian system are represented by precious stones: the Sun by a ruby (often at the center of the jewel), Venus by a diamond, Saturn by a sapphire, Ketu by a cat's-eye, Mars by coral, Mercury by an emerald, the Moon by a pearl, Rahu by a hyacinth, and Jupiter by a topaz. Wearing all nine stones in a single setting is thought to provide universal protection.[18]

Diamonds are considered poisonous, but other precious stones are ingested for medicinal purposes. A potion made with pearl powder, honey, and spices is still considered an effective tonic and remains in great demand as an aphrodisiac. Gold and silver leaf are added to food not only for decorative purposes but because of their supposed restorative properties.

The great Moghuls took ornamentation to unparalleled heights of refinement and exemplified the saying that the glory of a prince is made tangible by his buildings, his library, and his jewels. No fewer than three custodians tended the emperor Akbar's jewelry; his successor, Jahangir, kept his treasure in six forts.

The Moghuls helped popularize enameling, a craft technique that not only enhanced the play of light across gemstones but also saved on gold, a commodity always in short supply in India. The enamelers came from Punjab under a mandate to produce nothing but masterpieces. They graced their gorgeous bracelets and necklaces with enchanting combinations of colors, with names like pigeon's blood, parrot-feather green, mimosa-flower yellow, and deep peacock-neck blue.

The decorative styles of India run the gamut from baroque extravagance to abstract severity, and its techniques include forging and repoussé work, cutting and polishing of hard stones, granulation and filigree.

The Naga hill peoples of Assam reveal India at its most primitive: former head-hunters of Mongol descent who have been documented as far back as Ptolemy's time. For them, body adornment is a conspicuous indicator of social status and is so tightly interwoven with self-identification that some jewelry may not be removed until its owner has died. The right to wear certain ornaments is subject to rigid constraints and taboos. A Sema warrior may not wear the tusks of a boar he himself has killed. Only Sema who are headhunters may wear boar's-tusk necklaces. Hornbill feathers in an animal-fur headband identify warriors. Angami men may not wear hornbill feathers between millet-sowing time and the rice harvest. A Lhota man must purchase his ivory armlet through a go-between so that any evil in it will befall him, not the purchaser.[19]

And the list goes on: only certain Ao clans are entitled to wear bracelets cut from elephant tusk. For Konyak warriors, monkey skulls suspended from the neck have the same value as the number of human heads taken. They also make brass neck rings edged with round, head-shaped protrusions believed to represent shrunken-head trophies. The number of coveted hornbill feathers on a headdress gives a concise rundown of the wearer's deeds. The desirability of this ornament encourages competitiveness both in hunting and at celebrations that transform animal carcasses and barrels of rice beer into status-enhancing items. The V-pattern (probably symbolic of cattle horns) that the men engrave on their shell ear ornaments is similar to the tattoo markings on warriors' chests.

All of these decapitated heads, tiger's teeth, hornbill beaks, and spiked arm ornaments have an unmistakable aura of manliness. The women wear necklaces strung with variously mounted beads and mass their seed-bead necklaces in a way that sends supply twisting strands of red, green, yellow, and blue cascading down their necks. Some of their ample, multi-strand necklaces use rod-shaped spacers of bone, ivory, or horn—curiously, they bring to mind ancient Egyptian neck ornaments—while the clasps are fashioned from sections of conch shell from the Bay of Bengal. Carnelian, once a form of currency, is still in demand and combined with glass, rock crystal, brass, and ivory beads to create bold, kaleidoscopic compositions.

FROM THE ROOF OF THE WORLD

The peoples of the Himalayas—the snow-capped domain embracing Tibet, Nepal, Ladakh, and Bhutan—wear copious amounts of jewelry over their clothing. The itinerant Newari smiths of Nepal made repoussé, chased, and engraved metal jewelry for centuries, fostering cultural interaction with China and Mongolia as they trekked from village to village and tribe to tribe.

The luminous turquoise that graces so many pieces of Himalayan jewelry is considered a living stone; it shares the ultimate fate of the mortals that wear it. Because of its color—symbolizing water, the sky, and air—it is thought to counteract evil forces and make the wearer brave and invulnerable. Seeing it in a dream is believed to bring good luck.

The weighty headdresses favored by women in Ladakh—red fabric stretched across an oblong felt frame and studded with pieces of turquoise—are supposed to represent an erect, swollen-hooded cobra. They are braided into the wearer's hair and complemented by astrakhan ear flaps tacked to the hair. The bits of turquoise laid into the mosaic girandoles that Lhasa women wear are carefully matched for color.

Turquoise is also liberally used in the making of gold, silver, or copper amulet boxes, which can be round, square, oval or mandala-shaped. These charm cases contain spells or prayers designed to appease evil spirits, and their symbolic decoration is believed to strengthen the power of their sacred contents.

Coral, another prized substance, was thought to bring women strength and good luck and have a favorable effect on menstruation. The most desirable variety, Italian coral, was a scarce commodity worn only by members of the wealthiest class. Marco Polo noted that Tibetans ranked coral among precious stones and used it to adorn the necks of their women and idols. According to Buddhist belief, blue represents air and red represents light; jewelry that combines the blue of the sky and the glowing red of fire effects a fusion of natural energies.

Amber, an earth symbol, protects against jaundice and cures those afflicted with it. The most coveted amber came from an extinct species of conifer that flourished on the shores of the Baltic Sea during the Eocene period. Prized for its distinctive golden color, it was imported into the Himalayan region by way of Russia and Turkestan. If Baltic amber was unavailable, less desirable redder varieties were used.

The beads known as *dZi*, a prized and celebrated component of Himalayan necklaces, are believed to be of supernatural origin. According to one legend, these brown or black agate beads once adorned the gods, who discarded any that were found to have a defect. Other legends have it that they are petrified insects or the droppings of a mythical bird that feeds only on precious stones.

Jewelry from this part of the world has a rugged quality. Like its wearers, some of whom are nomadic, it must not only withstand the rigors of an itinerant life, but contend with the many forces that are lurking in the mountains and which talismans are expected to keep at bay.

The tribal peoples that came from southwestern China and settled in northern Thailand, Burma, and Laos scratch out an uncertain living but have developed rich and varied craft traditions, including jewelry and textiles. The women are often loaded down with massive amounts of silver ornaments. Everything—a pig, a horse, an opium crop, brideprice—is measured in terms of silver. Consequently, jewelry is considered a readily negotiable currency.[20]

Highland tribes have developed a keen feeling for purity of form, and its most familiar expression is the torc. Here, neck rings with clean, unbroken lines sound the dominant theme. A few days after the birth of a child, at the naming ceremony, the infant is given a torc which must be worn at all times because it keeps in the wearer's soul and protects against sickness. It also signifies that the child has entered the human world. If he or she should die before this ceremony can be performed, there will be no funeral, because the child still belongs to the spirit world. The original neck ring is often melted down so that the growing child can be fitted with a bigger one.

The Hmong or Meo hill people are partial to multi-tiered tubular neck rings and often attach lock-shaped pendants symbolically to prevent the soul from escaping. The Akha prefer flawlessly smooth, flat neck rings. The Lisu spangle their clothing with silver buttons and dangles.

The repertory of bracelets among highland groups is equally sophisticated. Here, too, forms and techniques can vary considerably and include specimens that are enameled, solid, hollow, wrought, and embellished with twisted or spiraled wire. In addition to this impressive array of silver, women wear a slender brass bracelet on the wrist at all times to help them keep their souls inside their bodies.

Although exposed to successive incursions reaching back to the Dongson period (Bronze Age) and continuing with India, China, and eventually the influence of Islamic religion, Indonesia has managed to preserve its rich and varied local cultures. Its spices lured merchants from all over mainland Asia. As traders from the subcontinent shuttled between the Far East and the Mediterranean, Java and Bali became Indianized. The Buddhist temple of Borobudur in Java shows people and trees alike bedecked with beads and gems, exuding sensuality.

Between the eighth and sixteenth centuries, local goldsmiths expanded their range to include finely detailed ear ornaments as well as rings that featured chased designs and cabochon-cut garnets, carnelians, amethysts, rock crystal, lapis lazuli, moonstones, sapphires, and emeralds.

The beads circulated by Indian and Muslim merchants were in such demand that as recently as the early twentieth century a slave could still be traded for a single multicolored bead. On the island of Borneo, Roman-period beads were worn on the wrist, or a symbolic design was tattooed on the wrist to prevent loss and thereby keep the soul from leaving the body.

Deft weavers and embroiderers, the peoples of Indonesia routinely enhance their textiles with beadwork to attract protective spirits and maintain harmony between humankind and the cosmos. A person can be transformed and made powerful by what he or she wears. Warriors on Sulawesi (formerly Celebes) crowned their headdresses with a daunting coiled ornament of polished bronze whose very gleam was thought to deflect the weapons of their enemies.

Indonesian women wear bulky, double spiral earrings, called *padung-padung*, that weigh more than two kilograms and need to be secured to their headdresses. These earrings, wrought from slender silver ingots and worn asymetrically, are brought out for major rites of passage and worn during sowing and harvest festivities.

Jewelry also figures in the elaborate system of exchange between so-called wife-givers and wife-takers. Wife-givers do not surrender their daughters and sisters to their duly appointed wife-takers without sending along an array of gifts ranging from textiles to raw or cooked food and blessings guaranteeing fertility. To balance out the marriage bargain, the wife-takers reciprocate with gold, jewelry, livestock, weapons, and the promise of physical protection.[21]

Jewelry designs inspired by houses, boats, and other man-made structures are a particular feature in Indonesia. On Timor old European coins were melted down and recast as bracelets with realistically detailed miniature houses. Replicas of boats adorn pendants worn by chiefs from Flores. In a curious turnabout, representations of neck rings are found adorning houses on Nias, and the objects called *mamuli*, which enhance contact with the spirit world but are also given as gifts, appear depicted on funerary stone slabs on Sumba.

The Chinese brought gold, silver, jade, and other goods to the Philippines. Glass beads, by far the most popular trade item among the natives, continued to arrive from Venice and Bohemia by way of the Spaniards. As itinerant craftsmen roamed the islands introducing beadwork, men took to wearing beads in ritual ornaments as indications of their status as warriors and headhunters. At certain wedding ceremonies, the groom's mother still drops two beads into a cup from which newlyweds drink so that they may remain together always.[22]

As one might expect in a region dotted with thousands of islands, sea shells of all kinds figure prominently in jewelry. On Mindanao, the Bagobo people believe that closed circles form an impenetrable barrier protects them from baleful influences and that no harm can come to them so long as they are wearing bracelets cut from shells. Mother-of-pearl adorns the headgear of unmarried men in northern Luzon as well as the belts or woven rattan chest ornaments that once were the prerogative of headhunters. One raw material can also masquerade as another: the crocodile teeth that headhunters suspended from their ceremonial necklaces might actually have been pieces of shell carved to look like the real thing.

Most forms of jewelry made few inroads into Japan. Even there, however, women of every station—ladies of the Imperial household, courtesans, average Japanese—traditionally placed metal or lacquered wood pins in their hair. Combs did more than just keep hairstyles from coming undone. In the seventeenth century, wood, tortoiseshell, or ivory combs became decorative and symbolic components of intricately twisted and knotted arrangements of hair held in place by an aloe-based paste. They were thought to protect brides and were worn for luck; to lose one was considered a bad omen. Such was the power invested in combs that a women wanting a divorce signaled her intention by throwing a comb at her husband's feet.

Bridal necklace from Yemen. Gilded silver. Length 34.5 cm.

Like their counterparts in many other cultures, Bedouin women receive a gift of jewelry from their family when they marry. Their wedding dowry remains their exclusive property.

OPPOSITE TOP:

Woman's necklace from Yemen. Silver and coral. Length 42 cm.

The distinctive jewelry style that developed in this relatively isolated part of the world influenced body adornment in nearby areas, including the Horn of Africa.

OPPOSITE BOTTOM:

Necklace from Yemen. Silver. Length 40.5 cm.

Amulet cases, like the three *herz* attached to this bridal necklace, usually contain verses from the Koran. Slender chains, filigree, and granulation are common denominators of jewelry in the Arabian peninsula, most of which was produced by Jewish smiths.

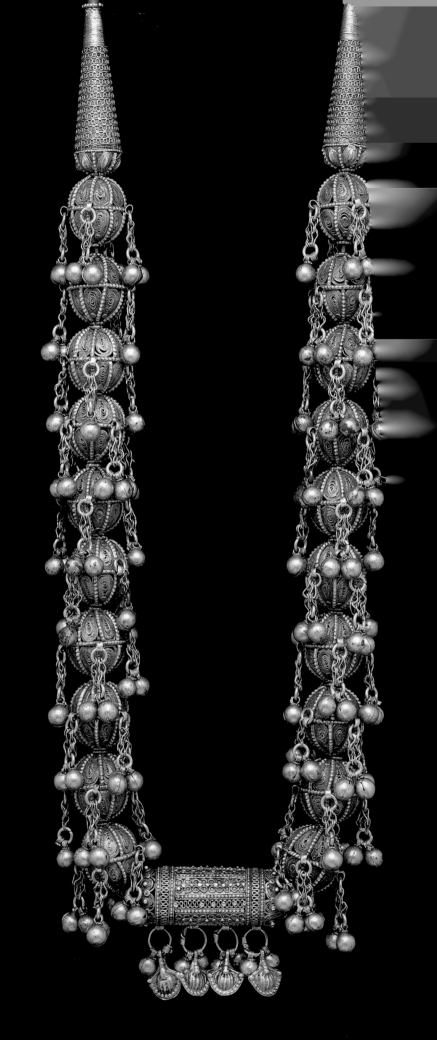

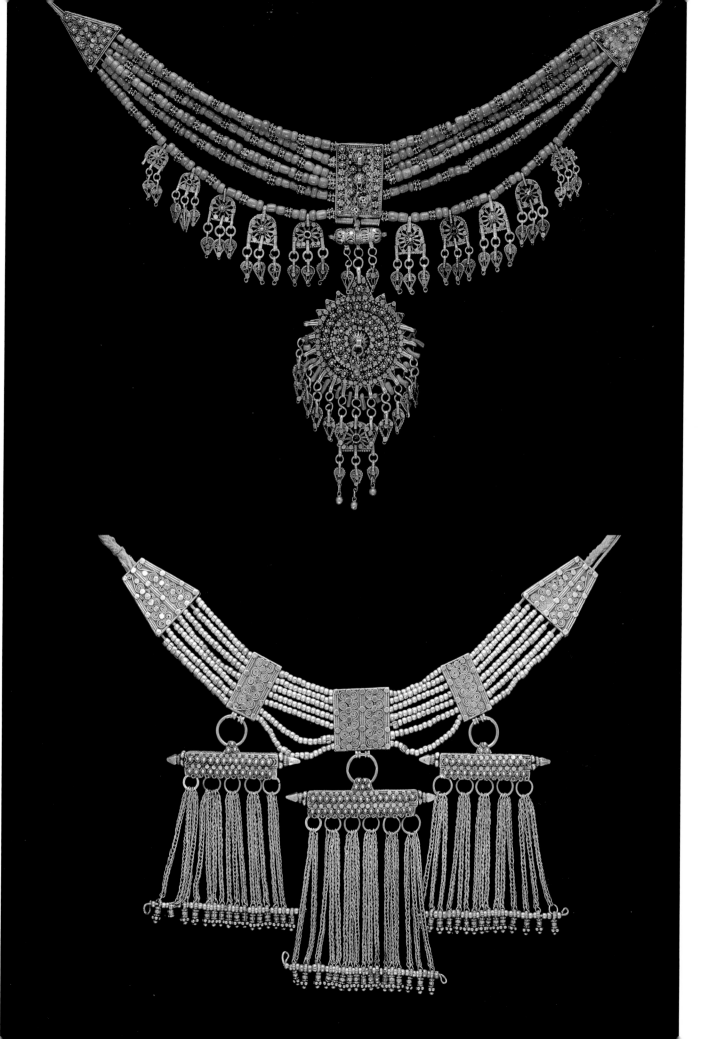

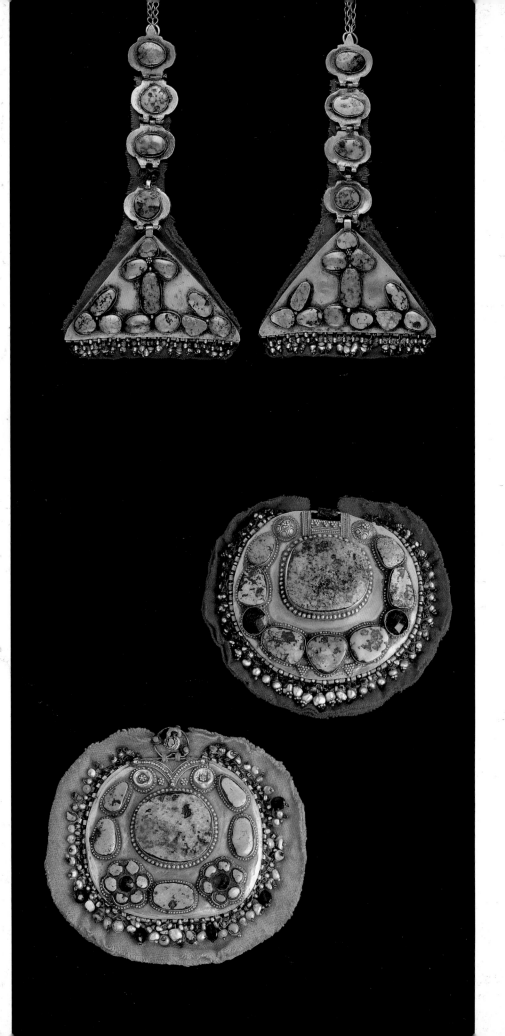

TOP:

Woman's headdress pendants from the Najd, Saudi Arabia (Bedouin). Gold, turquoise, and pearls. Height 16 cm.

Although the finest turquoise comes from Iran, the mineral can be found around Medina. Both of these ila-gah pendants are sewn onto red cloth backing and, when worn with a kaffa *(see bottom), make for a splendid decorative ensemble.*

BOTTOM:

Woman's forehead ornament from the Najd, Saudi Arabia (Bedouin). Gold, turquoise, pearls, and glass stones on cloth. Width 11.5 cm.

This kaffa *is fringed with pearls from the Persian Gulf.*

OPPOSITE LEFT:

Necklace from the Najd, Saudi Arabia (Bedouin). Gold, coral, and turquoise. Length 34 cm.

Red coral is very popular among the Bedouin because it symbolizes life. The biconical gold beads are remarkable both for their shape, probably derived from a very ancient prototype, and their exceptionally delicate granulation.

OPPOSITE RIGHT:

Women's necklaces from Yemen. Silver and coral. Length 28 cm. to 42 cm.

Yemeni necklaces often consist of several strands of silver and/or coral beads and usually include triangular or teardrop terminal spacers.

OPPOSITE TOP:

Woman's necklace from the Najd, Saudi Arabia (Bedouin). Gold and turquoise. Length 20 cm.

Because the Najd (literally, "high plateau") was inaccessible for centuries, local goldsmiths, influenced by ancient models, developed a distinctive style, as this necklace attests.

OPPOSITE BOTTOM:

Earrings from the Najd, Saudi Arabia (Bedouin). Gold, turquoise, and pearls.

Top: Width 6.7 cm.

Bottom: Height 4 cm.

ABOVE:

Amulet cases from Iran. Silver and turquoise (top), iron with gold inlay (bottom). Widest (without cords) 7.2 cm.

Worn above the elbow, these bazuband *contain a miniature Koran or selected holy verses associated with protection.*

Headdress and necklace from Oman (Bedouin). Silver and leather. Height 26 cm. (top) and width 45 cm. (bottom).

Slender pieces of braided leather festooned with silver elements make this headdress look like a wig. It is unusual to find one with its matching necklace.

BOTTOM:

Bracelets from Oman (two pairs at left), Saudi Arabia (top, bottom) and Yemen (top right). Silver. Largest diameter 8.3 cm.

This group hints at the wide variety of bracelets worn on the Arabian Peninsula.

LEFT:
Woman's necklace and earrings from Oman. Silver, gold leaf, and glass beads. Length 42 cm.

The two herz *(amulet boxes) attached to this necklace have an overlay of gold leaf applied by hammering, a common practice in Oman. As can be seen here, women sometimes suspend earrings from their necklaces.*

BOTTOM:
Necklace and earrings from Oman. Silver. Length 47.5 cm. (top) and height 17.3 cm. (bottom).

Maria Theresa dollars (thalers) were the most widely used form of barter currency between East and West Africa during the nineteenth century because of the high silver content. The necklace is the most important type of Omani necklace and is often worn with earrings (halaq).

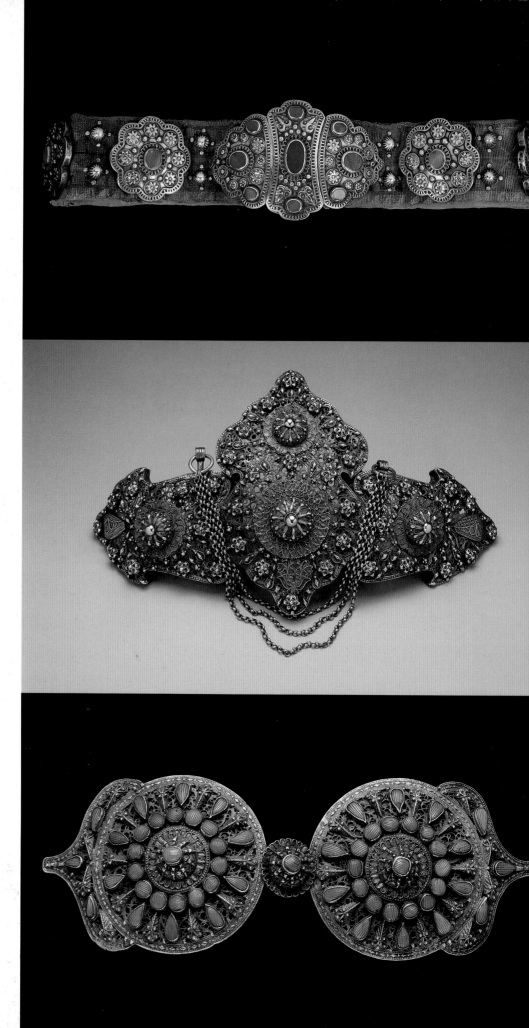

TOP:

Belt from Central Asia (Yomud Turkoman). Partly fire-gilded silver, carnelian, other materials. Total length 97 cm.

Except for an amulet or finger ring, this belt, with its large buckle and eight medallions, is one of the few pieces of jewelry a Yomud man might wear.

MIDDLE:

Belt buckle from Turkey. Late eighteenth century. Silver and enamel. Width 31.5 cm.

This type of silver buckle, with enameled domes and filigree, was worn in regions that were once part of the Ottoman Empire.

BOTTOM:

Belt buckle from Saphrampolis, Turkey. Nineteenth century. Gilded silver, coral, and enamel. Width 30 cm.

Although this type of belt buckle was common throughout the Balkans during the Ottoman period, it was valuable because of the materials and labor invested in it. Saphrampolis was one of Asia Minor's two jewelry-making centers.

OPPOSITE:

Woman's temple pendants from Central Asia (Yomud Turkoman). Partly fire-gilded silver and carnelian. Height 53 cm.

Turkoman women attached the adamlyk to each side of their headdresses to frame the face. The ornaments were displayed, however, only for special ceremonies.

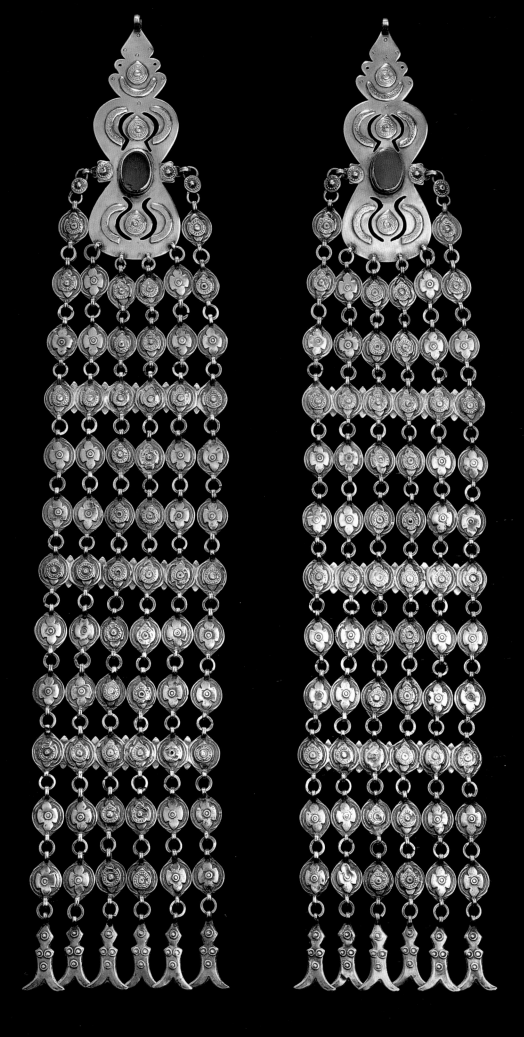

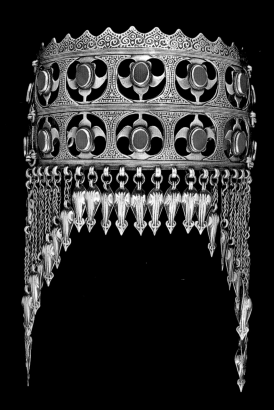

OPPOSITE TOP LEFT:

Diadem from Central Asia (Yomud Turkoman). Partly fire-gilded silver and carnelian. Height 29.5 cm.

This very rare example of a married woman's headdress is crowned with a distinctive feature: stylized bird heads. This diadem and the one to the right come from the same chieftain's family.

OPPOSITE TOP RIGHT:

Woman's diadem from Central Asia (Yomud Turkoman). Partly fire-gilded silver and carnelian. Height 21 cm.

OPPOSITE BOTTOM LEFT

Necklace (or diadem?) from Central Asia (Yomud Turkoman). Partly fire-gilded silver and carnelian. Total height 26 cm.

This may be a necklace (bukov), but the large central element, with its stylized double-headed bird motif, and its crown-like appearance suggest that it is a head ornament.

OPPOSITE BOTTOM RIGHT:

Breast ornament from Central Asia (Yomud Turkoman). Partly fire-gilded silver and carnelian. Total height 68.5 cm.

The stylized bird heads suggest that this breast ornament is probably an amulet.

ABOVE:

Women's bracelets from Central Asia (Turkoman). Partly fire-gilded silver and carnelian (except as noted below). Widest 9.8 cm.

Outer loop, clockwise from top right: Tekke, Yomud, Yomud, Tekke, Olam (silver), Yomud, Tekke, Olam (silver), Goklan(?), Tekke. Inner loop, clockwise from top right: Ersari (silver), Yomud, Goklan(?), and Olam (silver).

While bilezik usually consist of two to four bands, some have as many as five to eight. Single-band bracelets of this type are very rare.

123

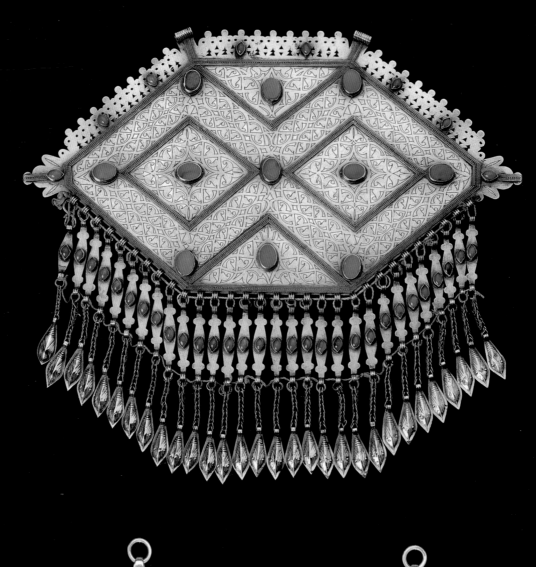

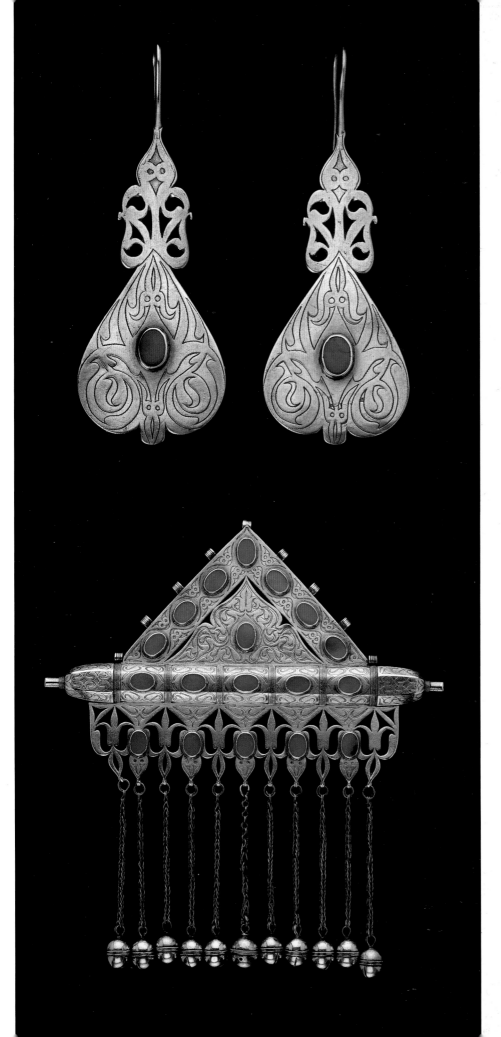

OPPOSITE TOP:

Breast ornament from Central Asia (Tekke Turkoman). Partly fire-gilded silver and carnelian. Width 36.5 cm.

This massive Tekke gonzuk, *or breast ornament, is but one component of a Turkoman woman's set of bridal jewelry, which can weigh between five and eight kilograms.*

OPPOSITE BOTTOM:

Pair of pendants from Central Asia (Yomud Turkoman). Partly fire-gilded silver and carnelian. Total height 34 cm., diameter 17.5 cm.

The exceptionally large size and ornate decoration of these pendants suggest that they belonged to someone of high status.

TOP:

Woman's earrings from Central Asia (Tekke Turkoman). Partly fire-gilded silver and carnelian. Height 13 cm.

This flawlessly shaped pair of tenecir *are examples of the earrings of Turkoman women, who mostly wear temple pendants attached with hooks to each side of their headdress.*

BOTTOM:

Amulet case from Central Asia (Tekke Turkoman). Partial fire-gilded silver and carnelian. Height 25.7 cm.

Amulet cases, tumar, *contain verses from the Koran. Turkoman women prize them above all other jewelry because of their supposed powers of protection. Some go so far as to wear one about their waists to ease the pain of childbirth.*

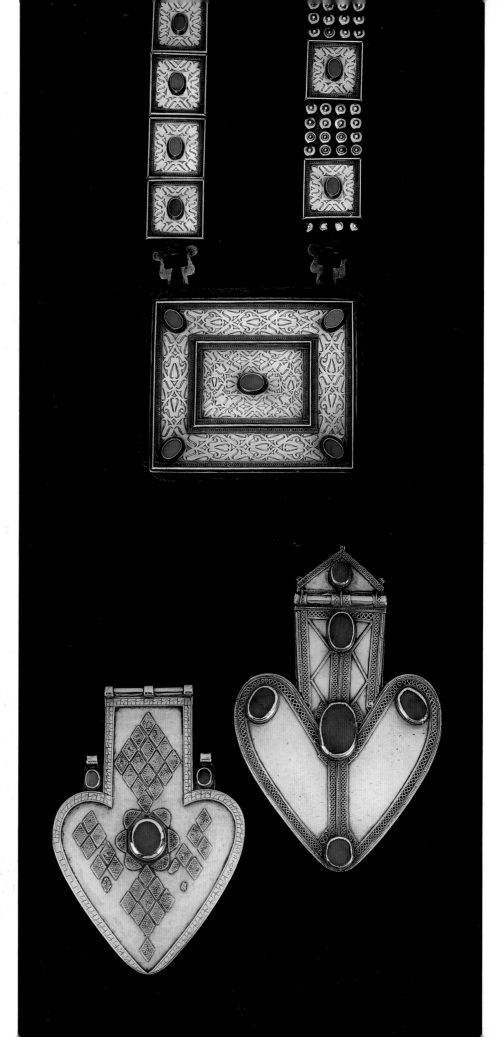

TOP:

Amulet pouch from Central Asia (Tekke Turkoman). Leather, partly fire-gilded silver, and carnelian. Total length 67 cm.

A cheikel, which older Tekke women sling across the shoulder, might contain a miniature Koran or sura (part of the Koran) as well as small personal possessions.

BOTTOM:

Right: Dorsal pendant from Central Asia (Saryk Turkoman). Silver and carnelian. Height 25 cm.

Left: Dorsal pendant from Iran (Yomud). Partly fire-gilded silver. Height 21.6 cm.

The gilding on the asyk from Iran is typical of Yomud jewelry. The Saryk never gild their ornaments.

OPPOSITE TOP:

Headdress tiara from Central Asia (Tekke Turkoman). Partly fire-gilded silver, carnelian, and other materials. Total length 43 cm.

Married Tekke women used to wear an imposing headdress tiara (egme) like this one until the birth of their first child and gradually reduced their jewelry as they got older. Once past childbearing age, they wore no silver ornaments at all. This egme, complete with original cloth backing, is a rare find.

OPPOSITE BOTTOM:

Woman's skullcap from Central Asia (Ersari Turkoman). Silver. Diameter 18.3 cm.

The same type of decorative elements are applied to Turkoman horse trappings. The attention that the horsemen of the steppes lavish on their mounts has been known to make women jealous.

126

THIS PAGE:

Temple pendants from Uzbekistan, Central Asia. Partly fire-gilded silver, turquoise, coral, and other materials. Height 36 cm.

These sumptuous temple pendants conjure up the world of the Arabian Nights *and hint at the opulence of the wearer's full set of jewelry.*

OPPOSITE TOP LEFT:

Woman's earrings from Bukhara, Central Asia. Gold, seed pearls, semiprecious stones. Longest 13 cm.

Oases in the khanate of Bukhara served as rest stops along the caravan routes that once crisscrossed Central Asia. Trading activity turned the region into a prosperous cultural center from the sixteenth to the early twentieth century. Local craftsmen, renowned for their textiles, also produced splendid jewelry.

OPPOSITE TOP RIGHT:

Man's belt buckles from Uzbekistan, Central Asia. Iron with gold inlay. Widest 10 cm.

Inlaid gold highlights in no way detract from the rugged boldness of these iron buckles. Decorative belts are worn by Uzbek men and women alike. Although floral and animal motifs predominate, strikingly arranged calligraphic inscriptions adorn many pieces of Islamic jewelry.

OPPOSITE BOTTOM:

Belt from Bukhara, Uzbekistan. Silver, gilded silver, and other materials. Total length 97 cm., buckle length 18 cm.

When Uzbek men wear several cloaks (chapans), the innermost one is belted with a kamar. Wars and revolutions have claimed many ornaments from the past, but surviving pieces suggest the wealth and luxury of cities like Bukhara and Samarkand.

TOP:
Pair of pendants from Uzbekistan, Central Asia. Gilded silver, turquoise, other materials. Height 4.6 cm.

Uzbek women hung pendants like these in their hair.

BOTTOM:
From Bukhara, Uzbekistan. Gold semiprecious stones, and baroque pearls.

Top: Forehead ornament. Height 6 cm.

Bottom: Necklace. Length 23.5 cm.

This Uzbek necklace is reminiscent of the Moghul jewelry of India.

OPPOSITE TOP LEFT:
Bracelets from Kazakstan, Central Asia. Silver. Maximum height 5.4 cm.

This group of bilezik *(bracelets) from various regions hint at a wide range of techniques that include casting, stamping, and granulation.*

OPPOSITE TOP RIGHT:
Earrings from Kazakstan, Central Asia. Partly fire-gilded silver. Height 30 cm.

OPPOSITE BOTTOM LEFT:
Chest ornament from Central Asia (Kazak). Partly fire-gilded silver. Height 50 cm.

Like the Turkoman, Kazaks marry off their daughters when they are between the ages of twelve and fifteen and bedeck them with a heavy array of ornate wedding jewelry.

OPPOSITE BOTTOM RIGHT:
Finger rings from Central Asia (Kazak). Silver and gilded silver. Height 3.4 to 9.3 cm.

The largest of these Kazak finger rings is a kudagi zhuzik, *which the bride's mother presented to the matchmaker; the double ring on the back symbolized the marriage.*

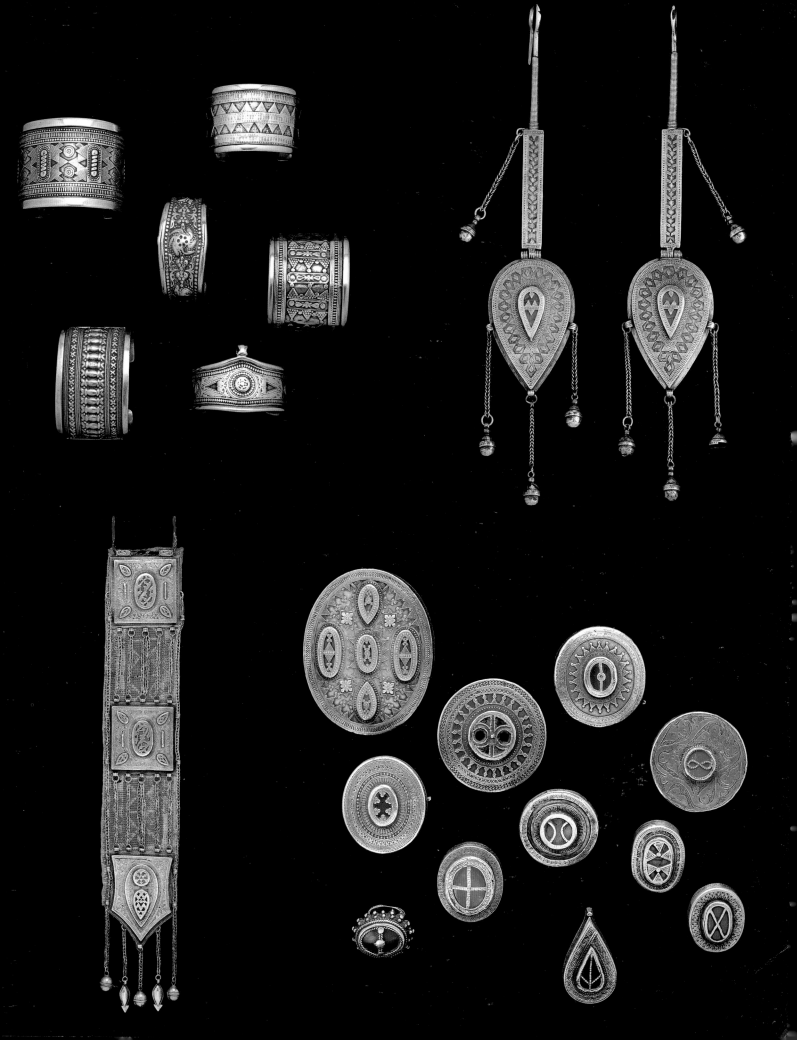

OPPOSITE TOP:

Bracelets from Dagestan, Russia. Silver and glass stones. Width 7.4 cm.

Aside from the medieval-looking cabochons, these women's bracelets are not unlike those worn in the vicinity of Aktyubinsk (western Kazakstan).

OPPOSITE BOTTOM:

Belt buckles from the Caucasus. Silver with niello decoration.

Top: Man's buckle. Width 22 cm.

Bottom: Woman's buckle. Width 28.5 cm.

Delicate curvilinear designs and flawless niello work are the hallmarks of silver ornaments from the Caucasus.

THIS PAGE:

Woman's pendant from Dagestan, Russia. Silver with niello decoration, and other materials. Length 30 cm.

Many indigenous peoples incorporate coins into their jewelry not only because of their intrinsic value, but for their decorative effect.

TOP:

Bracelets from India. Silver. Maximum height 14.4 cm.

Left to right: Karnataka, Orissa(?), Assam, Maharashtra, Gujarat, Madhya Pradesh.

This selection from various provinces suggests the wide range of bracelet shapes and sizes found in India, where there are more combinations of forms and materials than anywhere else on earth.

MIDDLE:

Neck rings from India and Pakistan (left) and Swat, Pakistan (middle and right). Silver. Largest 17 cm.

Although Indian and Pakistani tribal jewelry dates from the eighteenth century or later, it echoes a more distant past. The neck ring from Swat (right) shows the Greek influence that has been strong in the region since the invasion of Alexander the Great.

BOTTOM:

Woman's bracelets from Pakistan and India. Silver. Width 15 cm.

The aggressive appearance of these massive, but hollow gokhru clearly indicates that they were designed to protect the wearer from harm.

OPPOSITE TOP:

Neck ring from Kutch, Gujarat, India (Rabari). Silver. Width 20 cm.

Unmarried Indian women begin to amass their dowry jewelry when they are still children. This heavy silver varloh is the largest such piece.

OPPOSITE BOTTOM:

Neck rings from Rajasthan, India (Marwari). Silver. Width 15.6 cm. (top) and 17.7 cm. (bottom).

Although these hansli are made of silver, the sophisticated use of gilding, gemstones, and even diamonds tells us that only a wealthy person could have afforded them.

TOP:

Anklets from India. Silver. Maximum width 13.5 cm.

Each of these anklets is a model of Indian precious metalwork. They are worn in pairs by well-to-do women.

MIDDLE:

Anklets from India. Bronze. 28 cm.

The pair of unusually decorated anklets serve as a reminder that Indian jewelry includes a wide range of ornaments in bronze as well as in precious metals.

BOTTOM:

Anklets from Maharashtra, India. Silver. Diameter 8.5 cm. (right) and 14.5 cm. (left).

In India, a surprisingly diverse array of metal chains—some square, others as round and sinuous as a snake—are formed into belts, bracelets, and anklets.

OPPOSITE TOP:

Anklet from Rajasthan, India. Silver. Width 12 cm.

The lush contours of this anklet suggest the highly sensuous qualities of Indian art.

OPPOSITE BOTTOM:

Pair of woman's anklets from Kutch, India (Koli). Cast silver. Diameter 12.3 cm.

Utter simplicity of form gives these dowry k'dla a strikingly contemporary look.

THIS PAGE:

Necklace with pendant amulet case from Rajasthan, India. Silver, gilded silver, glass stones, and other materials. Length 49 cm.

The red pompons indicate that this woman's necklace from Jaisalmer is to be worn on a wedding day and other festive occasions.

OPPOSITE TOP LEFT:

Neck ring from Kanataka, India. Gold. Length 17 cm.

The style and condition of this hansli *mark it as an ancient piece of jewelry.*

OPPOSITE TOP RIGHT:

Pendant from Rajasthan, India (Marwari). Gold and precious stones. Width 8 cm.

Indians attach great importance to gold, the metal of the sun, and precious stones, which they associate with the planets.

OPPOSITE BOTTOM LEFT:

From India, eighteenth and nineteenth centuries.

Top left: Pendant. Jade, gold, and diamonds. Width 5 cm.

Middle: Pendant. Gold, precious stones, and pearls. Height 6.5 cm.

The combination of precious stones, enameling, and gold is typical of Moghul jewelry.

Right: Central element of a bazuband. *Gold, enamel, and precious stones. Height 4.4 cm.*

This bazuband—*an armlet worn above the elbow—features nine stones that represent the planets of the Hindu system.*

Bottom: Bazuband. Gold, enamel, stones, and silk cords. Width 6.1 cm.

Like all the objects above, this is an example of kundan *work, a method of gem-setting consisting of inserting gold foil between the stone and its mount. The backing adds brilliance while helping to conceal the irregular cut of the stone.*

OPPOSITE BOTTOM RIGHT:

Nose rings from India. Glass beads and gold.

Right: From Gujarat (Harijan). Width 6.2 cm. Left: From Uttar Pradesh (Bothia). Width 11.8 cm.

OPPOSITE:

From India. Gold, seed pearls, and precious stones. Maximum height 9 cm.

Top to bottom: Nose ornament from Gujarat; woman's earrings from Karnataka; nose ornament and woman's earrings from Gujarat.

Indian jewelry makes liberal use of pearls, which are associated with water and women. Pearls are believed to have healing powers.

TOP:

From India.

Left: Comb. Gilded silver and silver. Width 7.4 cm.

An epitome of the sensuality found in India is that the comb contains a well that drips perfume into the wearer's hair.

Right: Armlet. Gold and silver. Width 9 cm.

The armlet (bazuband) of silver with gold-leaf overlay bears an incised image of the elephant-headed god Ganesh, son of Shiva and Parvati.

BOTTOM

Belt buckle from the Deccan, India, eighteenth century. Iron and gold. Width 7.5 cm.

This remarkable piece of metalwork combines the intricacy of an elaborate foliate pattern with simplicity of form.

TOP:

Earrings from India. Gold. Height 2.2 to 5.3 cm.

These earrings from Kerala (top and second from top) and Rajasthan (middle and second from bottom) exude femininity and seductive appeal. Indian women often wear several different types of earrings simultaneously.

BOTTOM:

Necklaces from India. Gold. Maximum length 35 cm.

Top to bottom: Madhya Pradesh, Karnataka, Karnataka, Kerala, Tamil Nadu, and Kerala.

Regardless of her social stratum, an Indian bride receives a stridhana, or dowry, of precious metal jewelry from her family. A tangible insurance policy against disasters, it is the only form of property a woman may exclusively possess.

OPPOSITE:

Woman's necklace from Kerala, India. Gold. Length 18 cm.

The central pendant features stylized cobras that identify the wearer as a member of the Hindu community. Kerala's Muslim and Christian communities have their own distinctive jewelry styles.

142

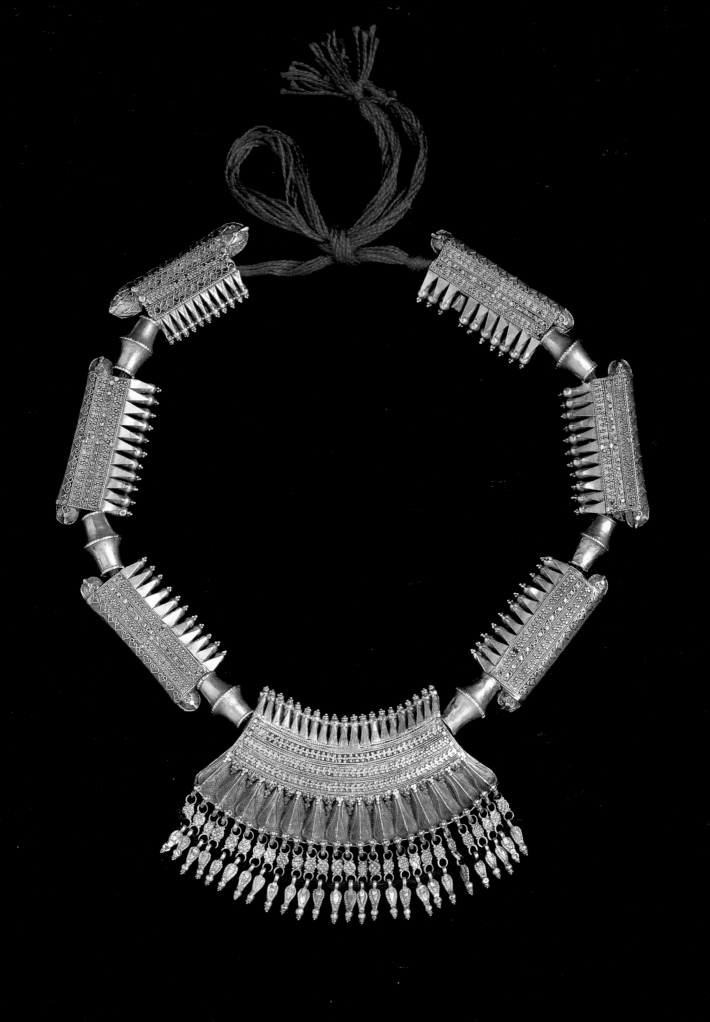

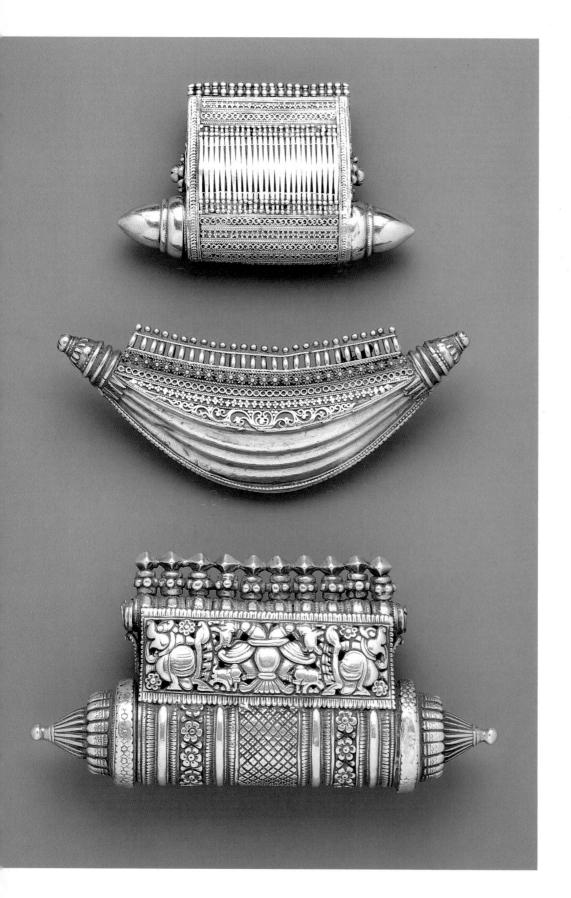

THIS PAGE:
Pendants from Kerala (top, middle) and Karnataka (bottom), India. Silver. Maximum width 12.5 cm.

These amulet cases (ta'viz) are tributes to the technical expertise of Indian metalworkers.

OPPOSITE TOP:
Belt from Andhra Pradesh, India. Silver. Total length 84 cm.

Delicate workmanship characterizes not only the articulated square medallions around the front of this heavy belt from Hyderabad, but the round medallions attached to the reverse of the bundled flat chains.

OPPOSITE BOTTOM:
Bracelet from Kerala, India. Silver. Diameter 14.5 cm.

Old examples like this symmetrical "sunburst" are small compared with modern bracelets like it that are made in gold and span as much as a foot in diameter.

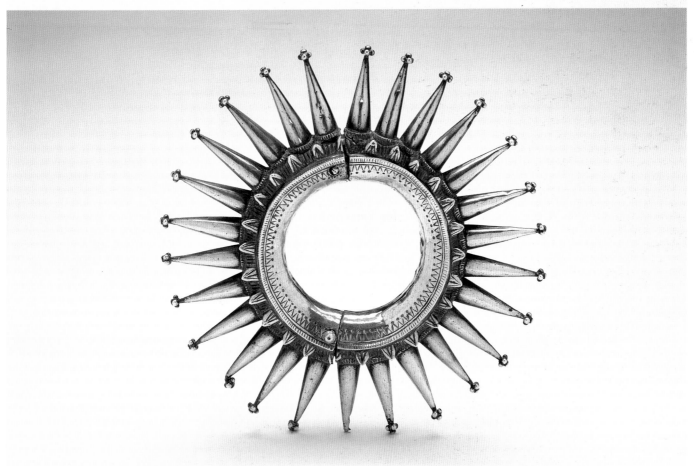

OPPOSITE:

Necklace from Tamil Nadu, India (Toda). Silver and cowrie shells. Total length 2.50 m., diameter of disk 33 cm., weight 11 kg.

This spectacular necklace is believed to decorate the horns of water buffalo during certain ceremonies, but the rituals are so secret that they have yet to be photographed or described. A smaller version of the same necklace is worn by men.

TOP:

Necklace from Tamil Nadu and Kerala, India. Gold, coral, and rubies. Length 31 cm.

Gold and coral: sun and life. This Brahmin necklace is a study in opulence and symmetry.

BOTTOM:

Woman's necklace from Tamil Nadu, India. Gold and precious stones. Diameter 32.5 cm.

Champakali necklaces represent the fragrant buds of the champa flower, which has been variously identified as jasmine, frangipani, and magnolia.

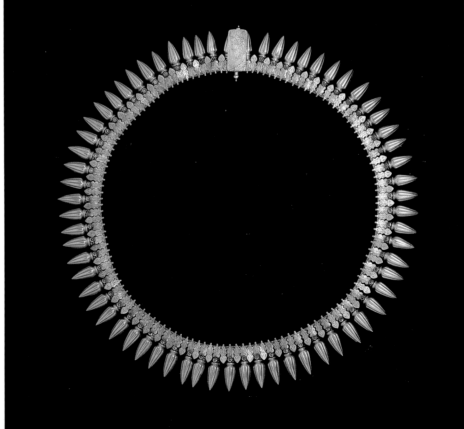

TOP:

Earrings from Tamil Nadu, southern India. Gold. Maximum height 4.8 cm.

An Indian woman might wear more than one pair of pampadam *at a time. Though lightweight, these hollow earrings can stretch the earlobe considerably. The pair at the top appear to represent birds, but they are in fact snakes.*

BOTTOM:

Marriage pendant from Tamil Nadu, India. Gold. Height 18.5 cm.

The equivalent of our wedding ring, a thali *is placed around a wife's neck when she marries and removed only when she becomes a widow. Indian marriage pendants come in a variety of shapes and sizes.*

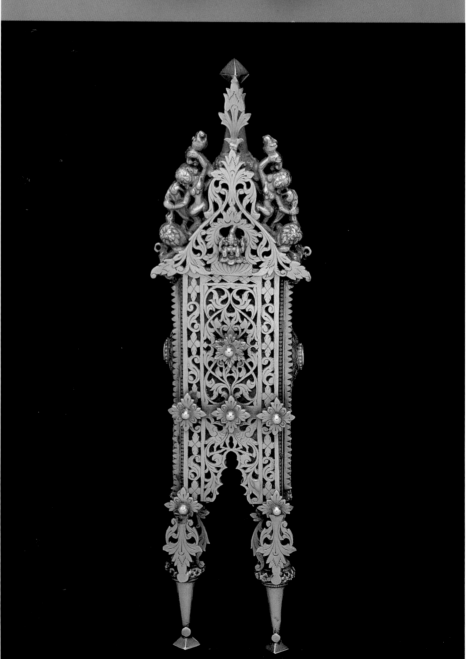

TOP:
Chest ornament from Tulu, southern India. Bronze. Width 23.5 cm.

Members of the Nalke caste wear this pectoral during an exorcism ritual known as the devil's dance.

BOTTOM:
Armlet from southern India. Bronze. Height 11.5 cm.

The cobra was venerated in Egypt at the time of the pharaohs and is revered in India as well. This bracelet is worn by men who belong to the Shivite community.

THIS PAGE:
Necklaces from Sri Lanka. Silver.
Length 24.3 cm. (top) and 47 cm.
(bottom).

The jewelry of Sri Lanka constitutes
a distinctive subgroup within the
context of Indian ornamentation,
except for certain bracelets and
small ornaments worn by the Tamil
of southern India.

OPPOSITE:
Necklace from Nagaland, India
(Angami). Conch shells, glass and
carnelian beads, bone, and brass.
Length 72 cm.

The Naga make use of a wide range
of materials, including conch shells
from the Bay of Bengal, carnelian,
glass, brass, ivory, bone, and rock
crystal.

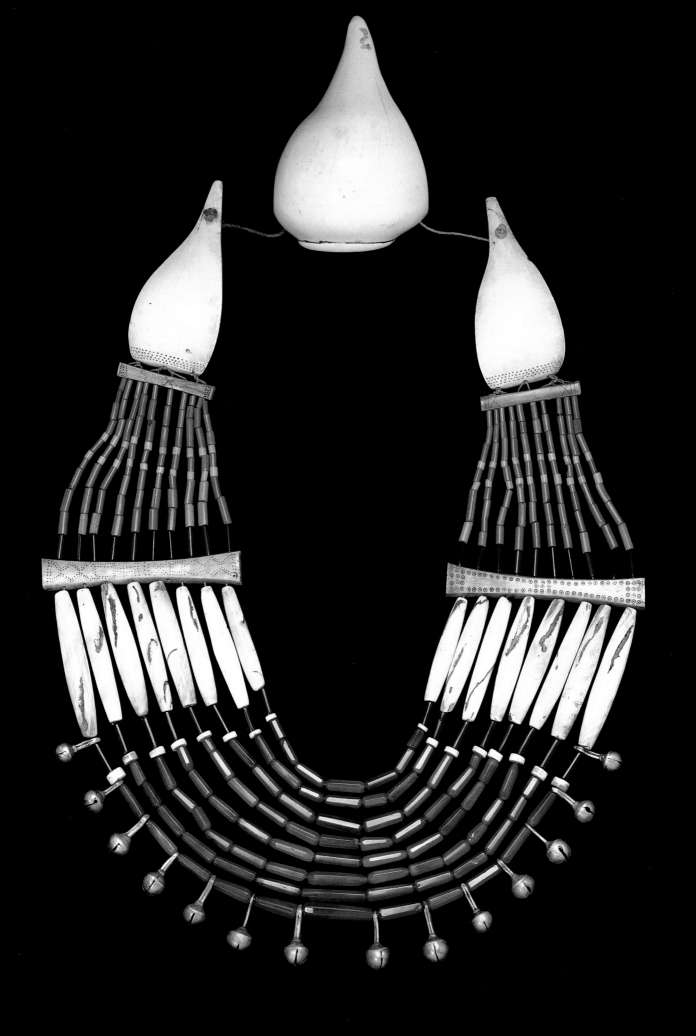

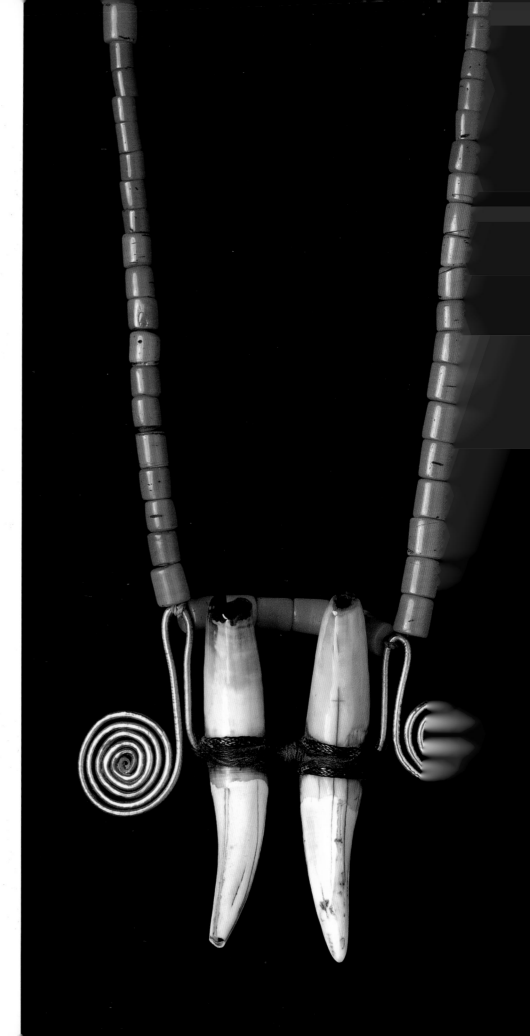

THIS PAGE:

Man's necklace from Nagaland, India (Konyak). Glass, [animal] teeth, and brass. Length 41 cm.

The wearing of tiger's teeth (or ivory imitations) indicates hunting prowess.

OPPOSITE TOP:

Woman's ear ornaments from Nagaland, India (Ao). Rock crystal. Width 4.7 cm.

Rock crystal or glass ear ornaments are a sign of wealth.

OPPOSITE BOTTOM:

Woman's necklace from Nagaland, India (Chang). Shell disks. Diameter of the central ornament 9.3 cm.

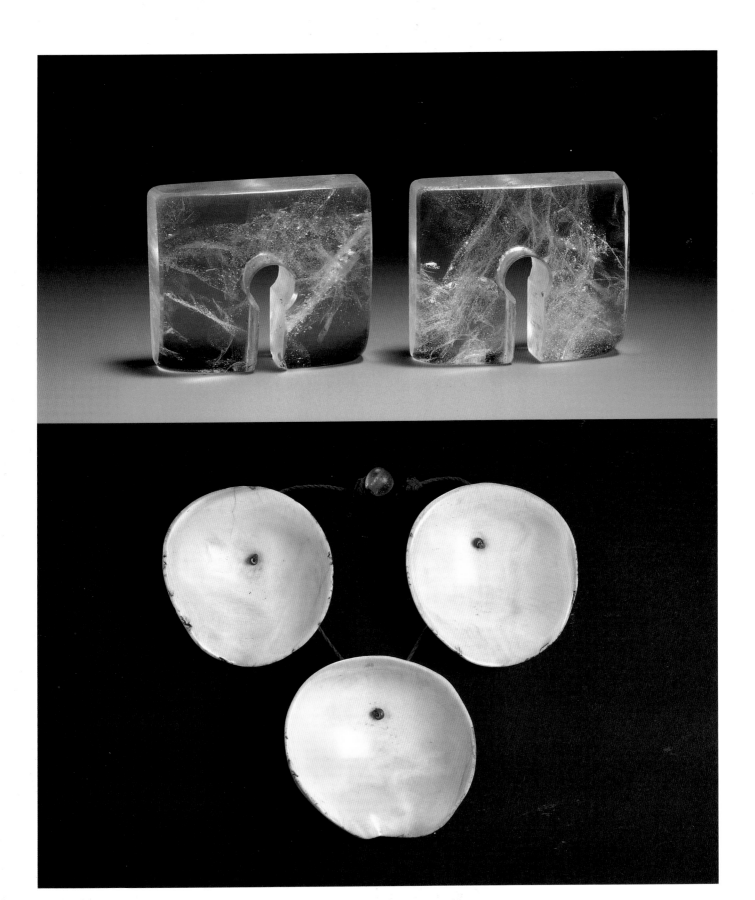

TOP:

Bracelets from Nagaland, India. Bronze. Height 4 cm. to 12.7 cm.

These heirloom arm ornaments—all cast by the lost-wax method—point to a long metalworking tradition. The bracelet at the top is reminiscent of bronzework from the Dongson period.

RIGHT:

From Nagaland, India (Konyak).

Top: Pendant. Bronze. Height 4.2 cm.

Bottom: Man's neck ring. Brass. Width 20.6 cm.

Head hunting allowed a village to increase its mio or "life force"—a power thought to be concentrated in the head—and thereby to drive away evil spirits.

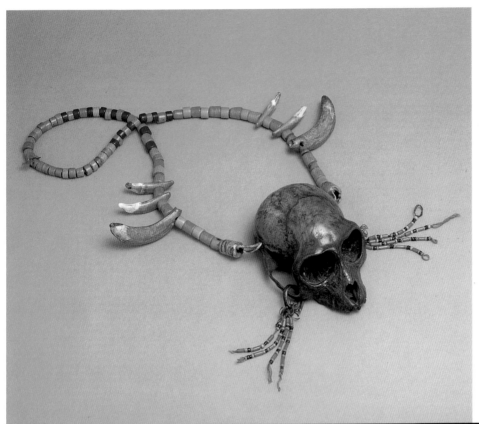

LEFT:

Man's necklace from Nagaland, India (Konyak). Monkey skull and glass beads. Length 39 cm.

For the Nagas, monkey skulls can represent the number of human heads taken. Occasionally carved from wood, the skulls also decorate headhunters' baskets.

BOTTOM:

Men's armlets from Nagaland, India (Konyak and Angami). Ivory. Width 10 cm. to 17 cm.

Worn by men above the elbow (except the bone one at far left), these ornaments indicated high status achieved through head-taking or feasting. Ivory used to be obtained locally.

OPPOSITE:
Woman's necklace from Nagaland, India (Ao). Glass beads, bronze, and shell. Length 67 cm.

TOP:
Chest ornaments and necklace from Nagaland, India (Konyak and Wancho). Brass, wood, and teeth. Height 6.4 cm. to 33.5 cm.

These ornaments indicate head-hunter status; most are Konyak (top, bottom center, and bottom left) or Wancho (right). The more head effigies, the greater the wear-er's prestige. One of the pendants (bottom middle) is in the shape of a conch shell.

MIDDLE:
Bracelets from Nagaland, India (left, Tangkhul; middle, Kabui; right, Konyak). Bronze. Width 6.2 cm. to 15 cm.

Naga ornaments boast a wide range of highly imaginative forms. The massive pair of bracelets on the left, intended for use as weapons, are incised with decorative patterns that resemble headhunters' tattoos.

BOTTOM:
Men's ear ornaments from Naga-land, India (Konyak and Ao). Shell and horn. Top: Height 7.9 cm.; middle 6.9 cm.; bottom 24 cm.

The Naga tribes of northeastern India live along the Burmese border, not far from China. However, they are of Mongolian descent and have no racial or cultural ties to Hindu India; they hold animistic beliefs and once practiced headhunting. The pattern repeated on both pairs of shell ear ornaments (top and middle) are similar to the tattoo markings on headhunters' chests. The very rare Ao ear ornaments (bottom) are in the shape of cattle horns.

TOP:

Necklace from Nepal (Newar). Claws, teeth, and other materials. Diameter 29 cm.

Worn to propitiate good health, the collar has even more beneficial effect if it is assembled and blessed by a holy man.

BOTTOM:

Man's wristband from Nepal. Wood. Width 19.5 cm.

This bracelet is designed to protect an archer's left wrist from the bow-string as it snaps back into place. According to Stone, this elaborately engraved wooden ornament is carved in the shape of a saddle.

OPPOSITE:

Woman's finger ring and necklace from Nepal (Newar). Gold and precious stones. Height of ring 2.6 cm; height of necklace's central element 5.6 cm.

The necklace is threaded with delicately engraved amulet cases.

TOP:

Woman's necklaces from Nepal (Gurung). Coral, turquoise, and gold. Length 60 cm. (top) and 72.5 cm. (bottom).

These two bhiru *are worn together.*

BOTTOM:

Woman's necklace from Nepal (Newar). Gilded copper and other materials. Length 38.5 cm.

Today this taillo (or tavo) *is worn only by a girl whom the priests and astrologer have selected at the age of four to be a living goddess.*

OPPOSITE TOP:

Ear ornaments and nose ring from Nepal. Gold. Height 4.2 cm. to 19.5 cm.

Top: Women of the Makalu region wear a nose ring daily.

Left and right: These ear ornaments, part of the ensemble that adorns the heads of Newar women on their wedding day, are attached to supporting hooks decorated with peacocks, symbols of fertility.

Center and bottom: These earrings are worn by Gurung women.

OPPOSITE BOTTOM:

Woman's necklace from Nepal (Limbu). Gold over lacquer with red felt spacers. Length 25.5 cm.

There are many types of konda, *which Limbu women always wear for the* mela, *a celebration during which families display their wealth.*

OPPOSITE FAR RIGHT:

Pendants from Ladakh (upper row, far right), Nepal (seventeenth century, far left) and Tibet (all others). Brass, copper, and bronze. Height 9 cm. to 15 cm.

Tibetans carry magic charms, fragments of a monk's robe, effigies of Buddha, and other religious relics in amulet boxes (gahu).

160

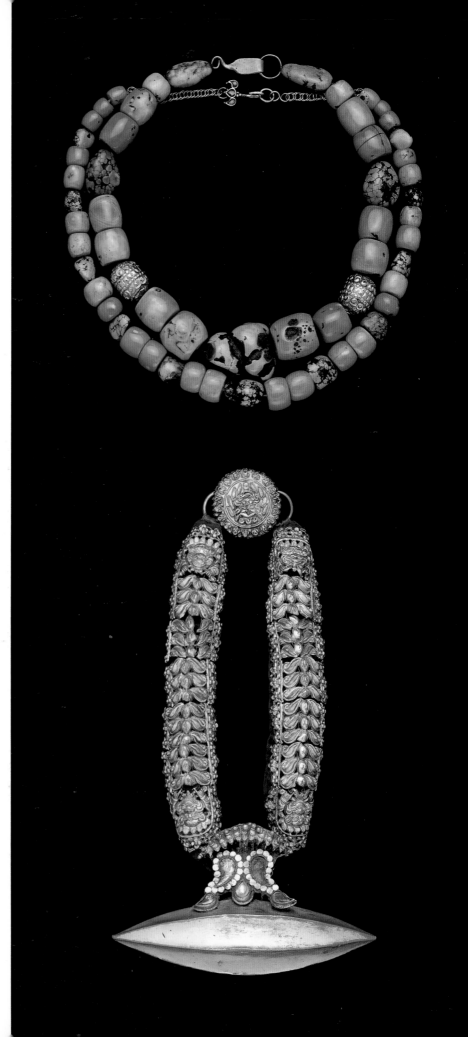

OPPOSITE:

Woman's necklace from Ladakh. Coral, turquoise, gold, and semi-precious stones. Length 22 cm.

Most Himalayan jewelry makes use of turquoise and coral: blue represents air and the sky, and red is associated with fire and light.

TOP:

Group of ornaments from Bhutan. Silver, gilded silver, coral, and turquoise. Height 6 cm. to 18.5 cm.

The Monpa people call the bracelets at the left (top and bottom) dobchu. The pair of fibulas (tingkhep, right top), believed to be older than the koma below, were used to fasten a garment at the shoulder.

BOTTOM:

Woman's necklace from Ladakh. Silver, amber, coral, and turquoise. Length 30 cm.

Turquoise, coral, and amber were highly valued jewelry materials in Ladakh, which had close ties with Tibetan culture. According to Corneille Jest, turquoise was considered "a living, perishable stone that shared its wearers' ultimate fate; it symbolized the vitality—and mortality—of man."

TOP:

Women's ornaments from Lhasa, Tibet. Eighteenth century. Gold, turquoise, and rubies. Height: 5.6 cm. (top, center), 8 cm. (left and right, and bottom).

Gahu—*prayer boxes containing religious relics or ritual incantations (mantras)—used to be worn by Tibetan noblewomen as pendants (bottom), headdress ornaments (top), or earrings (right, left). They could be plain or ornate and came in a wide range of shapes (round, oval, square) and materials (gold, silver, copper, iron).*

BOTTOM:

Belt from Tibet. Silver, gilded silver, and turquoise. Width 39 cm., length (including chain) 117 cm.

The gyenzen *once worn by high-ranking Tibetan women came equipped with sturdy end hooks to support the folded cloak they carried behind their skirts. Peacocks adorn the cloak pin at the end of the chain, which was fastened to the wearer's garment at the shoulder.*

OPPOSITE:

Woman's necklace from Tibet. Gold, turquoise, coral, and pearls. Length 28 cm.

This ornament was worn by noblewomen from Lhasa as a sign of prestige. A few of the elements in the necklace are agate dZi beads— some banded, others with "eyes" (mig)—that were thought to have magical power. Nine-eyed dZi were the most sought after.

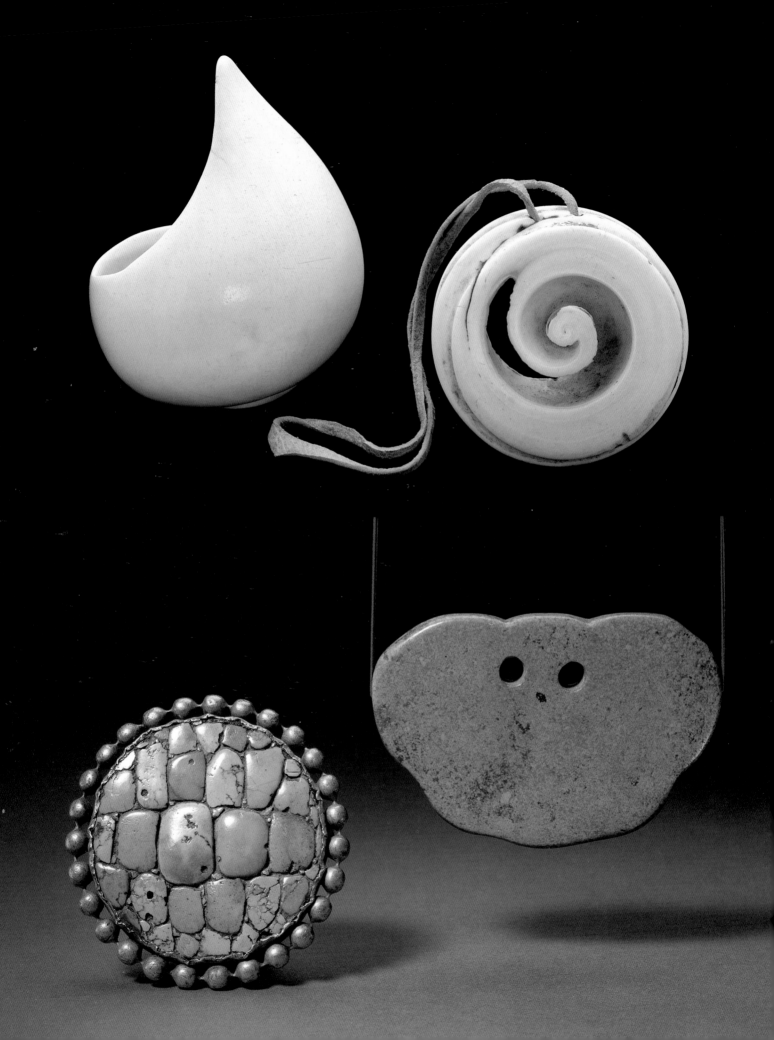

OPPOSITE TOP:

From Lhasa, Tibet.

*Left: Woman's bracelet. Shell.
Height 11.2 cm.*

*Right: Man's ear ornament. Shell.
Diameter 7.9 cm.*

*Women in Ladakh wear the same
type of bracelet, only smaller and
without a sharp protuberance. The
ear ornament is one of a pair worn
only by the most important Lamaist
shaman. It is particularly rare.*

OPPOSITE BOTTOM:

*Pendants from Tibet. Turquoise
and bronze. Width 8.5 cm. (right),
diameter 7.9 cm. (left).*

*The pendant on the right, carved
from a large piece of turquoise, is a
stylized representation of a bat, a
symbol of happiness and longevity.*

THIS PAGE:

*Pair of hair pendants. Lhasa, Tibet.
Gold and turquoise. Height 15 cm.*

*Only noblewomen from Lhasa
could afford ornaments of this size
and quality, which they displayed
on festive occasions.*

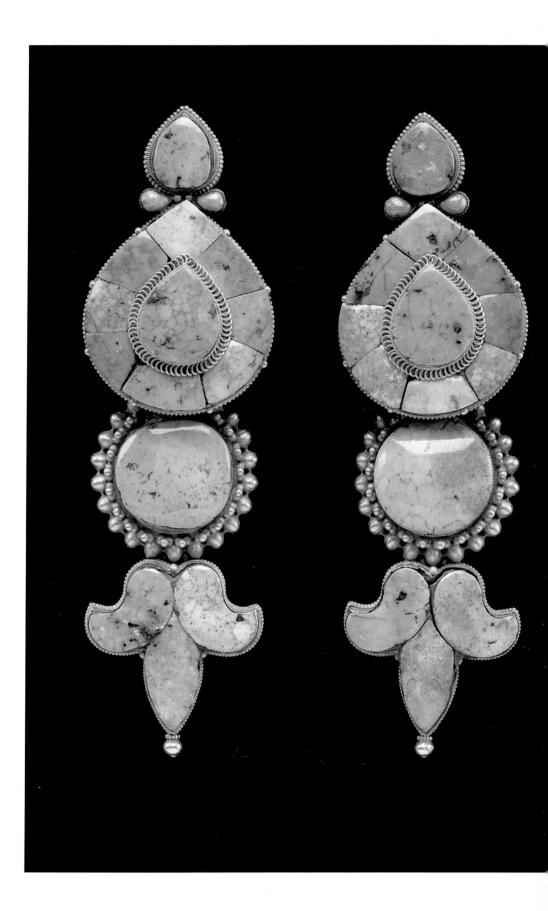

TOP:
Women's necklaces from Tibet. Amber and felt. Diameter 31 cm.

Tibetans credit amber with healing powers.

BOTTOM:
Fibula from Tibet. Bronze. Width 14 cm.

This ancient fibula, depicts the twelve animals of the Chinese zodiac and the eight auspicious Buddhist emblems.

OPPOSITE TOP:
Finger rings from Asia. Silver. Width 3 cm. to 4.8 cm.

Far left: Tibet. Diviner's ring with a "crown" of skulls.

Top left: India. An unusually large ring used as a seal.

Far right: Indonesia. A ring from Timor with a building shape.

Second from right: India. Ring decorated with an effigy of Siva's mount, Nandi, and two lingams.

Bottom: Indonesia. Balinese ring in the shape of a half-tiger, half-frog symbolizing complementary principles (male/female, power/fertility).

OPPOSITE MIDDLE:
Earrings from Tibet. Gold, turquoise, and glass. Length 18 cm. (bottom) and 5.5 cm. (middle).

The bottom ornament (shown with its case of silver-inlaid iron) was worn in the left ear as a mark of rank. The one in the middle was worn by wealthy laymen from Lhasa. According to Tibetan superstition, whoever wears no earring shall be reincarnated as a donkey.

OPPOSITE BOTTOM:
Pair of bracelets from eastern Tibet. Silver. Width 10.7 cm.

This type of wrought silver bracelet, worn for self-protection, is very rare.

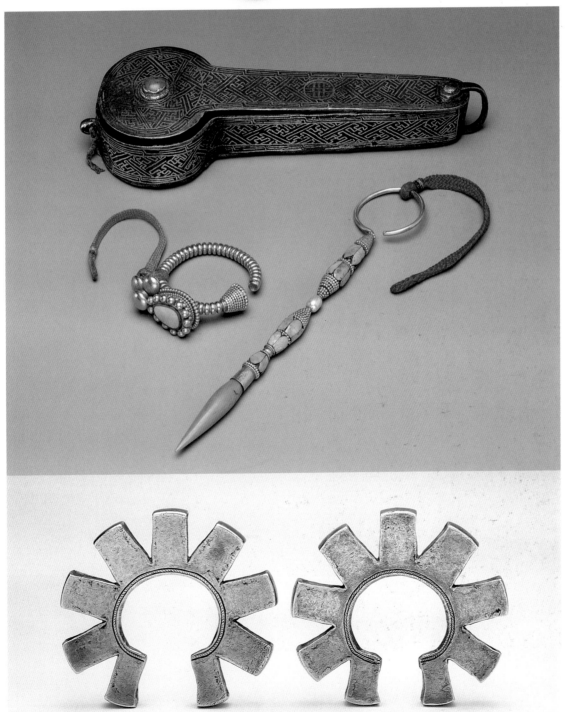

TOP:

Tinderbox and purse from Tibet. Leather, silver, brass, and coral. Width 16 cm. (left) and 14 cm. (right).

Tibetan men wear a me icags *on their belts as a sign of prestige; it contains flint and tinder to strike fire and is therefore believed to have great magical power. The* baghu *(right) is a woman's "purse."*

BOTTOM:

Finger rings and bracelets from Tibet. Silver and turquoise. Width 8 cm. (left and top right); height 3.4 cm. (center) and 2.4 cm. (bottom right).

The finger ring at bottom right, decorated with auspicious Buddhist symbols, was worn only by the official diviner. Tibetan women sometimes used a man's "saddle ring" (center) as a hair ornament.

OPPOSITE TOP LEFT AND RIGHT:

Woman's headdress from Khalkha Darkhan Beile, Mongolia. Front and back views. Silver, turquoise, and coral. Height 59 cm.

Hairstyles and headdresses are considered all-important in the Mongolian concept of female beauty. A married woman must remove her elaborate headdress set—along with the rest of her jewelry—when she becomes a widow.

OPPOSITE BOTTOM:

Hair ornament from Khalkha, Mongolia. (One of a pair, shown opened up.) Gilded silver, turquoise, coral, and seed pearls. Width 10.7 cm.

The extraordinary workmanship of this hair clasp can be credited to China. The Mongols were a rugged, nomadic people and did not excel at crafting ornaments or other objects in metal, though they worked well in wood and leather. Most of their jewelry came from Tibet and China or was made by itinerant artisans.

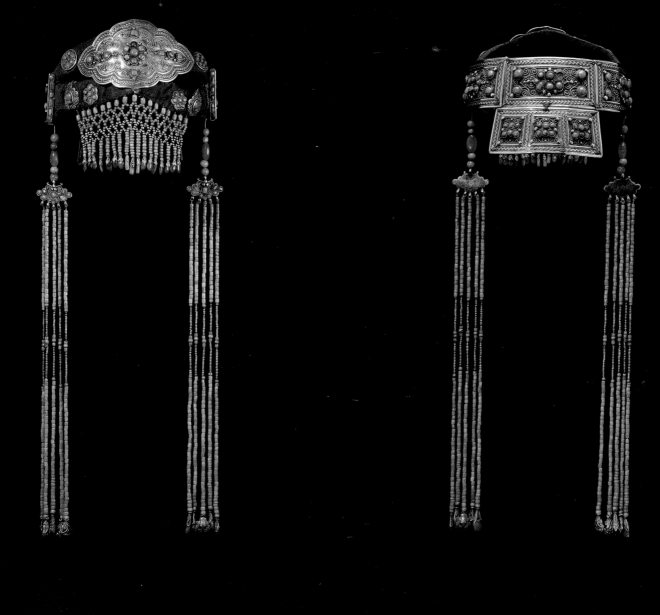

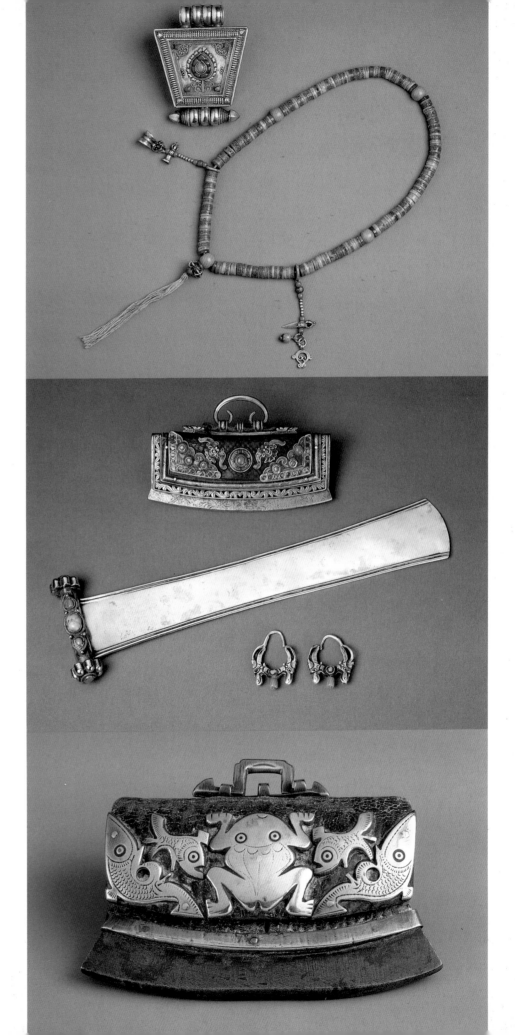

OPPOSITE:

Headdress pendants from Gulchagan Honichin, Mongolia. Silver, turquoise, coral, agate, and other materials. Height 19 cm.

Women in this region complement their headdresses with sparkling temple pendants like these, which are decorated with bits of coral and turquoise.

TOP:

From Mongolia.

Top: Pendant. Silver, turquoise, and coral. Height 8.8 cm.

Bottom: Buddhist rosary. Human bone, silver, and other materials. Length 35 cm.

A Buddhist rosary consists of 108 prayer beads, the number of the signs in the zodiac (twelve) times the number of planets (nine). In Buddhism, the number 108 also corresponds to the number of sinful desires that can be overcome by use of the prayer beads.

MIDDLE:

From Mongolia.

Top: Tinderbox. Leather, silver, enamel, coral, and other materials. Width 13 cm.

Middle: Hairpin. Silver and enamel. Length 28 cm.

Bottom: Earrings. Silver and enamel. Height 4.3 cm.

Mongolian ornaments often feature enamelwork and designs based on plants and animals.

BOTTOM:

Man's tinderbox from Mongolia. Bronze. Width 8.8 cm.

Considering that it was once used by a nomadic herdsman, the decoration on this tinderbox is well preserved. According to Martha Boyer, the fish on it may stand for constancy and tenacity, like "a carp which is fighting its way upstream against the current."

TOP:

*Necklace from Siberia(?). Bone.
Length 29 cm.*

Nothing is known of the function or
origin of this necklace, but its magical presence is bewitching.

BOTTOM:

*Counterweights from China. Ivory.
Height 2.1 cm. to 4.8 cm.*

Carved toggles like these were used
to suspend pipe pouches or personal
carrying cases by a cord from the
wearer's sash. Some experts believe
they inspired Japanese netsuke.

OPPOSITE TOP:

*Men's finger rings from China,
Ming dynasty to the nineteenth century. Jade except for glass at left,
center. Width 2.5 cm. to 3.3 cm.*

Jade was thought to have magical
power and has been prized in
China since ancient times. As far
back as the Han dynasty (200 B.C.–
A.D. 219), the dead were covered in
small jade plaques to keep their
bodies from deteriorating. Many of
the rings shown here, though
derived from a type once worn by
archers, were purely ornamental.

OPPOSITE BOTTOM:

*Belt buckle from China. Gilded
bronze, enamel, and tourmaline.
Width 6.5 cm.*

This type of buckle was highly valued in China during the Qing
dynasty (A.D. 1644–1911). The
number of buckles worn and the
materials from which they were
made indicated the wearer's rank.

174

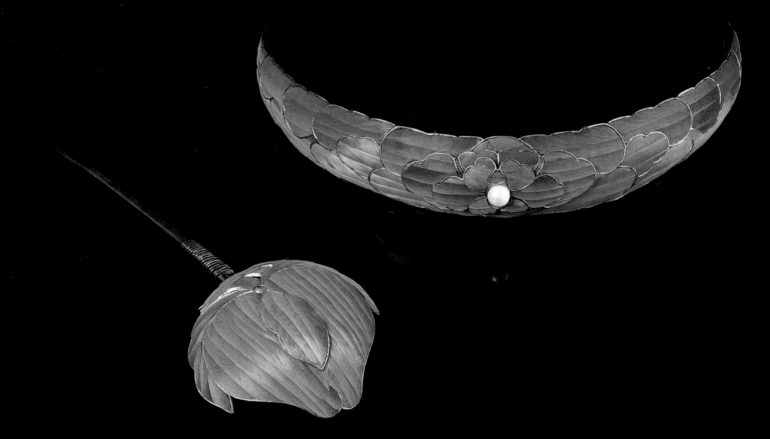

OPPOSITE TOP LEFT:

Mandarin chain and case from China. Peking glass beads, seeds, other materials. Length 116 cm.

So-called Mandarin chains were worn by the emperor and members of the nobility during the Qing dynasty (1644–1911). Those worn by the imperial family were strung on yellow silk because yellow was reserved to them. The necklaces contain a counterweight (left) that hung down the wearer's back, and exactly 108 beads—the same number as the Tibetan rosaries that inspired them. Some were made with precious or semiprecious stones, others with enameled metals, still others with carved seeds.

OPPOSITE TOP RIGHT:

Necklace from China. Silver. Length 24 cm.

Chinese women preferred stiff neck ornaments like this one to flexible bead necklaces. They also wore earrings, bracelets, and rings made of everything from jade, coral, and silver to kingfisher feathers.

OPPOSITE BOTTOM:

Hairpins from China. Gilded silver and feathers. Widest 16.5 cm.

The Chinese have made use of kingfisher feathers since the Han dynasty but did not begin to use them liberally in headdresses, hairpins, and ear ornaments until the nineteenth century. The kingfisher symbolizes happiness and marital fidelity. Patient craftsmanship went into arranging the feathers into complex mosaic patterns.

THIS PAGE:

Headdress pendants from China (Uighur or a Kazak minority). Silver, coral, glass, and other materials. Height 72 cm.

The silver elements in these temple pendants feature extraordinarily delicate granulation and filigree.

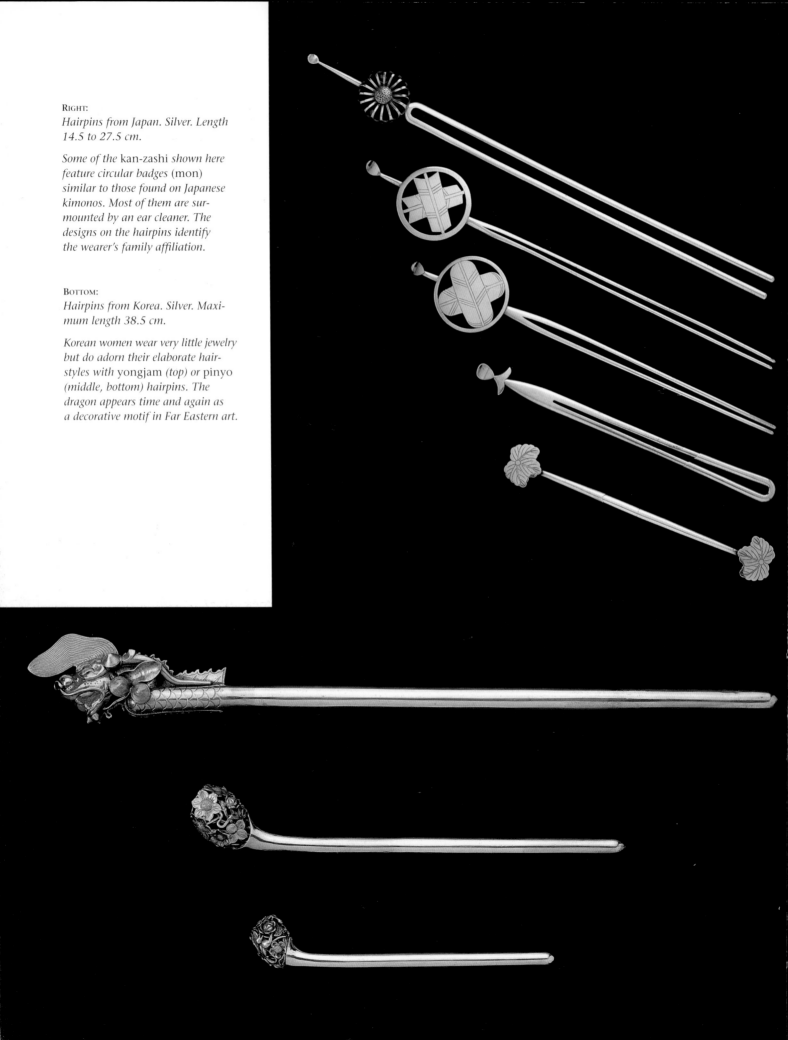

RIGHT:

Hairpins from Japan. Silver. Length 14.5 to 27.5 cm.

Some of the kan-zashi *shown here feature circular badges (mon) similar to those found on Japanese kimonos. Most of them are surmounted by an ear cleaner. The designs on the hairpins identify the wearer's family affiliation.*

BOTTOM:

Hairpins from Korea. Silver. Maximum length 38.5 cm.

Korean women wear very little jewelry but do adorn their elaborate hairstyles with yongjam *(top) or* pinyo *(middle, bottom) hairpins. The dragon appears time and again as a decorative motif in Far Eastern art.*

TOP:
Hairpins from Laos. Silver. Height 29.3 cm. to 34.4 cm.

These "pyramid" hairpins were also used to store tobacco—an example of jewelry that is also practical.

BOTTOM:
Comb from Vietnam. Ivory. Width 8 cm.

The design of this comb highlights the grain of the ivory.

OPPOSITE TOP:
Bracelets. Hmong (Meo). Silver. Tallest 10 cm.

Bottom right: Northern Thailand; top three: Burma; bottom center: Laos; all others: Chinese minorities.

Worn in pairs by both sexes, such bracelets are often described as Hmong (Meo), but the region is home to many groups, each with its own style.

OPPOSITE MIDDLE:
Finger rings from Thailand. Gold. Largest diameter 3 cm.

These ancient finger rings date from between the Dvaravati period (sixth–tenth centuries) and the Ayutthaya period (fourteenth–eighteenth centuries). It is thought that all such rings—whether from Thailand, Burma, Java, or Cambodia, and reserved for the royal court—are probably of Indian origin.

OPPOSITE BOTTOM:
Far left: Earring from East Sumba, Indonesia. Gold.

All others: Earrings/pendants from the Philippines. Gold. Height 2.5 cm. to 3.3 cm.

These ornaments (except top right) were worn as earrings or pendants by various ethnic groups of northern Luzon. Similar ones exist in silver, brass, and bronze. Artifacts with similar designs date back to 500 A.D.

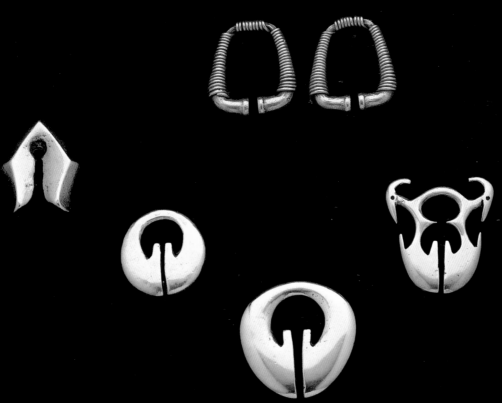

From the Philippines.

Top left: This Mandaya gelang *features alternating loops of clamshell and studded wood. Width 9.8 cm.*

Top right: Bagobo bracelet. Shell. Width 5.2 cm.

Bottom: Ifugao belt ornament. Diameter 11 cm.

The Ifugao fasten an upud, *a shell disk with mounted openwork horn decoration, to the front of their shell-disk belts (*ginutu*). Although this ornament is worn only by men, according to J.F. Safer it represents Pumupud, a deity believed to cause difficult births by blocking the birth canal, much as an operculum closes the opening of a shell.*

BOTTOM:

Belt from the Philippines (Bontoc). Shell and brass. Length 42 cm.

A brass spiral acts as a counterweight for this sangilot, *a woman's belt that can also be used as a pouch for personal possessions.*

TOP:

Armlet figure and complete armlet from the Philippines (Bontoc). Wood, boar's tusks, and human hair. Heights 17 cm. and 16.5 cm.

The tankil, *a Bontoc headhunter's ceremonial armlet, is also worn by other tribes in northern Luzon. Taking part in headhunting expeditions marked a young man's transition to adulthood.*

BOTTOM:

Necklaces from the Philippines (Ifugao). Bone, wicker, and mother-of-pearl. Longest 28.5 cm.

*This mother-of-pearl necklace (*palangapang, *right) is worn by both sexes.*

OPPOSITE:

Man's and woman's necklace from the Philippines (Isneg). Mother-of-pearl, glass beads, other materials. Total lengths 67 cm. (left) and 64 cm. (right).

Ceremonial sipatal *consist of several tiers of butterfly-shaped mother-of-pearl pendants* (bissin) *and, less frequently, silver dangles (right). Little shells are added to women's* sipatal *to symbolize fertility. Each of these impressive ornaments is suspended from an exquisite bead-work ribbon.*

TOP:

From the Philippines (Bontoc).

Left: Headband. Snake vertebrae. Diameter 21 cm.

Right: Headband. Glass beads and shell. Diameter 19 cm.

Whether it is made of snake verte-brae or glass beads and shell, a duli *is worn by women as protec-tion against lightning.*

BOTTOM:

From the Philippines (Bontoc).

Top: Belt ornament. Mother-of-pearl. Width 15.8 cm.

Bottom: Armlet. Monkey tails(?) and mother-of-pearl. Width 28 cm.

When mounted on a belt, the tikam *or* fikum *(top)—is called a* cabibi. *These engraved shells were worn by headhunters and noblemen.*

TOP:

Men's hats from the Philippines (Gaddang). Rattan, mother-of-pearl, brass, and beads. Diameters 10 cm. and 7.5 cm.

Young men sport a suklang, *or basketwork hat, to indicate that they are unmarried. A less elaborate version is worn by married men.*

BOTTOM:

Group of earrings from Kalimantan (top, second from top); Sarawak (far left, second from bottom); Sumatra (bottom); and Nias (far right). Bronze. Maximum height 10.5 cm. (far right), width 7.5 cm. (second from bottom).

Earrings of the Dayak people, when they do not feature abstract designs (far left), represent the aso, *a mythical half-snake, half-dragon that appears as a motif in all their decorative arts. The second pair from the bottom were suspended from two chains and originally served as counterweights for a gong. The earrings from Nias (far right) are in the shape of a plant. The Toba Batak earring (bottom) remains a mystery.*

OPPOSITE:

From Aceh, Sumatra, Indonesia. Enameled gold.

Top: Necklace. Length 21.5 cm.

Bottom: Pendants. Height 5.5 cm.

*This woman's necklace and matching purse pendants, fashioned from enameled gold set with gemstones (*intan*), are characteristic of jewelry from the former sultanate of Aceh.*

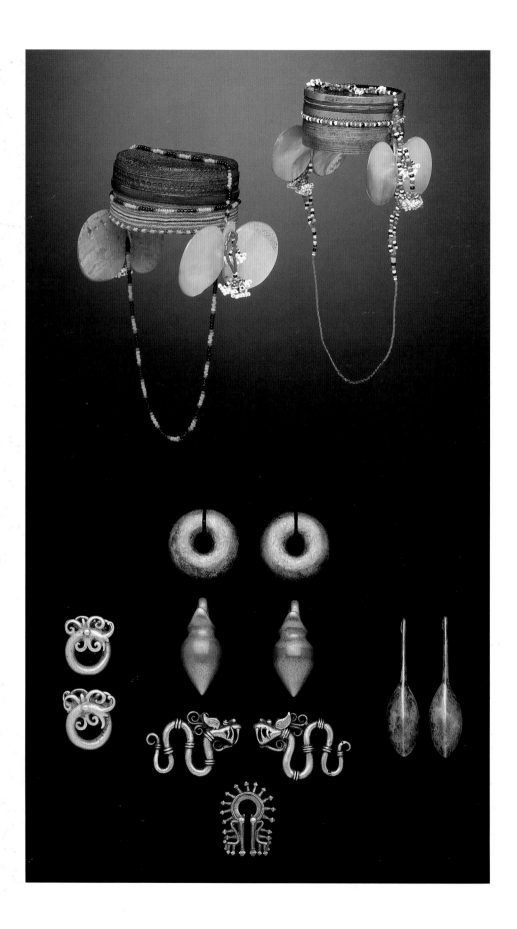

OPPOSITE LEFT:

*Amulet-pendant(?) from Sumatra,
Indonesia (Toba Batak). Bronze.
Height 15.2 cm.*

*The Toba Batak developed a bold
jewelry style and managed to keep it
alive for centuries despite foreign
influences, primarily from India.*

OPPOSITE TOP:

*Bracelet and finger ring from Sumatra,
Indonesia (Toba Batak). Bronze. Width
10.5 cm. (left) and 5.2 cm. (right).*

*This bracelet and finger ring were
believed to protect the man who wore
them. The* singa *motif—a mythical
beast combining elements of snakes
and elephants—reappears elsewhere
in local decorative art, particularly on
the supporting piers of* adat *houses.*

OPPOSITE BOTTOM:

*Man's bracelet from Sumatra,
Indonesia (Toba Batak). Bronze.
Width 9.5 cm.*

*This bracelet is believed to have
protective powers and is handed
down as part of a family's treasure.*

TOP:

*Belt buckle from Sumatra, Indonesia
(Minangkabau). Silver with niello
decoration. Width 30.7 cm.*

*Impressive size and exquisite niello
work make this an outstanding
example of a man's belt buckle, or
pandieng. Islam began to spread
into Sumatra late in the thirteenth
century and, as this ornament demonstrates, influenced the decorative arts.*

BOTTOM:

*Earrings from Sumatra, Indonesia
(Karo Batak). Silver. Height 18 cm.*

*Although it is hard to believe that
anyone could have worn this pair of
heavy* padung padung *in their
ears—even attached to a headdress
for additional support—a number of
old photographs prove otherwise.*

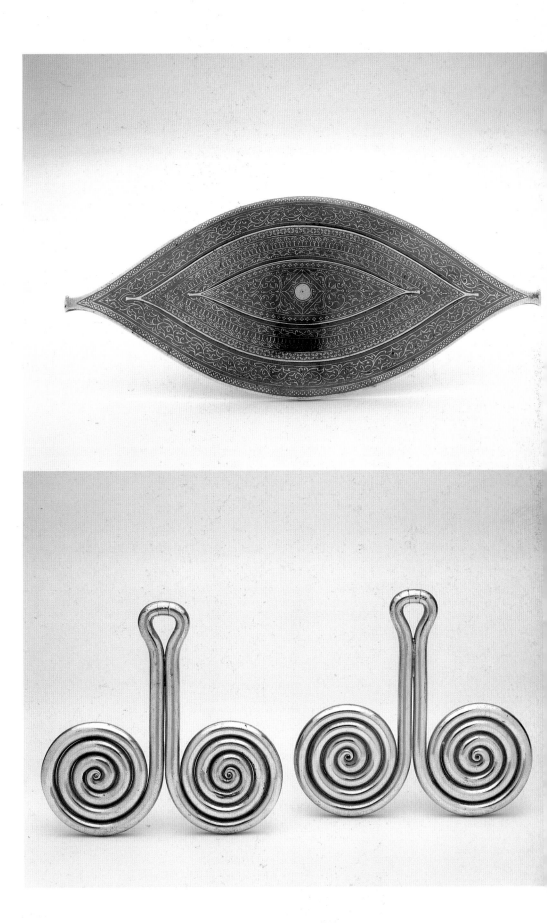

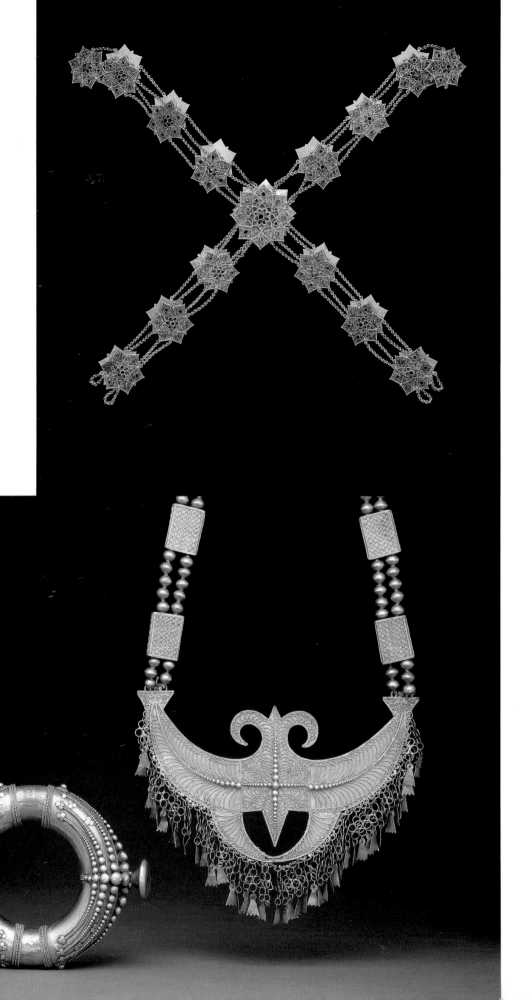

RIGHT:

Breast and back ornament from Aceh, Sumatra, Indonesia. Gold, enamel, and precious stones. Length 48 cm.

Married women wore this impressive criss-cross simplah *over the chest and back. An Islamic context can be discerned in the exquisite metalwork and geometric patterns.*

BOTTOM:

From Sumatra, Indonesia (Karo Batak).

Right: Necklace. Gilded silver. Length 37 cm.

Left: Bracelet. Gilded silver. Width 13.3 cm.

The pendant suspended from the wedding necklace or bura *(right) represents both water buffalo horns and the* adat *house. The bracelet at left is worn by Karo priests, village chiefs, and other men of high rank.*

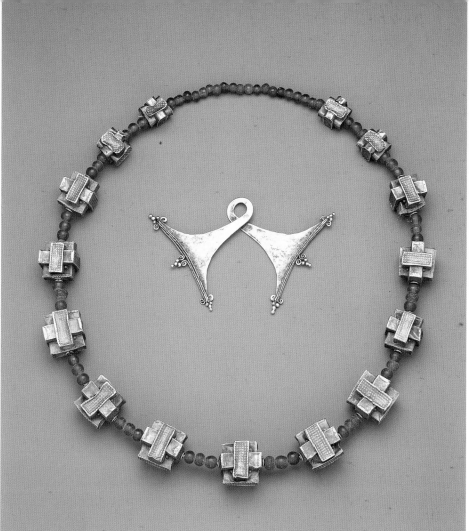

LEFT:

Top: Woman's necklace from Sumatra, Indonesia (Minangkabau). Gold with glass beads. Diameter 23 cm.

Center: Pendant from Tanimbar(?), Indonesia. Gold. Width 10.5 cm.

Very similar to pendants in a double-axhead shape from Flores as well as to Sumbanese marangga, *this* taka *could have been made by Savu smiths in Sumba and it may have been a trade item between islands.*

BOTTOM:

Top: Bracelet from Sumatra, Indonesia (Minangkabau). Gold. Height 8.3 cm.

Bottom left: Pendant from Sumbawa, Indonesia (Bugis). Gold. Width 8 cm.

Bottom right: Earrings from Sumbawa, Indonesia (Bugis). Gold. Length 8.5 cm.

These beautifully executed pieces of jewelry were probably made by itinerant Bugis craftsmen.

LEFT:

Combs from Indonesia. Tallest 18.5 cm.

These combs represent a wide range of materials, including horn (top) and tortoiseshell (far left and right) from Timor. The Toba Batak of Sumatra fashion combs of wood and bamboo (center) or wood and bone (bottom) made in the shape of the chests in which the people keep their treasured possessions.

BOTTOM:

Bracelets from Indonesia. Ivory. Diameter 10.4 cm. to 13 cm.

Few raw materials were as highly prized as ivory, particularly in the Sunda and Molucca Islands, from which all these bracelets come except for the one at far left. That bracelet is from Sumatra. Ornaments like these were used as currency for important transactions such as bridewealth payments. Although elephant tusks could be obtained from Borneo and Sumatra, they were brought in by ship from India as far back as the days of the Dutch East India Company.

TOP:

Headdress ornament from Java, Indonesia. Gold. Width 5.7 cm.

The sleek lines of this ancient ornament are astonishingly modern.

MIDDLE:

Finger rings from Java, Indonesia. Gold. Width 2.8 cm. to 3.6 cm.

These rings were worn at the Javanese court. Buddhist culture flourished in the middle of the island between the eighth and tenth centuries. The center of power then shifted to East Java, where a Hindu kingdom held sway between the eleventh and fifteenth centuries.

A considerable number of finger rings with semiprecious stones date from the earlier period. Some (top left and top right) represent the rice goddess Sri, symbol of abundance and fertility.

BOTTOM:

Earrings from Java, Indonesia (sixthth to fifteenth century). Gold. Height 1.5 cm. to 3 cm.

The influx of Indians into Indonesia (chiefly Java) began early in the Christian era. As their influence spread, jewelry-making enjoyed unprecedented development and metalworking techniques became highly sophisticated. Production of Indo-Javanese (Majapahit) jewelry came to a halt when Islam, and Islamic motifs, infiltrated the region in the fifteenth century.

OPPOSITE TOP LEFT:

Man's neck ring from Nias, Indonesia. Coconut shell and brass. Diameter 33 cm.

A symbol of high prestige, the kal-abubu was worn only by men who had killed an enemy and brought his head back to the village, thereby attracting protective forces to his community.

OPPOSITE TOP RIGHT:

Bracelet from Enggano, Indonesia. Silver. Height 9 cm.

This bracelet was found on Enggano, a small island off the southwest coast of Sumatra. Some think it represents a water buffalo, a symbol of wealth and high status; others see an architectural motif.

OPPOSITE BOTTOM:

Bracelets from Indonesia. Clam-shell. Height 3.2 cm. to 8.8 cm.

These men's bracelets come from Nias Island (far left and two at right) in the Indonesian archipelago and Sarawak, Borneo (all others).

TOP:

Necklace from Flores, Indonesia. Gold. Height 52 cm. Width (boat pendant) 12.3 cm.

One might be tempted to call this ornament "boat of the sun." An important theme in Indonesian lore since ancient times, boats were believed to transport the souls of the dead to the other world.

BOTTOM:

Headdress ornament from Kalimantan, Indonesia (Dayak). Brass. Height 14 cm.

This ornament with a stylized human figure was worn across the forehead, probably for protection.

TOP:

Earrings from Sumba, Indonesia. Gold. Maximum height 7 cm.

Worn as earrings or pendants, mamuli, *like* marangga *(page 26, top), are passed down through the family line as heirlooms and kept in an* adat *house as part of its sacred treasure. There are many types of Sumbanese* mamuli, *particularly in the eastern part of the island. These ornaments were worn on important ceremonial occasions by members of a raja's family or by his slaves.*

BOTTOM:

Pendant(?) from West Sumba, Indonesia. Gold. Height 4.3 cm.

The exact purpose of this unusual piece, called a madaka, *has yet to be determined.*

OPPOSITE:

Group of earrings from Flores (bottom two rows), Nias (top right), and the Moluccas (all others), Indonesia. Gold. Maximum height 10 cm.

Some of these earrings (left, second from bottom) are credited with magical power and figure prominently in the family gift exchanges that precede a marriage.

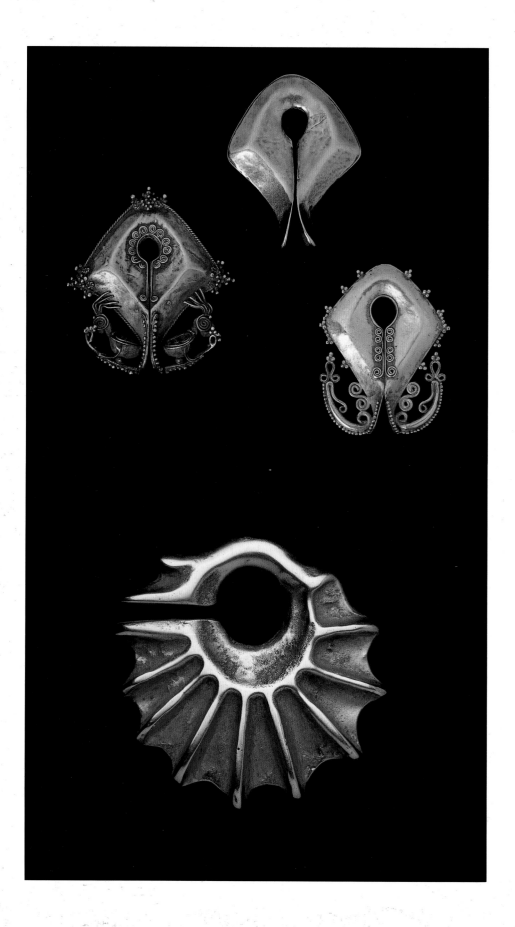

198

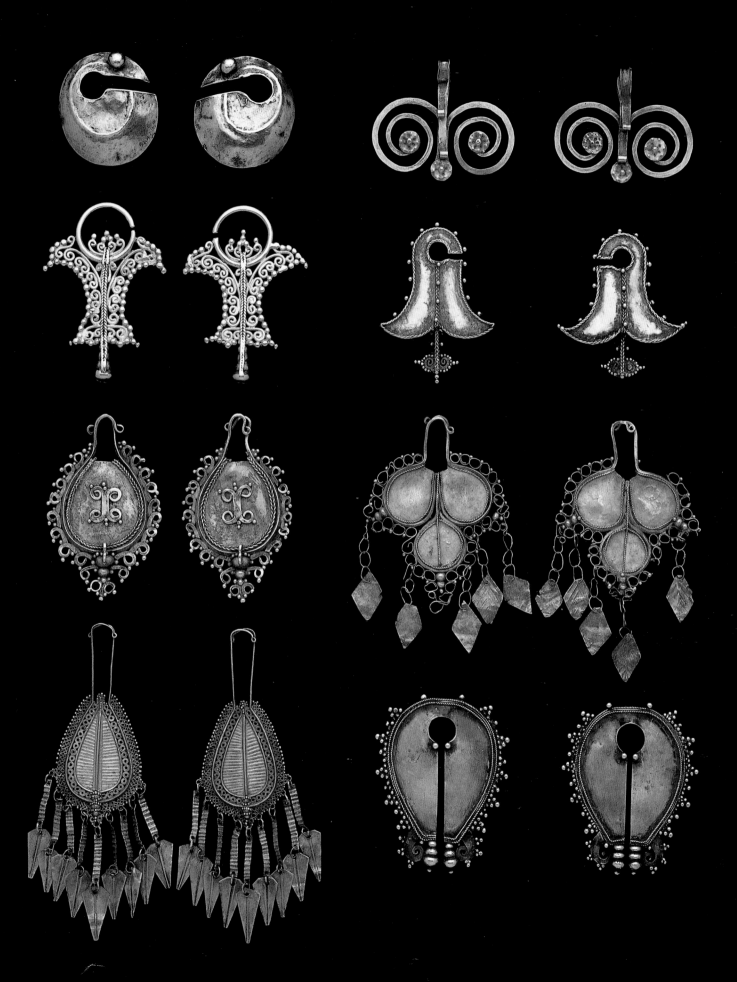

TOP:

Bracelets from Timor, Indonesia. Silver. Maximum height 10.8 cm.

These bracelets (niti) feature extraordinary decorative elements: houses symbolizing the cosmos, male and female figures. Timor boasts a wide range of silver and bronze bracelets and other jewelry made from old European coins. Most of these ornaments are believed to come from the central highlands (Belu), but they may have been made by the accomplished smiths that lived on the adjacent islands of Ndao and Roti.

BOTTOM:

Comb from Timor, Indonesia. Horn. Width 26.7 cm.

Combs like this one, with boat motifs, were often decorated with Dutch coins.

OPPOSITE TOP:

Man's necklace from Tanimbar, Indonesia. Shells and rattan. Length 23 cm.

Shells have been a medium of exchange in Indonesia since time immemorial.

OPPOSITE BOTTOM LEFT:

Man's earring from Tanimbar, Indonesia. Ivory. Height 8.6 cm.

This unusually large ear ornament, worn only by men, is very rare.

OPPOSITE BOTTOM RIGHT:

Mask from Tanimbar, Indonesia. Gold. Width 4.2 cm.

This little mask may have been attached to a headdress.

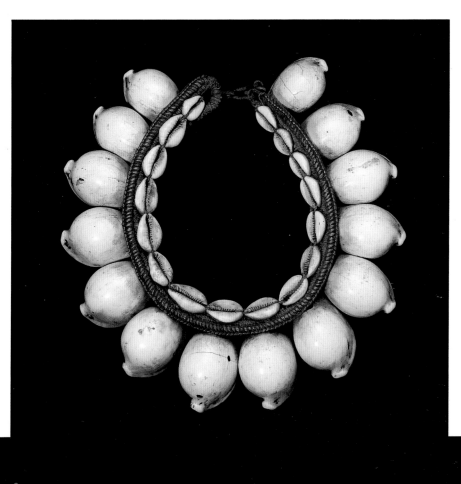

Bracelet from Sulawesi, Indonesia (Bugis). Gold. Height 14 cm.

Pairs of ponto karro karro tedong *were among the most spectacular ornaments worn by Bugis brides. The Bugis, remarkable merchants, crisscrossed the Indonesian archipelago and established a flourishing mercantile state whose influence reached beyond Sulawesi to Sumbawa (Bima). These sophisticated pieces of jewelry were among the items they traded. According to R. Wassing-Visser, the bracelet got its name from the ribbed pattern, which recalls the folds of a water buffalo's neck.*

OPPOSITE TOP:

Man's necklace from Sulawesi, Indonesia (Toraja). Crocodile teeth and wild boar fangs. Total length 55.5 cm.; fang length 17 cm.

The tora tora *is a headhunter's necklace.*

OPPOSITE BOTTOM:

Head ornament from Sulawesi, Indonesia (Toraja). Brass. Width 23.1 cm.

The crowning ornament, sanggori, *of a Toraja warrior's headgear is believed to be a source of magical protection.*

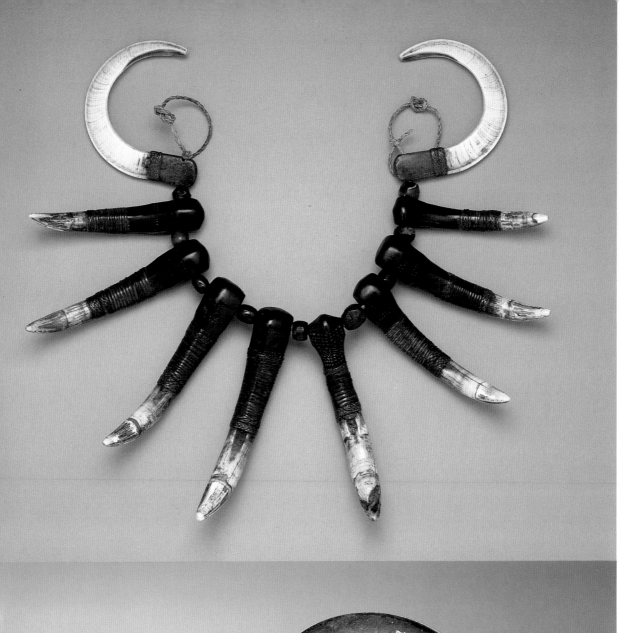

OPPOSITE TOP:

Earrings from Flores (top), Alor (bottom right), and the Moluccas (all others), Indonesia. Gold. Height 2 cm. to 4.6 cm.

Here is a sampling of the ornaments that men and women alike place on their ears in the Malay archipelago. Earrings like these play a key role in marriage exchanges.

OPPOSITE BOTTOM:

Pendants from Sulawesi, Indonesia. Brass. Height 4.1 to 7.2 cm.

The uses and meanings of taiganja vary from region to region. Believed to have considerable supernatural power, these pendants are kept in treasure chests and brought out only for certain ritual occasions.

TOP:

Pectoral from Kisar, Moluccas, Indonesia. Gold. Diameter 12.3 cm.

Men's disk-shaped chest ornaments depicting dolphins have been found in both the Sunda Islands and the Moluccas.

BOTTOM:

Pectoral from Babar, Moluccas, Indonesia. Gold. Width 25 cm.

According to Rodgers, the dish-like breast ornaments worn by Moluccan women were usually round.

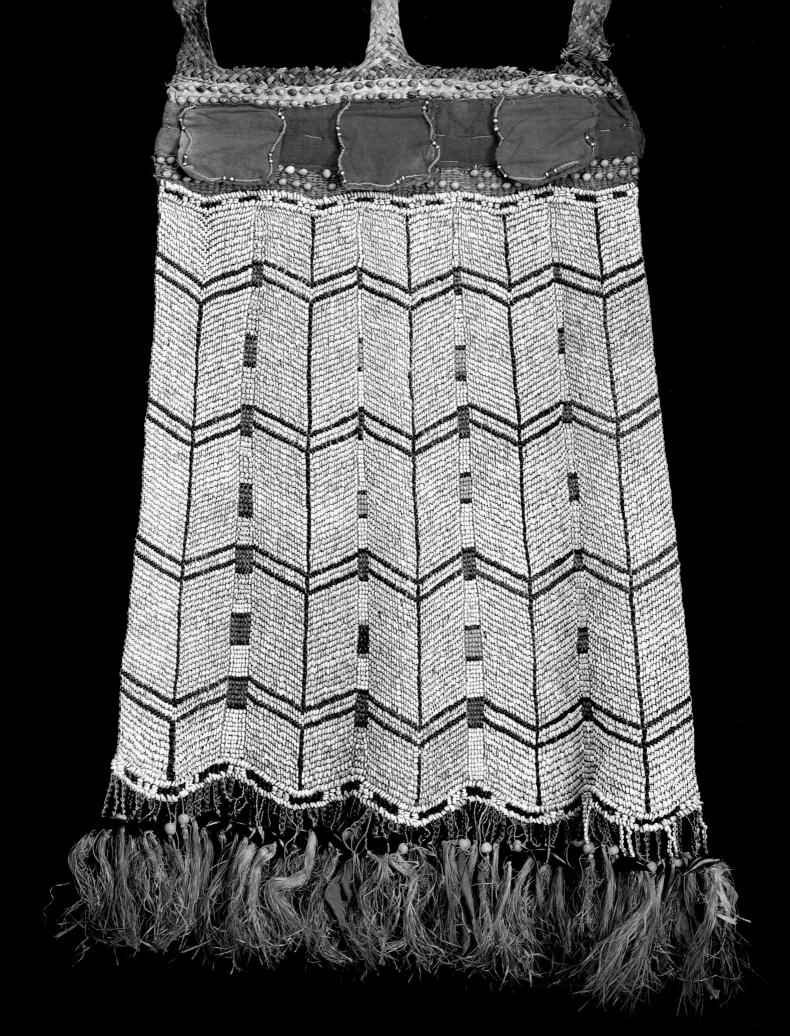

OCEANIA

Oceania, with its thousands of islands, has fostered pronounced local characteristics that make for a complex geography of styles. One thing the archipelagos of the Pacific do share, however, is a passion for self-decoration on a monumental scale. Big, bulky ornaments are commonplace. Asmat men of New Guinea, for example, think nothing of wearing an entire skull as a pectoral. The same decorative exuberance responsible for Japanese tattoos—the most elaborate on earth—informs all aspects of self-embellishment.

The alterations that Oceanic peoples perform on the living body are no less violent for being self-inflicted. Human beings transform themselves into creatures that only a Hieronymus Bosch could have dreamt up. Natives insert huge ornaments through holes they make in their noses, turning themselves into forbidding apparitions that look neither wholly man nor wholly beast. The human body is as aggressively altered after death as it is in life. In New Guinea, people cover ancestors' skulls with clay and decorate them with painted designs. The Maori of New Zealand use a kind of mummification process to preserve facial skin.

Male ornament predominates in Oceania, perhaps more so than anywhere else on earth. It is the men who enact the myths in ritual dramas; they even take the female parts. The women are often kept on the sidelines during these performances.

As one might expect from their geographic setting, these island-dwellers turn primarily to shells and other marine substances for raw materials. They fashion impressive nose ornaments from pieces of giant clam shell. Slices of melon shell serve as loincloths. Ivory from walruses and sperm whales is also used; a sperm-whale tooth might be worn as a pectoral. A pendant mounting of creamy white clamshell can set off the fragile intricacy of an openwork design cut from a thin sheet of tortoiseshell.

Even the humblest materials can be transfigured by the way they are assembled. Solomon Islanders insert tiny rodent teeth into elaborate wickerwork hairnets whose secret meanings have faded from memory. Men in the Highlands of New Guinea wear breastplate tallies down their chests like neckties: each piece of bamboo represents a set of five to ten prized pearl shells that the owner has given away during exchange ceremonies.

Shells—the preeminent insignia of social status—are extremely versatile. They have been used to make dye, containers, weapons, and tools. Giant clam shells are as hard and durable as marble. It is a difficult material to work, and only a handful of New Guinea craftsmen still know how to cut it. Those without modern equipment use a traditional tool set of bamboo and abrasive stone right out of the Stone Age; but time and patience make up for it. Months of labor can go into making even the simplest bracelet.[23]

In Oceania that familiar medium of exchange, the cowrie shell, reappears. Cowries are small, portable, long-lasting, hard-wearing, and difficult to counterfeit. Because they are relatively uniform in size and shape, they make a convenient

Man's loincloth from the Admiralty Islands, Papua New Guinea. Shell beads, glass trading beads, seeds, plant fiber, and cloth. Height 67 cm.

As a rule, the bak is worn only by men; however, an exception might be made for the wife of a very wealthy chief. These ceremonial loincloths, composed of thousands of minute shell beads, take months to make.

standard measure and a ready gauge of wealth alongside more perishable, less portable items of value, such as pigs or other live animals.

The peoples of New Guinea have used more than ten species of shell as mediums of exchange, and their value varies with locality. The Chambri (or Tchambuli) rate individual green turban shells according to their history, size, sex, shape, color, and markings. Pearl shell crescents can be used both to display wealth (on public or ceremonial occasions) and as a form of currency. These shells serve both purposes during gift-giving competitions, similar to the potlatch of northwestern coastal North America, when individuals jockey for social and political status. A person can raise his standing by giving more than he receives.

Pearl shell is assessed in terms of color and iridescence. Red or orange specimens are especially prized, and they are often rubbed with ocher to enhance their color. Although these shells may not be used to purchase purely utilitarian items, and are not money as we would define it, they may be exchanged for pigs or for the services of orators and sorcerers, and they may be paid as compensation to aggrieved parties for such things as insults or injuries. Pearl shells of white and green, although not considered part of an individual's wealth and prestige, are coveted ceremonial ornaments. Wearing white pearl shell for decorative purposes is thought to make a person look more impressive and give him an edge over rivals.

The intrinsic worth of shells eludes precise definition. A number of factors can affect their value: how hard they are to obtain, their purported healing properties, and the beliefs about the waters in which they are found, or their mythical origins. Some shells have specific functions. One variety, for example, is used exclusively during marriage negotiations. In the Sepik River region of Papua New Guinea, only a pearl shell crescent may be given as bridewealth payment and its value is greater than twenty green turban snail shells.

Other varieties of shell figure in initiation rites that mark the transition from childhood to maturity. Arapesh women wear the green tusk shell to indicate that they are married. In the Admiralty Islands, egg cowrie shells are the prerogative of nobles, who attach them to their belts, houses, and canoe prows. A warrior may hang some from his loincloth or wear one on his penis, but only when dancing or going into battle. Around Humboldt Bay of Papua New Guinea, a pectoral festooned with a species of tiny freshwater basket shell is believed to protect warriors in battle. On New Ireland, pendants fashioned from pierced tortoiseshell disks superimposed on clamshell disks—called kap kaps—may be worn only by men during celebrations commemorating the dead. They are handed down as family heirlooms, and their value is determined by both the size of the clam shell disk and the intricacy of the decorative openwork tortoiseshell design. The only thing a man from the Santa Cruz Islands values more than his pearl shell nasal ornament is his pectoral: making one used to be a long process that required the use of stone or shell tools and patient polishing with the skin of sharks or rays, pumice, or abrasive plants.

In Oceania one expects to find a profusion of shells in their natural state. In some regions, however, native artisans have been known to go to great lengths not to leave them as originally found. Shell beads are considered highly desirable because of the time and labor that go into making them. In the past, a stone tool was used to break the shell into pieces which were then sized by means of a perforated board. A hole was drilled into each disk with a flint boring tool and the shell was then polished with sand and water.

Shells are also used to imitate other materials. The Asmat people so prize wild boar's tusks that artisans contrive tusk-shaped nose ornaments from melon shell and pitch. Initiated men in the Maprik region, however, use actual tusks in their decorative back pendants. These pendants were once carried in the mouths of warriors as battle ornaments to make them look like charging boars, thereby proclaiming their fighting spirit and creating an impression of invulnerability.

Oceania's wealth of animal imagery is complemented by a marked tendency to simplification and even abstraction. The tortoiseshell wristbands used in ceremonial gift exchanges in the Sepik River region have plaited plant-fiber "clasps" with stylized animal designs, such as crocodiles. Few objects are as abstract as the jadeite or nephrite ear ornaments of New Zealand: unembellished, patiently polished rods, they are said to contain the *mana*, or magic power, of all who have worn them in the past.

Extreme simplicity of form also typifies the hook- or tongue-shaped neck ornaments from the Hawaiian Islands that are carved from a sperm-whale tooth or walrus tusk and suspended by slender loops of laboriously plaited human hair. Captain Cook brought back similar pendants in wood from one of his journeys to the South Seas. Australian aborigines fashion pubic pendants from pearl shell, a material they routinely use in their sorcery, and incise them with geometric patterns symbolizing rain.

Thus do the peoples of Oceania interpret the order of the cosmos.

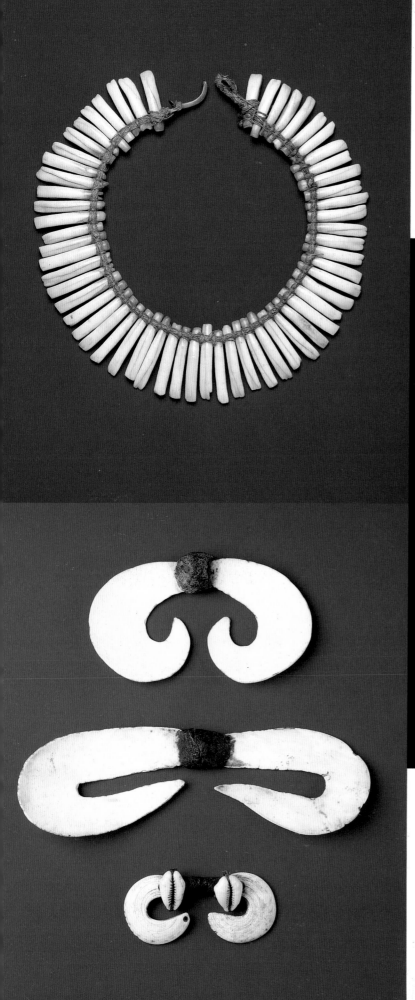

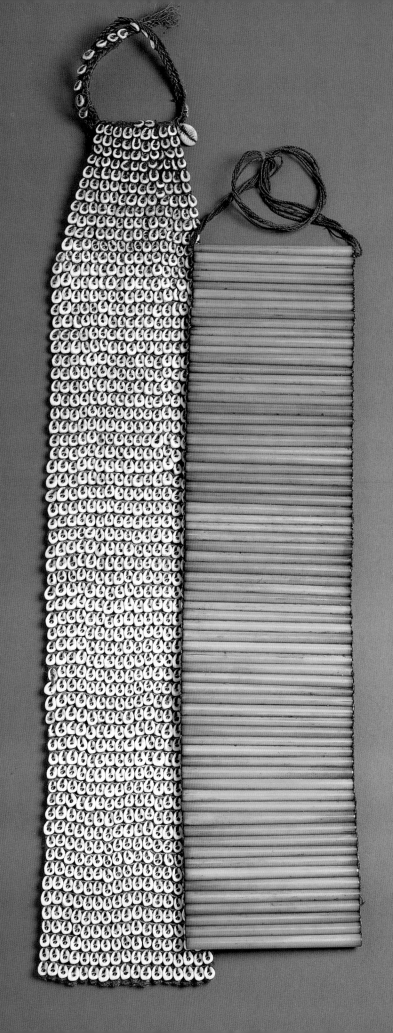

OPPOSITE TOP:
*Necklace from Irian Jaya (Asmat).
Diameter 18.5 cm.*

*This necklace is fashioned from
boar's teeth. The wild pig is held in
high regard in Oceania.*

OPPOSITE BOTTOM:
*Nose ornaments from Irian Jaya
(Asmat). Shell. Widest 19.8 cm.*

*Bipaneu carved in the shape of
boars' tusks were worn only on
important ceremonial occasions.*

OPPOSITE NEAR RIGHT:
*Necklace from Irian Jaya (Dani).
Bamboo with shell beads. Length
44 cm.*

*The Dani prize this type of necklace
because its materials are so costly.*

THIS PAGE:
*Left: Man's chest ornament from
Irian Jaya (Dani). Shell beads and
plant fiber. Height 46 cm.*

*Nassa shells—tiny basket shells
that live in fresh water or estuaries
—are widely used in Melanesian
and Indonesian body adornment.*

*Right: Man's breastplate from
Mount Hagen, Papua New Guinea.
Bamboo and plant fiber. Height
37.3 cm.*

*Only a high-ranking man is entitled
to wear an omak, a tally of bamboo slats, each of which represents
a set of pearl shells he has given
away during exchange ceremonies.*

Nose ornaments from Irian Jaya (Asmat). Cassowary or boar bone. Widest 16.4 cm.

Before they can wear an otsj, young initiated males must undergo a painful procedure to pierce the nasal septum.

Necklaces from Papua New Guinea and Tonga. Shell beads, Job's-tears, and teeth. Length 26 cm. to 62 cm.

Five necklaces from New Guinea (from top) and one from Tonga (bottom) demonstrate the varied uses of beads made from shell (bottom), seeds (third from bottom), and teeth (second from bottom). The necklace from Tonga is worn only by the king.

Pectoral from Humboldt Bay, Papua New Guinea. Boar's tusks, basket shells, seeds, and string. Height 40 cm.

Men display this impressive ornament at major celebrations. It is also worn in battle to deflect enemy arrows.

THIS PAGE:

Chest ornament from Papua New Guinea (Mendi). Shell. Height of shell 22.8 cm.

More often worn by men than by women, this ceremonial pakol covers nearly the entire chest.

OPPOSITE TOP LEFT:

Pendants and bracelet from Papua New Guinea (Sepik). Shell and tortoiseshell. Width 9.5 cm. (left), 10.2 cm. (top right), and height 13 cm. (bottom right).

Worn as pendants, these ornaments can also be incorporated into a cassowary-feather headdress. The mounted tortoiseshell designs can be abstract or representational.

OPPOSITE TOP RIGHT:

Chest ornament and case from Papua New Guinea (Foi). Pearl shell and tree bark. Width of left case 22.5 cm.

Kina *can be worn as body ornaments (right) or used as a means of payment (left). Spotted, red-stained pearl-shell pectorals are made only by the Foi people. The bark carrying cases, painted red and embellished with designs, are works of art in their own right.*

OPPOSITE BOTTOM LEFT:

Nose ornaments.

Top: From Papua New Guinea. Pearl shell. Width 10.2 cm.

Middle: From Papua New Guinea. Ivory. Width 8.5 cm.

Bottom: From Santa Cruz, Solomon Islands. Tortoiseshell. Height 5.3 cm.

Here, as in Africa, nose ornaments protect the wearer from both evil spirits and physical ailments.

OPPOSITE BOTTOM RIGHT:

Man's necklace from Papua New Guinea. Shell, feathers, and plant fiber. Width 38 cm.

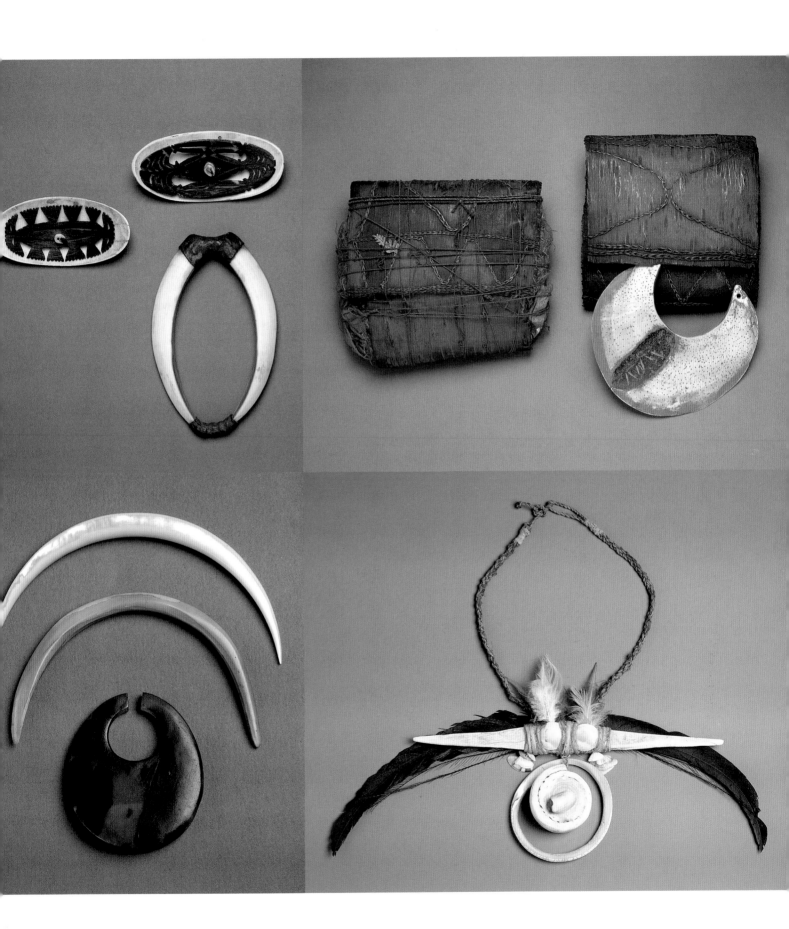

OPPOSITE TOP LEFT:

Chest ornament from Papua New Guinea. Pearl shell, pitch, and plant fiber. Height of shell 18 cm.

OPPOSITE TOP RIGHT:

Bottom right: Penile ornament from the Admiralty Islands, Papua New Guinea. Egg-cowrie shell. Height 8.4 cm.

All others: Necklace and pendants from the Solomon Islands. Shell. Width 7 to 13 cm.

The pendants are made of giant clamshell. The egg-cowrie-shell ornament is worn only by noblemen when they are dancing or fighting and is kept in a pouch suspended from the neck when not in use.

OPPOSITE BOTTOM LEFT:

Necklace from Papua New Guinea. Conus and nassa shells, plant fiber. Length 66 cm.

In New Guinea, ornaments may be worn variously on the body. A necklace might also be worn as a head-dress, a belt, or even a cache-sexe.

OPPOSITE BOTTOM RIGHT:

Top, left and right: Pendants from New Ireland, Papua New Guinea. Giant clamshell and tortoiseshell. Diameter 6.8 cm. and 8.8 cm.

The value of ceremonial kap-kaps varies with the diameter of the giant clamshell disk and the intricacy of the mounted openwork tortoiseshell design.

Bottom, left and right: Pendants from the Solomon Islands. Shell. Diameter 6 cm. and 6.1 cm.

These pendants are decorated with stylized frigate birds (left) and bonito (right).

THIS PAGE:

Necklace from Papua New Guinea. Shell beads, animal teeth, and plant fiber. Diameter 23.5 cm.

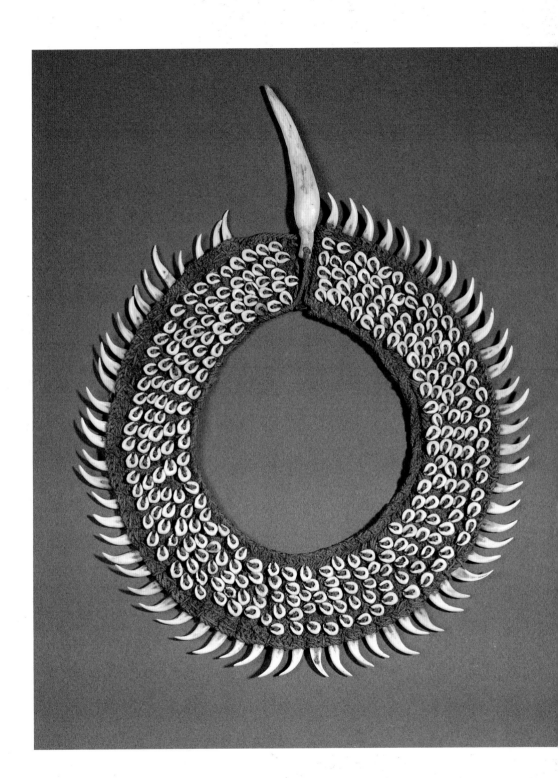

THIS PAGE:
Armband from Papua New Guinea. Tortoiseshell, plant fiber, and cowrie shells. Width 18.5 cm.

In the Sepik region, tortoiseshell armbands often feature decorative designs of woven plant fiber. The crocodile figures prominently in creation myths.

OPPOSITE TOP LEFT:
Man's armlet from Papua New Guinea (Mendi). Bamboo and string. Height 25.5 cm.

Only wealthy men may wear sekip, *one above each elbow.*

OPPOSITE TOP RIGHT:
Man's belt from Papua New Guinea. Tree bark. Diameter 21.5 cm.

Men wear this ceremonial ore *after they have been initiated. The designs engraved into the bark are high-lighted with whitewash. The stylized "head" represents an ancestor.*

OPPOSITE BOTTOM LEFT:
Kneeband from Papua New Guinea. Shell beads and plant fiber. Height 18 cm.

Worn by male dancers, this knee ornament resembles a similar type of funeral mask that represents the spirit of an ancestor.

OPPOSITE BOTTOM RIGHT:
Necklace from Papua New Guinea. Marsupial jaws. Diameter 25 cm.

Australia and New Guinea are home to the world's highest concentration of marsupial animals. The number of jaws comprising this necklace increase its potency as a source of strength and protection.

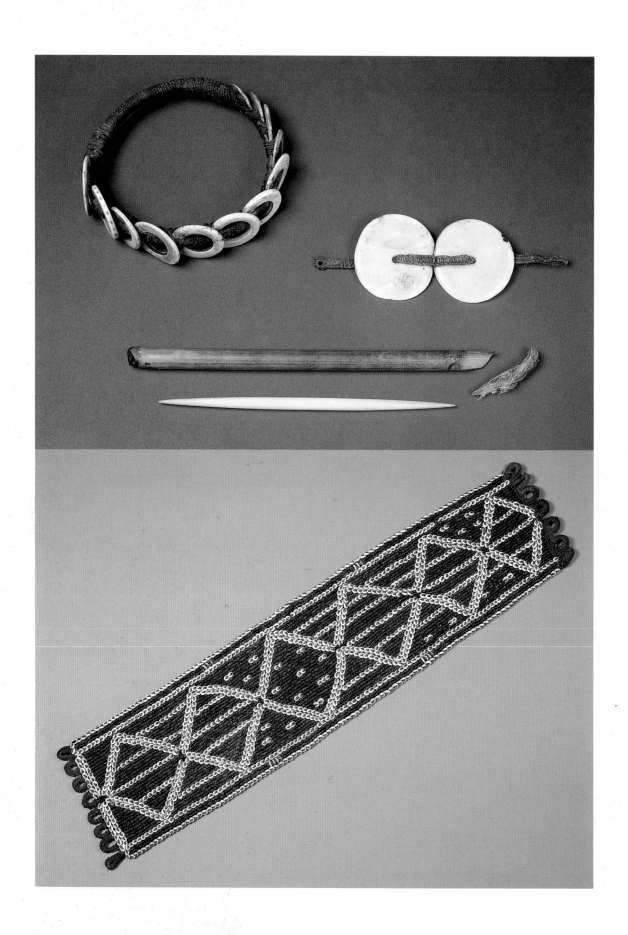

OPPOSITE TOP:

Top: Bracelets from Papua New Guinea. Shell. Diameter 12.6 cm. (left), width 15 cm. (right).

Bottom: Nose ornament from Santa Cruz, Solomon Islands. Shell. Width 17 cm.

Usually worn by men only, niale are commonly found throughout Melanesia.

OPPOSITE BOTTOM:

Belt from Papua New Guinea. Coconut fiber, shell beads, and plant fiber. Length 70.5 cm.

BOTTOM:

Chest ornament from the northeast coast of Papua New Guinea. Shells and plant fiber. Height 40 cm.

This pendant, decorated with several different kinds of shells, attests to the diversity of body adornment in New Guinea.

RIGHT:

Man's dorsal pendant from Papua New Guinea (Abelam). Tusks, shell beads, plant fiber, and feathers. Height 56 cm.

Warriors once held the kara-ut *in their mouths to frighten their enemies. This anthropomorphic ornament, believed to embody ancestral spirits, is now worn by high-ranking men as part of their daily attire.*

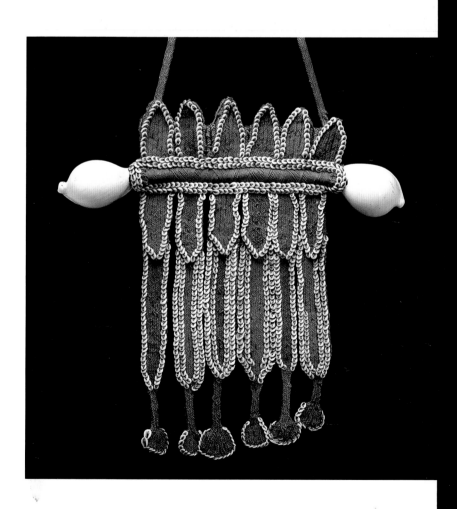

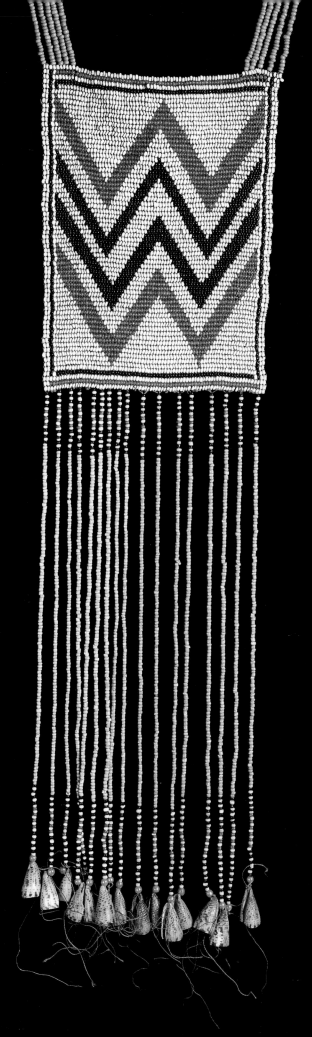

THIS PAGE:

Necklace from the Solomon Islands. Glass trade beads and shell beads. Total length 83 cm.

Solomon Islanders traded provisions and other items for European glass beads. Earlier versions of this type of marriage necklace were probably made completely of shells and represented great wealth. Indigenous peoples, however, are proud of possessions from the outside world. One old photograph shows a Solomon Islander with an alarm clock in his earlobe.

OPPOSITE TOP LEFT:

Armband from Vanuatu (formerly New Hebrides). Coconut fiber and shell beads. Height 19.5 cm.

This armband and the belt from New Guinea (page 220, bottom) feature the same kind of abstract design and contrasting colors even though the islands are hundreds of miles apart.

OPPOSITE TOP RIGHT:

Necklace from Nauru. Pearl shell and shell beads. Length 25 cm.

In Micronesia wood is scarce and sculpture rare. Most surviving jewelry from Nauru is made of plant material, shells, and frigate-bird feathers—fragile substances that impart a delicacy largely missing from Melanesian ornaments.

OPPOSITE BOTTOM:

From the Solomon Islands. Animal teeth, glass trade beads, and shell beads.

Left: Headband. Diameter 20 cm.

Right: Earrings. Height 2.5 cm.

Men wore headbands like this as an indication of wealth. Weaving row upon row of cuscus teeth into plant fiber was a time-consuming process that has since died out. The charming little earrings demonstrate the skill of basketweavers, who were better known for combs.

OPPOSITE TOP:

Belt from the Solomon Islands. Tree bark. Diameter 25.5 cm.

Like many ornaments and small personal objects from Melanesia, this belt is decorated with pyro-graphic designs probably inspired by local flora.

OPPOSITE BOTTOM:

Left: Bracelet from Choiseul, Solomon Islands. Shell. Diameter 7.3 cm.

This bracelet was buried alongside its owner and therefore has the characteristic look of ancient shell jewelry.

Right: Bracelet from Papua New Guinea. Tortoiseshell. Height 11 cm.

Unusual decoration sets this bracelet apart from others of its type, commonly worn on the northeast coast of New Guinea. The maker incised the design using rodent teeth and then steam-bent the tortoiseshell into shape.

THIS PAGE:

Chest ornaments from the Solomon Islands. Pearl shell. Height 13 cm. (top) and width 22.5 cm. (bottom).

These pectorals exemplify Solomon Islanders' preference for understated ornamentation. Much more elaborate assemblages are favored by New Guinea tribesmen.

TOP:

Man's chest pendant from Santa Cruz, Solomon Islands. Giant clamshell and plant fiber. Height 19.3 cm.

Cut from giant clamshell, this *tepatu* is worn by men as a part of daily attire. Its impressive size notwithstanding, it is worth less than clamshell disks with mounted openwork tortoiseshell designs.

BOTTOM:

Chest pendant from Santa Cruz, Solomon Islands. Shell, tortoiseshell, and plant fiber. Diameter 13.7 cm.

The considerable time and effort invested in making objects like this *tema* conferred considerable prestige on the man who wore them. The mounted tortoiseshell designs represent some bonito and a frigate bird.

OPPOSITE TOP LEFT:

Man's pubic pendant from Australia (Pitjantjara). Pearl shell. Height 17.3 cm.

The ocher-reddened patterns symbolize rain or indicate ethnic affiliation. The pendant may be suspended from a belt of human hair or used in exchange for goods.

OPPOSITE TOP RIGHT:

Man's ear ornament from New Zealand (Maori). Nephrite. Height 12.5 cm.

Handed down from generation to generation, each kuru mahora supposedly contained the magic power of all who had worn it.

OPPOSITE BOTTOM:

Pectoral from the Solomon Islands. Pearl shell. Width 19.6 cm.

A spectacular ornament like this was the prerogative of young men. Older men wore kap-kaps, nose ornaments, and earrings.

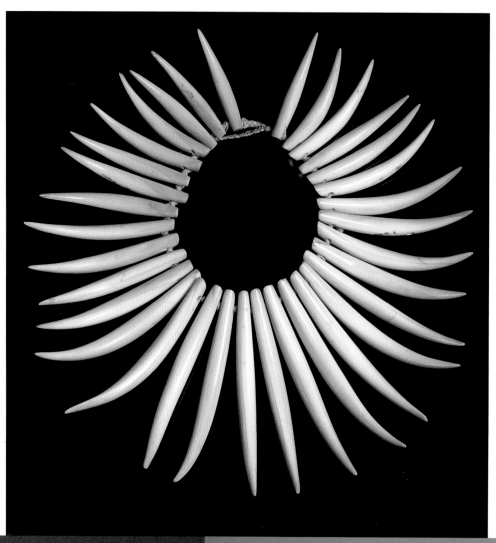

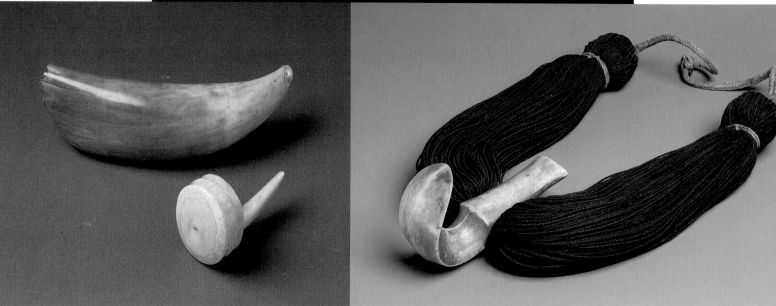

Necklace from Fiji. Sperm-whale ivory. Diameter 32 cm.

The wasekaseka, *a prestigious chief's necklace, was also worn on Samoa and Tonga.*

Opposite bottom left:

Top: Man's pectoral from Fiji. Sperm-whale tooth. Width 21 cm.

The chief's pendant is a complete sperm whale tooth suspended from a thick cord of plaited coconut fiber.

Bottom: Ear ornament from the Marquesas Islands. Whale ivory. Width 8.7 cm.

Ha'akai, *pairs of ear ornaments carved from single pieces of ivory, were worn by high-ranking men on festive occasions.*

Opposite bottom right:

Neck ornament from Hawaii. Sperm-whale ivory and human hair. Length 26 cm., ivory 11 cm.

It is easy to see why the lei niho palaoa *ranks as Hawaii's most prestigious body ornament. Only persons of high status were entitled to it.*

Top:

From the Marquesas Islands.

Right: Headdress or necklace. Teeth, glass beads, and plant fiber. Diameter 22 cm.

Left: Earrings. Teeth, tortoiseshell, and glass beads. Height 9 cm.

This set of women's ornaments was occasionally worn by men. Glass beads imported from Europe gradually replaced fish vertebrae; the teeth are of porpoises.

Bottom:

Necklace from Hawaii. Shells. Diameter 23 cm.

Worn on the head or around the neck, this woman's lei *is made up of thousands of tiny shells.*

229

Certain facets of Pre-Columbian civilizations completely vanished without any tangible vestiges or documentation. Time took its toll on feathers and other perishable materials, leaving us with serious gaps in the history of self-adornment in this region. One fact, however, is indisputable: its peoples were passionately interested in precious metals. They developed sophisticated metalworking traditions. This was, after all, the birthplace of the legend of El Dorado, the man covered from head to toe with gold dust, plates of gold, and golden crowns.[24] The peoples of Mesoamerica believed that gold was the sweat of the sun. In Peru, silver was thought to be the tears of the moon.

Smiths utilized forging techniques and the lost-wax casting process to produce highly prized gold status symbols that accompanied their owners to the grave. Some nose ornaments were so large that they covered the wearer's mouth. Round labrets enlarged the lips, and chests were emblazoned with pendants decorated with highly stylized human and animal figures, exquisitely detailed illustrative scenes, and spirals and other geometric motifs.

When the Spaniards first arrived in the New World, they were dumbfounded by the profusion and sumptuousness of indigenous jewelry, some of which was documented by travelers and artists. In addition to precious metals, beautiful minerals were used, and they, too, had other meanings: jade, for example, symbolized the flesh of rain gods and came to be associated with purity and newborn children. Body ornamentation was the preeminent art form of Pre-Columbian America and in some cases, as with the Tairona people, the remaining artifacts serve as our sole concrete links to an entire culture.

That the indigenous peoples of the Americas, North and South alike, have used more feathers than anyone else is a point few would argue. Birds were hunted or domesticated expressly for their plumage, which was used on everything from tools and ritual artifacts to headdresses, earrings, and armbands. Among the Kayapo of Amazonia and a number of other societies, dancers literally transform themselves into "bird men" by covering their bodies with a mixture of latex, crushed eggshell, and down.[25] For some peoples, certain kinds of feathers are a means of self-identification. Elsewhere, a person's standing in the community may be gauged by how skillfully he or she can trim, combine, arrange, or bind feathers together. In one group a novice shaman is considered to be initiated once his winged spirit has taken leave of his body.

In some American cultures men and women alike dress up as birds to mark important ceremonies: after the loss of virginity, after a murder, at initiations, or at celebrations related to crops or food supply. At funerals, the deceased may be given feathers so that he can take wing, to expedite his journey from the village of the living to the realm of the dead. Diverse though these feather-related practices may be, they must not distract us from the ubiquitous criterion of self-embellishment. Wearing ritual attire does not make a man any less intent on showing off.

Pendant from Colombia (Tairona),
A.D. 900–1550. Gold. Height 3.2 cm.

THIS PAGE:
From Colombia.

*Left: Ear ornament. Quimbaya,
A.D. 400–1100. Gold. Diameter
4.3 cm.*

*Right: Nose ornament. Tairona,
A.D. 900–1550. Gold. Height 3 cm.*

OPPOSITE TOP:
*Chest ornament from Tairona,
Colombia, A.D. 900–1550. Gold.
Width 17.7 cm.*

*The name Tairona means "gold-
worker," and their jewelry marked
the culmination of a long goldwork-
ing tradition in Colombia. Their
techniques included both hammering
(as exemplified by this pectoral)
and lost-wax casting (see page 230).*

OPPOSITE BOTTOM :
*Chest ornament from Sinu region,
Colombia, A.D. 900. Gold. Width
26 cm.*

*Pre-Columbian artisans were adept
at hammering sheet gold into decorative objects, like this large pectoral.*

The desire of tribal peoples to acquire the beauty and power of highly respected animals relates closely to their totemic beliefs. In some parts of South America it is thought that a person can magically absorb the violent strength of the fearsome harpy eagle, which is regarded as a mythical creature. The same holds for the jaguar, which has always fascinated the peoples of the Americas, who believed it gave fire to humankind and made civilization possible. Several Amazonian peoples claim descent from a woman who was raped by a jaguar, the cat that epitomizes strength as surely as the lion does in other cultures. Because jaguars hunt by day and by night, they came to be associated with movement between different levels of the cosmos. Regarded as mediators, they were the shaman's favorite totem animal; their fur, teeth, and claws became emblems of power.

In addition to adorning their bodies, the people also alter them; earlobes are pierced to create a symbolic second aural opening. Men have their lower lips pierced in the belief that this will improve oratorical skills. Piercing the nose is thought to enhance the sense of smell. By changing their bodies in these and other ways the men and women of the Americas sought ways to abet their senses and greatly increase the influential power of speech.

Some of the indigenous peoples scattered throughout the sprawling Amazonian rain forest are still cut off from the outside world. Presumably, therefore, certain ancestral forms of adornment have been replicated for centuries with relatively consistency. The Navajo and Zuni peoples of North America, however, so famous for their wrought jewelry, are thought to have learned metalworking techniques from Spanish smiths. These Indians went on to become masters of silverwork, often adding turquoise, a possible resurfacing of an age-old tradition of using the luminous, sky-blue stone in mosaic and inlay. Their brooches, belt buckles (probably modeled on the decorative fittings of Spanish saddles and bridles), finger rings, and hairpins are constant reminders of European influences, proof of adept acculturation.

OPPOSITE TOP:

Men's and women's earrings from Chile (Mapuche). Silver. Height 3.7 cm. to 12 cm.

Documents from the thirteenth century describe the Mapuche, also called Araucanians, as being richly adorned with silver jewelry.

OPPOSITE BOTTOM:

Cloak pins from Chile (Mapuche). Silver. Height 22 cm. to 42 cm. Largest diameter 19 cm.

Mapuche women wear long cloak pins when they go into town, or to funerals and other special ceremonies. They shine their jewelry once a year.

OPPOSITE NEAR RIGHT:

Woman's cloak pin from Chile (Mapuche). Silver. Length 38 cm. (pin) and height 35 cm. (pendant).

Although fibulas and pendants come in a wide range of shapes and sizes, those produced by Mapuche artisans feature articulated assemblages of geometrically shaped elements. Making jewelry is men's work—and their only form of manual labor.

TOP:

Man's necklace from Mato Grosso, Brazil. Teeth and cotton. Length 32.5 cm.

Like many other peoples, some South American natives believe that wearing an animal's claws and fangs imparts its strength to the wearer. The right to wear certain kinds of teeth is determined by rank in the community.

BOTTOM:

Necklaces from Brazil. Top to bottom: Mother-of-pearl (Xingu); snake vertebrae (Rio Negro); shell (Xingu); teeth (Xingu River). Length 35 cm. to 48.5 cm.

Even today, peoples living in remote regions cling to traditional body adornment.

OPPOSITE TOP:

Ear ornaments from Brazil.
Feathers. Height 14.5 cm.

Certain tribes, such as the Kayapo,
believe that ear piercing and the
ability to hear, understand, and
remember orally transmitted
knowledge are linked.

OPPOSITE BOTTOM:

From Xingu, Brazil (Mekragnoti).

Left: Bracelet. Seeds, plant fiber,
and glass beads. Width 22 cm.

Right: Ear ornaments. Feathers.
Height 12.5 cm.

TOP:

Necklace and ear ornaments from
Amazonia, Brazil. Feathers, seeds,
and cotton. Length: 43 cm. (left),
and height 26 cm. (right).

Feathers, like other forms of body
adornment, constitute a language
indicating ethnic affiliation, age,
social status, and wealth.

BOTTOM:

Feather jewelry from Amazonia,
Brazil (Txicao).

Top: Headdress. Diameter 21 cm.

Bottom left: Armband. Width 17 cm.

Bottom right: Pair of ear ornaments.
Height 9 cm.

The same type of headdress is worn
by the Jivaro of Peru.

237

TOP:

*Man's headdress from Upper Xingu,
Brazil (Kamaiura). Feathers and
plant fiber. Height 63 cm.*

The akangitat *is customarily worn
by men, but women wear it during
the* yamaricuma, *one of only two
ceremonies in which women take
a leading part.*

BOTTOM:

*Necklace from Amazonia (Brazil).
Feathers. Length 28 cm.*

*Materials like feathers and seeds
are perishable in the tropics. That
is why so few examples of older
decorative featherwork, like the
one shown here, have survived.*

OPPOSITE TOP:

*Man's pendant from Mato Grosso,
Brazil. Animal claws and cotton.
Width 23 cm.*

*Although a similar kind of cotton
binding occurs in work produced
by the Bororo of Mato Grasso, the
provenance of this pendant has
not been positively identified.*

OPPOSITE BOTTOM:

*Basket from Brazil (Kaiabi). Straw
and feathers. Width 36 cm.*

*This container was used to store
and protect feathered ornaments
and small personal possessions.*

Opposite:

Necklace and earrings from the southwestern United States (Navajo). Silver. Length 40 cm. and 6.5 cm.

Squash-blossom necklaces are worn by both sexes. The earliest Navajo silver jewelry was influenced by Spanish smiths, which accounts for the pomegranate-shaped beads and the crescent-shaped pendant. The earliest examples of Navajo silver-work are typically quite understated and do not contain turquoise.

Top:

Finger rings from the southwestern United States. Height 3 cm. to 5.3 cm.

Far right, center, and top left: Navajo. Silver and turquoise.

All others: Zuni. Silver, turquoise, jet, and shell.

Turquoise—which the Indians call sky stone—symbolizes good luck, health, and happiness, has religious significance, and is believed to have magical powers.

Bottom:

Bracelets from the southwestern United States (Navajo). Silver and turquoise. Width 6 cm. to 7.5 cm.

The earliest Navajo silver jewelry is said to date from the 1860s. Anything made before the 1920s is considered very old. Most of these bracelets were made during that period.

RIGHT:

RIGHT:

Necklaces from the southwestern United States (Santo Domingo Pueblo). Turquoise and shell. Length 48 cm.

These necklaces consist of disk-shaped heishi *beads interspersed with pieces of turquoise. The* heishi *happen to be of shell, but they can be made from various materials. Pueblo women used to wear a pair of long ornaments* (joclas) *in their ears, but now they dangle them from their necklaces.*

BOTTOM:

From the southwestern United States (Navajo).

Left: Wristband. Silver, leather, and turquoise. Height 11.3 cm.

Right: Belt buckle. Silver and turquoise. Width 9.4 cm.

The concha *(right), probably inspired by Spanish prototypes, and* ketoh *(archer's wristband, left) are among the oldest types of body ornaments attributed to the Navajo.*

As is true in many other native cultures, Navajo silver and turquoise jewelry can be used as currency.

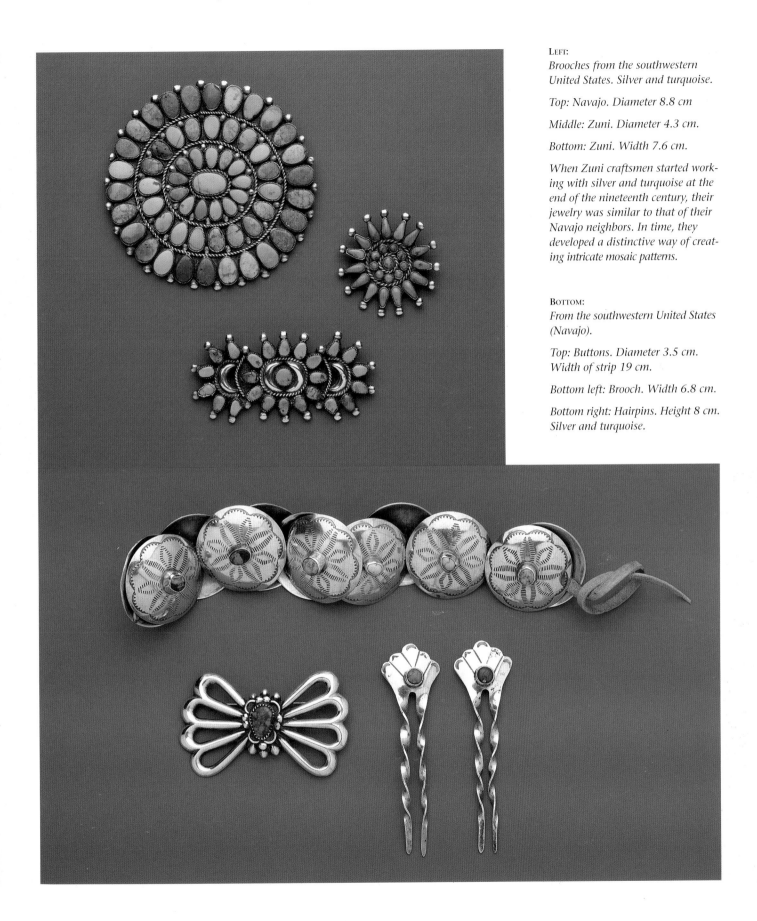

LEFT:
Brooches from the southwestern United States. Silver and turquoise.

Top: Navajo. Diameter 8.8 cm

Middle: Zuni. Diameter 4.3 cm.

Bottom: Zuni. Width 7.6 cm.

When Zuni craftsmen started working with silver and turquoise at the end of the nineteenth century, their jewelry was similar to that of their Navajo neighbors. In time, they developed a distinctive way of creating intricate mosaic patterns.

BOTTOM:
From the southwestern United States (Navajo).

Top: Buttons. Diameter 3.5 cm. Width of strip 19 cm.

Bottom left: Brooch. Width 6.8 cm.

Bottom right: Hairpins. Height 8 cm. Silver and turquoise.

JOURNEY'S END

As we range through this vast world, the importance—the vital importance—of something we might idly dismiss as trivial or superfluous becomes all too apparent. No culture fails to lavish time and energy on the making and wearing of body adornments. Every culture invests it with meaning, and turns it into an iridescent language that can be passed on from one generation to the next.

All civilizations express themselves through body ornamentation whether or not they have developed writing. It is anything but a subsidiary or marginal means of communication. Seldom has a language thrived on so many materials, colors, forms, and technical skills. Every conceivable resource, every available substance, from the crudest to the most sophisticated, is used. The body becomes a kind of book that chronicles not only life's routine activities, joyous occasions, and momentous rituals, but death and our ceremonial attempts to lessen the sting of its finality.

Over the millenia, ornaments have been the human body's constant companion, from the moment wailing newborns enter the world to the moment the wizened and timeworn breathe their last. People have taken these prized possessions with them to the grave or cremation pyre, a final escort to help them negotiate such momentous transitions as may await them in the hereafter. These treasures are as fabulous as the hoard in Ali Baba's cave, only they are scattered all over the world. How do things stand with them now?

Nostalgia is growing for cultures that are no more, for those essential objects once so tightly woven into the fabric of life and which would have long since faded into oblivion had collectors and museums not taken them under their wing. Think of the many cultures that have died away, forsaking that which is most intimate, yet most public about them: their jewelry. Jewelry invariably embellished its wearers, whether it was worn to seduce, or flaunted as insignia of power; whether it absorbed the warmth of their bodies or, as was sometimes the case, injured or maimed them. Jewelry reached into every facet of life and encoded a bewildering complex of meanings—codes to which we have all too often lost the key.

We have lost tangible artifacts, but the loss in terms of symbolic content is no less grievous. The absence of perishable materials has left gaps in the history of humanity. Once copious wellsprings of imagery have dried up. The collective memory of nonliterate peoples, their oral traditions, are apt to fade away.

Man's necklace from the Plains region of the United States. Fur, grizzly bear claws, and brass beads. Diameter 38 cm.

Necklaces like this signified hunting prowess and conferred considerable prestige on the wearer. Bear claws were so highly prized that when the grizzly population dwindled in the late 1800s, imitation claws carved from all sorts of materials became popular.

The mythologies of Africa or Oceania hold as many riches as ancient Greece or Rome. Their true depth and range become apparent when we examine the scraps of knowledge that alert, receptive ethnologists like Marcel Griaule and Michel Leiris just barely managed to rescue from oblivion. A blind Dogon elder named Ogotemmeli once told Griaule how human speech is like weaving, how the ornaments women wear—a circlet of green beads about the head, a necklace, two red beads at the corners of the nostrils—represent jewelry that adorns the Nommo, or water spirit. Their copper bracelets are supposed to represent the spirit's bones; rows of beads on the right ankle stand for his tail; rings on the first, third, and little finger symbolize his body. The elder made a point of mentioning that "no rings should be worn on the toes, because the Spirit has no feet."[26]

This story exemplifies a trove of remarkable lore that is as rich as children's stories, as rich as literature, as rich as the world's major religions. Of course, an ethnologist has to be something of a poet to decode key information that spells out in great detail how a highly developed culture predicates its craft traditions on myth—unless, that is, the process works the other way around.

Once prolific, ethnic craft traditions have been reduced to a few scattered pockets of activity. A source of growing concern is that international standardization may be having a leveling effect on traditions that still combine technical expertise and imaginative design. Cargo upon cargo of beads flooded Africa in the nineteenth century, but natives adapted them to regional styles and altered and rearranged them to suit individual tastes.

As things now stand, some of the world's capacity to make ethnic jewelry is irretrievably lost. Much of what is still being produced is geared to the tourist trade. Age-old craft traditions are slipping away; nothing, or precious little, is taking their place. All the more reason to cherish the Ghysels Collection, which has so diligently gleaned these illuminating fragments of culture over the decades.

1. For an exhaustive discussion of this subject, see William Rubin (ed.), *"Primitivism" in 20th-Century Art: Affinity of the Tribal and Modern*. New York: Museum of Modern Art, and Harry N. Abrams, Inc., 1984.

2. See *Picasso et les choses*. Paris: Grand Palais, 29 September–28 December 1992 (exhibition catalogue).

3. *A Visage découvert*. Paris: Flammarion-Fondation Cartier, 1992.

4. See Renate Wente-Lukas, *Die materielle Kultur der nicht-islamischen Ethnien von Nordkamerun und Nordostnigeria*, p. 241.

5. *Sculptures nègres, 24 photographies précédées d'un avertissement de Guillaume Apollinaire et d'un exposé de Paul Guillaume*. Paris, 1917.

6. Limited space precludes a comprehensive discussion of geographical subdivisions. See, for example, Angela Fisher, *Africa Adorned*. See also Denise Paulme and Jacques Brosse, *Parures africaines*.

7. Carol Beckwith and Marion van Offelen, *Nomads of Niger*.

8. See France Borel, *Le Vêtement incarné*.

9. Fisher, *Africa Adorned*, page 137.

10. Also spelled *accory, akori, eygri, aigris*.

11. See Lois Sherr Dubin, *The History of Beads from 30,000 B.C. to the Present*.

12. Timothy F. Garrard, *Gold of Africa: Jewellery and Ornamentation from Ghana, Cote d'Ivoire, Mali and Senegal in the Collection of the Barbier-Mueller Museum*.

13. Mungo Park, *Travels in the Interior Districts of Africa*, London, 1799. New York: Arno Press, 1971. p. 304.

14. Garrard, *Gold of Africa*.

15. Garrard, *Gold of Africa*.

16. Garrard, *Gold of Africa*.

17. Dubin, *History of Beads*.

18. Momin Latif, *Bijoux Moghols-Mogol Juwelen-Mughal Jewels*. Brussels: La Société Générale de Banque, 21 January–28 February, 1982 (Exhibition catalogue).

19. Julian Jacobs, with Alan Macfarlane, Sarah Harrison, and Anita Herle, *The Nagas, Hill Peoples of Northeast India: Society, Culture, and the Colonial Encounter*.

20. Paul and Elaine Lewis, *Peoples of the Golden Triangle: Six Tribes in Thailand*.

21. Susan Rodgers, *Gold and Power: Jewelry from Indonesia, Malaysia, and the Philippines from the Collection of the Barbier-Mueller Museum, Geneva*.

22. Dubin, *History of Beads*.

23. See Jane Fearer Safer and Frances McLaughlin Gill, *Spirals from the Sea: An Anthropological Look at Shells*.

24. See *Gold of El Dorado*, text by Warwick Bray. New York: American Museum of Natural History, 1979. (Exhibition catalogue, November 13, 1979–March 18, 1980).

25. Gustaaf Verswijver, *Kaiapo-Amazonie*.

26. Marcel Griaule, *Conversations with Ogotemmeli: An Introduction to Dogon Religious Ideas*. Oxford: International African Institute, Oxford University Press, 1965. pp. 73, 80–81.

BIBLIOGRAPHY

GENERAL

Al-Jadir, S. *Arab and Islamic Silver*. London: Stacey International, 1981.

Biebuyck, D. P., and Van Den Abbeele, N. *The Power of Headdresses*. Brussels: Tendi, 1984.

Borel, F. *Le Vêtement Incarné*. Paris: Calmann-Lévy, 1992.

Buschan, G. (ed.) *Illustrierte Völkerkunde*. (2 Bd.) Stuttgart: Strecker, and Schröder, 1923.

Buschan, G. (ed.) *Die Sitten der Völker*. (3 Bd.) Stuttgart: Union Deutsche Verlagsgesellschaft, no date.

Daniels, G. *Folk Jewelry of the World*. New York: Rizzoli, 1989.

Dubin, L. S. *The History of Beads from 30,000 B.C. to the Present*. New York: Harry N. Abrams, Inc., 1987.

Ebin, V. *The Body Decorated*. London: Thames and Hudson Ltd., 1979.

Erikson, J. M. *The Universal Bead*. New York: Norton and Co., 1969.

Gerlach, M. *Primitive and Folk Jewelry*. New York: Dover Publications, 1971.

Gladiss, A., von. *Traditioneller Silberschmuck der Islamischen Welt*. Hannover: Kestner-Museum, 1986 (exhibition catalogue).

Haenni, J. J., and Dufour Chr. "L'ambre de la Baltique dans la Mythologie, l'histoire, l'artisanat, la médecine, et l'industrie." *Les Fantômes de l'ambre*. Neuchâtel: pp. 11–13, Musée d'Histoire Naturelle, 1992.

Hammerton, J. A. (ed.) *People of All Nations*. 6 volumes, London: Fleetway House, no date.

Hasson, R. *Later Islamic Jewelry*. Jerusalem, L. A. Mayer Institute for Islamic Art, 1987.

Heiniger, E. A. and J. *Le Grand Livre des Bijoux*. Lausanne: Edita, 1974.

Herion, P. *La Parure*. Königsbach-Stein: Verlag Hans Schöner, 1985.

Hoffman, E., and Treide, B. *Parures des Temps Anciens, des Peuples Lointains*. Paris: Aux Quais de Paris, Librairie G. Kogan, 1977.

Hutchinson & Co. (ed.) *Living Races of Mankind*. 2 volumes, no date.

Hutchinson, W. (ed.) *Customs of the World*. 2 volumes, London: no date.

Jenkins, M. and Keene, M. *Islamic Jewelry in the Metropolitan Museum of Art*. New York: The Metropolitan Museum of Art, 1982.

Klever, K. and U. *Exotischer Schmuck*. Munich: Mosaik Verlag, 1977.

Mack, J. *Ethnic Jewelry*. New York: Harry N. Abrams Inc., 1988.

Musée d' Ethnographie de Genéve (ed.) *La parure dans le Monde*. 1949.

Musée Royal de l'Afrique Centrale. Choix d'objets de Parure de Cinq Continents. Tervuren: Musée Royal de l'Afrique Centrale, no date.

Palazzo Ducale. *Ambra oro del Nord*. Venice: Alfiere Edizioni d'Arte, 1978 (exhibition catalogue).

Phelps, S. *Art and Artifacts of the Pacific, Africa and the Americas*. The James Hooper Collection, London: Hutchinson, 1976.

Rabineau, P. *Feather Arts*. Chicago: Field Museum of Natural History, 1979.

Safer, J. F., and Gill, F. M. *Spirals from the Sea*. New York: Clarkson N. Potter Inc., 1982.

Sleen, W. G. N., van der. *A Handbook on Beads*. Liège: Librairie Halbart, 1973.

Stone, G. C. *A Glossary of the Construction, Decoration and Use of Arms and Armor*. New York: J. Brussel, 1961.

Tait, H. (ed.) *Jewelry, 7000 Years*. New York: Harry N. Abrams, Inc., 1991.

Thomas, N. W., and Athol Joyce, T. *Women of All Nations*. 2 volumes, London: Cassell and Co., no date.

Untracht, O. *Metal Techniques for Craftsmen*. New York: Doubleday & Co., 1975.

Untracht, O. *Jewelry Concepts and Technology*. London: Robert Hale Ltd., 1982.

Verneau, R. *L'homme*. Paris: Larousse, 1931.

AFRICA

African-American Institute, The. *Traditional Sculpture from Upper Volta*. New York: The African-American Institute, 1978.

Amrouche, P. and Thiam, A. *Art Moba du Togo*. Paris: Pierre Amrouche, 1991.

Bachinger, R. and Exler, H. *Die Hand: Schutz und Schmuck in Nordafrika*. Frankfurt: Galerie Exler Co., 1981 (exhibition catalogue).

Bachinger, R., and Schienerl, P. W. *Silberschmuck aus Agypten*. Frankfurt: Galerie Exler Co., 1984 (exhibition catalogue).

Balandier, G., and Maquet, J. *Dictionnaire des Civilisations Africaines*. Paris: Fernand Hazan, 1968.

Bastin, M. L. *Museu do Dundo: Art Décoratif Tshokwe*. Lisbon: Companhia de Diamantes de Angola, 1961.

Beckwith, C., and Fisher, A. *African Ark*. New York: Harry N. Abrams, Inc., 1990.

Beckwith, C., and Saitoti, T. O. *Maasai*. New York: Harry N. Abrams Inc., 1980.

Beckwith, C., and van Offelen, M. *Nomads of Niger*. New York: Harry N. Abrams, Inc., 1983.

Benouniche, F. *Bijoux et Parures d'Algérie*. Alger: Art et Culture, 1982.

Bertrand, A. *Tribus Berbères du Haut Atlas*. Lausanne: Edita, 1977.

Besancenot, J. *Bijoux Berbères du Maroc*. Paris: Galerie de l'Orfèvrerie Christofle, 1947.

Besancenot, J. *Bijoux Arabes et Berbères du Maroc*. Casablanca: Editions de la Cigogne, 1953.

Blandin, A. *Bronzes et Autres Alliages*. Marignane: A. Blandin, 1988.

Bliss, F. "Bahriyan Jewelry and its Relation to the Nile Valley." *Ornament*, 1982, vol. 6, no. 2 pp. 10–14, 44–45.

Boujibar, N. K. *Bijoux et Parures du Maroc*. Casablanca: Royal Air Maroc, 1974.

Brincard, M.-Th. (ed.) *The Art of Metal in Africa*. New York: The African-American Institute, 1982 (exhibition catalogue).

Brincard, M.-Th. (ed.) *Beauty by Design: The Aesthetics of African Adornment*. New York: The African-American Institute, 1984 (exhibition catalogue).

Burssens, H., and Guisson, A. *Mangbetu*. Bruxelles: Kredietbank, 1992 (exhibition catalogue).

Camps-Fabrer, H. *Les Bijoux de Grande Kabylie.* Paris: Arts et Métiers Graphiques, 1970.

Camps-Fabrer, H. *Bijoux Berbères d'Algérie.* Aix-en-Provence: Edisud, 1990.

Carey, M. *Beads and Beadwork of East and South Africa.* Aylesbury: Shire Publications Ltd., 1986.

Center for African Art, The (ed.) *Art/Artifact.* New York: 1988 (exhibition catalogue).

Champault, D., and Verbrugge, A. R. *La Main.* Paris: Musée National d'Histoire Naturelle, 1965.

Collart, R., and Celis, G. *Burundi 1900–1930.* Ramegnies-Chin: no date.

Cornet, J. *Art Royal Kuba.* Milan: Edizioni Sipiel, 1982.

Creyaufmuller, W. (introduction by) *Silberschmuck aus der Sahara.* Tuareg und Mauren, Frankfurt: Galerie Exler & Co., 1982 (exhibition catalogue).

Creyaufmuller, W. *Völker der Sahara.* Mauren und Tuareg, Stuttgart: Linden-Museum, 1979.

Elliott, A. *The Magic World of the Xhosa.* London: Collins, 1970, reprinted 1975.

Elsen, J. *Beauté Fatale: Armes d'Afrique Centrale.* Brussels: Crédit Communal, 1992 (exhibition catalogue).

Eudel, P. *Dictionnaire des Bijoux de l'Afrique du Nord.* Paris: Ernest Leroux, 1906.

Fagg, W. *Yoruba Beadwork.* New York: Rizzoli, 1980 (exhibition catalogue).

Fedders, A., and Salvadori, C. *Turkana Pastoral Craftsmen.* Nairobi: Transafrica, 1977.

Fischer, E., and Himmelheber, H. *Gold aus Westafrika.* Zurich: Museum Rietberg, 1975 (exhibition catalogue).

Fisher, A. *Africa Adorned.* New York: Harry N. Abrams, Inc., 1984.

Flint, B. *Forme et symbole dans les arts du Maroc, Bijoux amulettes I.* Tanger: B. Flint, 1973.

Forster, T., and Homberger, L. *Die Kunst der Senufo.* Zurich: Museum Rietberg, 1988.

Gabus, J. *Oualata et Gueïmaré des Nemadi: Rapport brut des Missions Ethnographiques en R. I. de Mauritanie du 19 Décembre 1975 au 29 Mai 1976.* Neuchâtel: Musée d'Ethnographie.

Gabus, J. *Au Sahara: Arts et Symboles.* Neuchâtel: A la Baconniére, 1958.

Gargouri-Sethom, S. *Le bijou traditionnel en Tunisie.* Aix-en-Provence: Edisud, 1986.

Garrard, T. *Gold of Africa: Jewellery and Ornamentation from Ghana, Côte d'Ivoire, Mali and Senegal in the Collection of the Barbier-Mueller Museum.* Munich: Prestel, and Geneva: Musée Barbier-Mueller, 1989.

Goldwater, R. *Senufo Sculpture from West Africa.* New York: The Museum of Primitive Art, 1964.

Grossert, J. W. *Zulu Crafts.* Pietermaritzburg: Dhuter & Shooter, 1978.

Himmelheber, H. *Negerkunst und Negerkünstler.* Braunschweig: Klinkhardt und Biermann, 1960.

Holas, B. *Animaux dans l'Art Ivoirien.* Paris: Librairie Orientaliste, Paul Geuthner S.A., 1969.

Jereb, J. "The Magical Potency of Berber Jewelry."

Ornament, winter, 1989, pp. 40–43, 69 and 73.

Johannesburg Art Gallery, (ed.) *Art and Ambiguity: Perspectives on the Brenthurst Collection of Southern African Art.* Johannesburg, 1991 (exhibition catalogue).

Kalter, J. *Schmuck aus Nordafrika.* Stuttgart: Linden-Museum, 1976.

Kennedy, C. *The Art and Material Culture of the Zulu-Speaking Peoples.* Los Angeles: University of California, 1978 (exhibition catalogue).

Kolb, E. de. *Soothsayer Bronzes of the Senufo.* New York: Gallery d'Hautbarr, 1968.

Laburthe-Tolra, Ph., and Falgayrettes-Leveau, Ch. *Fang.* Paris: Musée Dapper, 1991.

Langmuir, E. C. *Ethiopia: The Christian Art of an African Nation.* Salem: The Peabody Museum, 1978 (exhibition catalogue).

Lehuard, R. "Omakipa. Parure en Ivoire des Femmes Cuanhama." *Arts d'Afrique Noire,* 1982, no. 42, pp. 20–24.

Lehuard, R. *Statuaire du Stanley-Pool.* Villiers-le-Bel: Arts d'Afrique Noire, 1974.

Leopoldo, B. *Oasis d'Amun-Siwa.* Geneva: Musée d'Ethnographie, 1986.

Leuzinger, E. *Wesen und Form des Schmuckes afrikanischer Völker.* Zurich: E. Lang, 1950.

Levinsohn, R. *Art and Craft of Southern Africa.* Craighall: Delta Books Ltd., 1984.

Meyer, P. *Kunst und Religion der Lobi.* Zurich: Museum Rietberg, 1981 (exhibition catalogue).

Moore, E. *Ethiopia, Jewelry.* Ethiopian Airlines.

Morin-Barde, M. *Coiffures Féminines du Maroc.* Aix-en-Provence: Edisud, 1990.

Musée de L'Homme (ed.) *Ethiopie d'aujourd'hui.* Paris: Musée National d'Histoire Naturelle, 1975.

Musée des Arts Décoratifs (ed.) *Dura dji: Visages et Racines du Zaire.* Paris: no date (exhibition catalogue).

Musée d'Israël. *La Vie Juive au Maroc.* Jerusalem: 1973, cat. no.103.

Northern, T. *The Sign of the Leopard: Beaded Art of Cameroon.* Storrs: The William Benton Museum of Art, The University of Connecticut, 1975 (exhibition catalogue).

Northern, T. *The Art of Cameroon.* Washington: Smithsonian Institution, 1984 (exhibition catalogue).

Palais des Beaux-Arts (Société des Expositions, ed.) *Utotombo: L'Art d'Afrique Noire dans les Collections Privées Belges.* Brussels: 1988 (exhibition catalogue).

Paulme, D., and Brosse, J. *Parures Africaines.* Paris: Hachette, 1956.

Perrois, L. *Art Ancestral du Gabon.* Geneva: Musée Barbier-Mueller, 1985.

Picard, J., and R. *Beads From the West African Trade.* Los Prados Carmel: Picard African Imports, 1986–1991.

Poncet, M. *Les Bijoux d'argent de Tunisie.* Maison Tunisienne de l'Edition, 1977.

Ratton, Ch. *Fetish Gold.* Philadelphia: University Museum, 1975.

Raunig, W. *Religious Art of Ethiopia.* Stuttgart: Institut für Auslandsbeziehungen, 1973 (exhibition catalogue).

Riefenstahl, L. *Les Nouba.* Paris: Chêne, 1973–1976.

Riefenstahl, L. *Les Nouba de Kau.* Paris: Chêne, 1976.

Rouach, D. *Bijoux Berbères au Maroc.* Paris: ACR Edition, 1989.

Roy, Chr., *Art of the Upper Volta.* Meudon: A. et F. Chaffin, 1987.

Schaffar, J. J. *Trésor et Mystère des Berbères du Maroc.* Milan: Art World Media, 1990.

Schiemerl, P. W. "The Twofold Roots of Tuareg Charm-Cases." *Ornament,* Summer,1986, pp. 54–57.

Sieber, R. *African Textiles and Decorative Arts.* New York: Museum of Modern Art, 1972 (exhibition catalogue).

Sijelmassi, M. *Les Arts Traditionnels au Maroc.* Paris: Flammarion, 1974.

Spring, Chr. *African Arms and Armour.* London: British Museum Press, 1993.

Sugier, C. *Bijoux Tunisiens: Formes et Symboles.* Tunis: Editions Cérès Productions, 1977.

Sugier, C. *Symboles et Bijoux Traditionnels de Tunisie.* Tunis: Editions Cérès Productions, 1967.

Wente-Lukas, R. *Die materielle Kultur der nicht-islamischen Ethnien von Nordkamerun und Nirdostnigeria.* Wiesbaden: Franz Steiner Verlag, 1977.

Vangroenweghe, D. *Mongocultuur.* Sint-Niklaas: Gemeentekrediet, 1984 (exhibition catalogue).

ASIA

Abdullayev, T.; Fakhretdinova, D.; Khakimov, A. *A Song in Metal: Folk Art of Uzbekistan.* Tashkent: Gafur Gulyam Art and Literature Publishers, 1986.

Asian Art Museum of San Francisco (ed.) *Beauty, Wealth, and Power: Jewels and Ornaments of Asia.* 1992 (exhibition catalogue).

Bartolomew, M. K. *Thunder Dragon: Textiles from Bhutan.* Tokyo: Shikosha, 1985.

Bernard, P., and Huteau, M. *Karennis: Les Combattants de la Spirale d'or.* L' Harmattan, "Partir là-bas," 1988.

Boyer, M. *Mongol Jewellery: Nationalmuseets Skrifter.* Copenhagen: Etnografisk roekke, 1952.

Campbell, M. *From the Hands of the Hills.* Hong Kong: Media Transasia, 1978.

Casal, G.; Regaldo Trota, J. jr.; Casino, E. S.; Ellis, G. R.; Solheim II, W. G. *The People and Art of the Philippines.* Los Angeles: Museum of Cultural History, 1981 (exhibition catalogue).

Chiang, L. P. *Among the Dayaks.* Singapore: Graham Brash, 1989.

Denver Art Museum. *Secret Splendors of the Chinese Court.* Denver: Editors Marlene Chambers, Carol Rawlings, and Margaret Ritchie, 1981.

Dupaigne, B. "Le Grand Art Décoratif des Turkmènes." *Objets et Mondes.* Paris: 1978, tome 18 fascicule 1–2, pp. 3–30.

Fakhretdinova, D. *L'Art de la Joaillerie d'Ouzbekistan (enrusse).* Tashkent: Gafur Gulyam Art and Literature Publishers, 1988.

Firouz, I. A. *Silver Ornaments of the Turkoman.* Teheran: 1978.

249

Frances, P. jr. "Beads of the Philippines," *Arts of Asia*, Nov–Dec, 1990, pp. 97–107.

Gabriel, H. "The Cheptisoon, Traditional Nepalese Ear Ornament." *Ornament*, 1981, vol. 5 no. 1, pp. 26–27.

Hasibuan, J. S. *Batak: Art et Culture*. Djakarta: Total Indonésie, 1985.

Hawley, R. *Omani Silver*. London & New York: Longman, 1978.

Heissig, W., and Müller, C. C. (ed.) *Die Mongolen*. Innsbruck: Pinguin-Verlag, 1989.

Hibi, S. *Japanese Tradition in Color and Form: Dress*. Tokyo: Graphic Sha Publishing Company Ltd., 1987.

Janata, A. "A Distinctive Kind of Caucasian Belt Buckle." *Ornament*, 1982, vol. 5 no. 5, pp. 4–5.

Janata, A. *Schmuck in Afghanistan*. Graz: Akademische Druck-u Verlagsanstalt, 1981.

Jasper, J. E., and Pirn, M. *Mas Pirndadie: De Inlandsche Kuntsnijverheid in Nederlandsche Indie*. Deel IV De goud-en zilversmeedkunst, 1927. s'Gravenhage: De Boek and Kunstdrukkerij v/h Moton and Co.

Jenkins, B. W. R. *The Greek Ethos: Folk Art of the Hellenic World*. Los Angeles Craft and Folk Art Museum and the UCLA Center for Medieval and Renaissance Studies, 1979.

Jessup, H. I. *Court Arts of Indonesia*. Catalogue of the exhibition held at The Asia Society Galleries, New York: The Asia Society, 1990.

Jest, C. *La Turquoise de Vie: Un Pèlerinage Tibétain*. Paris: Editions A.M. Metailie, 1985.

Kalter, J. *Aus Steppe und Oase*. Stuttgart and London: Hansjörg Mayer, 1983.

Lewis, P. and E. *Peoples of the Golden Triangle: Six tribes in Thailand*. London and New York: Thames and Hudson, 1984.

Liu, R. K. "Asian Glass Ornaments." *Ornament*, May 1985, pp. 25, 28–29.

Liu, R. K. "Asian Glass Ornaments, Part II, China." *Ornament*, August, 1985, pp. 34–36, 47.

Liu. R. K. "Chinese Toggles." *Ornament*, Summer, 1989, pp. 30–31.

Lobsiger-Dellenbach, M. *Népal*: Catalogue de la Collection d'ethnographie Népalaise du Musée d'ethnographie de la ville de Genève, Ville de Genève: 1954.

Miksic, J. N. *Old Javanese Gold*. Singapore: Ideation, 1990.

Miksic, J. N. *Small Finds: Ancient Javanese Gold*. Catalogue of exhibition held in Singapore at the National Museum, Southeast Asian Gallery, 1988.

Moor, M. de, and Kal, W. H. *Indonesische Sieraden*. Amsterdam: Het Tropenmuseum, 1983.

Müller, C. C., and Raunig, W. *Der Weg zum Dach der Welt*. Innsbruck: Pinguin-Verlag, 1982.

Munneke, R. *Van Zilver, Goud en Kornalijn*. Leiden/ Breda: Rijksmuseum voor Volkenkunde, 1990.

Musée Ethnographique des peuples de l'U.R.S.S. *Joaillerie*. Leningrad: Editions d'art Aurora, 1988.

National Palace Museum (ed.) Catalogue of the Exhibition of Ch'ing Dynasty Costume Accessories, Taipei: 1986.

Newark Museum, The. Catalogue of the Tibetan collection and other Lamaist articles, vol. V. Newark, New Jersey: 1950.

Regents of the University of California, The. *The People and Art of the Philippines*. Los Angeles: Museum of Cultural History, 1981 (exhibition catalogue).

Reynolds, V. *Tibet: A lost world*. The Newark Museum Collection of Tibetan Art and Ethnography, New York: The American Federation of the Arts, 1978.

Rodgers, S. *Power and Gold: Jewelry from Indonesia, Malaysia, and the Philippines*. From the collection of the Barbier-Mueller Museum, Geneva: 1985 (exhibition catalogue).

Roma, V. *Etnografia de Filipinas*. Barcelona: Ayuntamiento de Barcelona: Fundación Folch, 1986 (exhibition catalogue).

Ross, H. C. *The Art of Bedouin Jewellery: A Saudi Arabian Profile*. Fribourg: Arabesque Commercial S. A., 1981.

Ross, H. C. *Bedouin Jewellery in Saudi Arabia*. London: Stacey International, 1978.

Rudolph, H. *Der Turkmenenschmuck*. Sammlung Kurt Gull, Stuttgart, London: Hansjörg Mayer, 1985.

Schletzer, D. and R. *Old Silver Jewellery of the Turkoman*. Berlin: Dietrich Reimer Verlag, 1983.

Schoffel, A. *Arts Primitifs de l'Asie du Sud-Est*. Meudon: ed. A. et F. Chaffin, 1981.

Sibeth, A. *Mit den Ahnen Leben: Batak-Menschen in Indonesien*. Edition Hansjörg Mayer, und Linden Museum, 1990.

Srisadavi, B. C. *The Hill Tribes of Siam*. Bangkok: Odeon Store, 1963.

Sychova, N. *Traditional Jewellery from Soviet Central Asia and Kazakhstan*. Moscow: Sovetsky Khudozhnik Publishers, 1984.

Tokhtabayeva, S. Z. *Kazakh Jewellery*. Alma-Ata: FNER, 1985.

Tropenmuseum, The (ed.) *Budaya-Indonesia: Arts and Crafts in Indonesia*. Exhibition catalogue from the Tropenmuseum's collection, Amsterdam: 1987.

Völger, G.; Welck, K.; and Hackstein, K. *Pracht und Geheimnis. Kleidung und Schmuck aus Palästina und Jordanien*. Katalog der Sammlung Widad Kawar, Koln: Rautenstrauch-Joest-Museum, 1987.

Volkenkundig Museum Nusantara (ed). *Nias: Tribal Treasures*. Delft: 1990.

Wassing-Visser, R. *Sieraden en lichaamsversiering uit Indonesie*. Delft Volkenkundig Museum Nusantara, 1984 (exhibition catalogue).

Weihreter, H. *Schmuck aus dem Himalaja*. Graz: Adeva, 1988.

Weir, S. *Palestinian Costume*. London: The Trustees of the British Museum, 1989.

Wilson, V. *Chinese Dress*. London: Victoria and Albert Museum, 1986.

Windisch-Graetz, S. and G., de. *Trésors de l'Himalaya*. Lausanne-Paris: La Bibliothèque des Arts, 1982.

Wrigglesworth, L. *The Accessory: China*. London: 1991.

Ziesnitz, S., and Lester, G., "Japanese Combs and Hairpins." *Arts of Asia*, March–April 1990, pp. 86–95.

INDIA

Barbier, J. P. *Art du Nagaland*. Geneva: Musée Barbier-Mueller, 1982.

Brijbhushan, J. *Masterpieces of Indian Jewellery*. Bombay: Taraporevala, 1979.

Brunel, F. *Jewellery of India: Five Thousand Years of Tradition*. New Delhi: National Book Trust, 1972.

Bunting, E.-J. W. *Sindhi Tombs and Textiles: The Persistence of the Pattern*. Albuquerque: The Maxwell Museum of Anthropology, The University of New Mexico Press, 1980.

Dhamija, J. (ed.) *Crafts of Gujarat*. New York: Mapin International Inc., 1985.

Elson, V. G. *Dowries from Kutch*. Los Angeles: Los Angeles Museum of Cultural History, UCLA, 1979.

Elwin, V. *The Art of the North-East Frontier of India*. Shillong: North East Frontier Agency, 1959.

Fürer-Haimendorf, Chr., von. *Return to the Naked Nagas*. London: John Murray, new ed., 1976.

Gabriel, H. "Shell Jewelry of the Nagas," *Ornament*, August 1985, pp. 37–41.

Ganguli, M. *A Pilgrimage to the Nagas*. New Delhi: Mohan Primlani, 1984.

Havell, E. B. "Art Industries of the Madras Presidency," *The Journal of Indian Art and Industry*, vol. 5, October 1892.

Hendley, T. H. "Indian Jewellery," 2 volumes. Delhi: Cultural Publishing House, 1909, reprinted 1984.

Höpfner, G., and Haase, G. *Metallschmuck aus Indien*. Berlin: Museum f. Völker-kunde, 1978.

Hutton, J. H. *The Angami Nagas*. London: Macmillan & Co., 1921.

Hutton, J. H. *The Sema Nagas*. London: Macmillan & Co., 1921.

Jacobs, J.; Mcfarlane, A.; Harrison, S.; and Herle, A. *The Nagas, Hill People of Northeast India: Society, Culture and the Colonial Encounter*. London and New York: Thames and Hudson, 1991.

Jain, J., and Aggarwala, A. J. *Museums of India: National Handicrafts and Handlooms Museum*. New Delhi, Ahmedabad, Mapin Publishing Pvt. Ltd.,1989.

Kalter, J. *Swat: Bauern und Baumeister im Hindukush*. Stuttgart: Edition Hansjörg Mayer, 1989.

Latif, M. *Bijoux Moghols*. Brussels: Catalogue d'exposition présentée par la Societé Générale de Banque, 1982.

Nath, A., and Waziarg, F. *Les Arts Traditionnels du Rajasthan*. Geneva: Olizane.

Pressmar, E. *Indian Rings*. Ahmedabad: New Order Book, Co., 1982.

Stronge, S.; Smith, N.; and Harle, J. C. *A Golden Treasury: Jewellery from the Indian Subcontinent*. London: Victoria and Albert Museum and Mapin Publishing Pvt. Ltd., 1988.

Untracht, O. "Nava-Ratna: Manifestation of the Divine." *Ornament*, Summer 1989, pp. 58–64.

Untracht, O. "The Nava-Ratna" *Islamic and Hindu Jewellery*. London: Spink and Son, 1988, pp. 17–30.

Untracht, O. "The Body Encrusted: Traditional Jewelry of India." *American Craft*. August/September 1980, pp. 42–49.

Welch, S. *India, Art, and Culture: 1300–1900*. New York: The Metropolitan Museum of Art. Holt, Rinehart, and Winston, 1985 (exhibition catalogue).

NORTH AMERICA

Bedinger, M. *Indian Silver: Navajo and Pueblo Jewelers*. Albuquerque: University of New Mexico Press, 1973.

Frank, L. *Indian Silver Jewelry of the Southwest: 1868–1930*. Boston: New York Graphic Society, 1978.

Jacka, J. D., and Hammack, N. S. *Indian Jewelry of the Prehistoric Southwest*. Tucson: The University of Arizona Press, 1975.

King, D. S., and Mera, H. P. *Indian Silver*. Tucson: Dale Stuart King, 1976–1977.

Lincoln, L. (ed.) *Southwest Indian Silver from the Doneghy Collection*. Austin: University of Texas, The Minneapolis Institute of the Arts, 1982 (exhibition catalogue).

Orchard, W. C. *Beads and Beadwork of the American Indians*. New York: Museum of the American Indian, Heye Foundation, 1975.

Rosnek, C., and Stacey, J. *Skystone and Silver*. Englewood Cliffs, New Jersey: Prentice Hall Inc., 1976.

Woodward, A. *Navajo Silver*. Flagstaff: Northland Press, 1971.

Wright, M. *Hopi Silver*. Flagstaff: Northland Press, 1972.

SOUTH AMERICA

Bisilliat, M. *Indiens du Xingu*. Paris: Chêne/Hachette, 1979.

Bray, W. *The Gold of El Dorado*. London: The Royal Academy, 1978 (exhibition catalogue).

Hartmann, G. *Gold + Silber*. Berlin: Dietrich Reimer Verlag, 1988.

Hartmann, G. *Silberschmuck der Araukaner, Chile*. Berlin: Museum für Völkerkunde, 1974.

Maison de l'Amérique Latine. *L'or du Pérou*. Paris: Maison de l'Amerique Latine, 1987 (exhibition catalogue).

Metropolitan Museum of Art, The. *The Art of Precolumbian Gold*. New York: 1985, (exhibition catalogue).

Musée d'Ethnographie de Genève. *L'art de la Plume. Brésil:* 1985 (exhibition catalogue)

Museu de Etnologia (ed.) *Indios da Amazonia*. Lisbon: Museu de Etnologia 1986 (exhibition catalogue).

Museum of Mankind London (ed.) *The Hidden Peoples of the Amazon*. London: British Museum Publications Ltd., 1985.

Schindler, H. "Silver Jewelry of the Mapuche," *Ornament*. February 1985, pp. 32–37.

Seiler-Baldinger, A. *Indianer im Tiefland Südamerikas*. Basel: Museum für Völkerkunde, 1987 (exhibition catalogue).

Trupp, F. *Les Derniers Indiens*. Paris: Fournier Diffusion, 1982.

Verswijver, G.; Braeke, V.; Turner, T.; and Vidal, L. *Kaiapo: Amazonie: Plumes et peintures corporelles*. Tervuren: Musée Royal de l'Afrique Centrale, 1992.

OCEANIA

Chauvet, S. *Les Arts Indigènes en Nouvelle-Guinee*. Paris: Société d'Editions Geographiques, Maritimes et Coloniales, 1930.

Clunie, F. *Yalo i Viti*. Suva: Fiji Museum, 1986.

De Deckker, P., and F. *Ta'aroa*. L'Univers Polynésien. Brussels: Crédit Communal, 1982.

Dodd, E. *Polynesian Art*. London: Hale, 1967.

Force, R. W. and M. *The Fuller Collection of Pacific Artifacts*. London: Lund Humphries, 1971.

Grunne, B., de. *Art Papou*. Brussels: LME, 1979 (exhibition catalogue).

Heermann, I. and Menter, U. *Schmuck der Südsee*. Munich: Prestel Verlag, 1990 (exhibition catalogue).

Kaeppler, A. L. "Artificial Curiosities," Honolulu: Bishop Museum Press, 1978 (exhibition catalogue).

Kaufmann, C. *Ozeanien*. Basel: Museum für Völkerkunde und Schweizerisches Museum für Völkerkunde, 1979.

Koch, G. *Kultur der Abelam*. Berlin: Museum für Völkerkunde, 1971.

Koch, G. *Materielle Kultur der Santa Cruz-Inseln*. Berlin: Museum für Völkerkunde, 1971.

Konrad, G. and U., and Schneebaum, T. *Asmat. Life with the Ancestors*. Glashütten/Ts: Herausgegeben von, F. Bruckner, 1981 (exhibition catalogue).

Liu, R. K. "Lei Niho Palaoa. A Classic Hawaiian Ornament." *Ornament*. August 1985, pp. 21–25, 66.

Nevermann, H. *Die Admiralitäts-Inseln*. Ergebnisse der Südsee-Expedition 1908–1910. Hamburg: Friederichsen, De Gruyter and Co. GmbH, 1934.

Parkinson, R. *Dreissig Jahre in der Südsee*. Stuttgart: Strecker und Schröder, 1907.

Rose, R. G. *Hawaii: The Royal Isles*. Hawaii: Bishop Museum Press, 1980.

Santa, E., della. *Mélanésie*. Brussels: Editions de la Connaissance, 1954.

Starzecka, D. C. *Hawaii: People and Culture*. London: British Museum Publications Ltd., 1975.

Starzecka, D. C., and Cranstone, B. A. L. *The Solomon Islanders*. London: British Museum Publications Ltd., 1974.

Stöhr, W. *Kunst und Kultur aus der Südsee*. Sammlung Clausmeyer Melanesien: Koln Rautenstrauch-Joest-Museum für Völkerkunde, 1987.

Tischner, H. *Dokumente verschollener Südsee-Kulturen*. Nurnberg: Naturhistorische Gesellschaft, 1981.

Wassing-Visser, R. *Sieraden*. Delft: Volkenkundig Museum Nusantara, 1984.

INDEX

Page numbers in italics refer to illustrations and captions.

A

Abelam, *221*
Aceh, *188, 189, 192*
adamlyk, *120, 121*
adat, *26*
ade, *19*
Admiralty Islands, 208; *206, 207, 216, 217*
adrim, *8, 9*
Africa, 16, 18, 21, 24, 31, 35–103, 246; Sahel, 38; *94*; Songhai, 38. *See also* North Africa; West Africa; *specific country*
aggrey beads, Africa, 36
aghraw, *8, 9*
Aguaruna, *24, 25*
akal-e-ngo, *73*
Akan, 38; *82, 84, 93*
Akbat, 107
Akha, 109; *180, 181*
Algeria, *49*; Beni Yenni (Great Kabylia), *6, 7, 52, 53*; Tuareg, *96*
amazonite, *49*
amber: Africa, 41; *42, 43, 62, 63*; Himalayan, *108*; *168*
Americas, 230–44. *See also specific country*
amerouan, *96*
amesluh, *52*
amulet containers, *112, 113*; Central Asia, *125, 126*; India, *138, 144*; Iran, *117*; Ladakh, *108*; Nepal, *158, 159*; Oman, *119*; Tibet, *160, 161*
amulet-pendant, Indonesia, *190, 191*
amulets: Central Asia, *122, 123*; India, 27; Nigeria, *80, 81*; North Africa, 30, 40; Turkoman, 105
Angami, 107; *150, 151, 155*
Angola, *100, 101*; Tshokwe, *71*
anklets, 18; Africa, 24; Algeria, *52*; Burkina Faso, *88*; Chad, *56*; Gabon, *73*; India, 106; *136, 137*; Ivory Coast, *82, 83, 84*; Liberia, 40; *87*; Mali, *92, 93*; Mauritania, *48, 49*; Morocco, *44*; Niger, 39–40; Nigeria, *78, 79, 80, 81*; Tunisia, *54*; Zaire, *69*
Ao, 107; *152, 153, 156, 157*
aprons, South Africa, *102, 103*
Arapesh, 208
Araucanians. *See* Mapuche
armbands. *See* armlets
armlets: Americas, 231; Brazil, *237*; Burkina Faso, *88, 89*; Chad, *56*; Gabon, *73*; India, 107; *138, 139, 141, 149, 155*; Kenya, *63*; Nigeria, *76, 77, 92, 93*; Papua New Guinea, *218, 219*; Philippines, *185, 187*; Sudan, *56, 57*; Vanuatu, *222, 223*
arm rings, Burma, *16, 17*
Asante, 38
Ashanti, *82, 93*
Asia, 27. *See also* Central Asia; *specific country*
Asmat, 207, 209; *210, 211, 212*
assrou n'swoul, *50, 51*
asyk, *2, 4, 126*
Australia, 209; Pitjantjara, *226, 227*
Azande, *56, 68, 69*
azrar, *6, 7*

B

back ornaments, Indonesia, *192*
baghu, *170*
Bagobo, 110–11; *184*
bak, *206, 207*
Bakelite, *53*
bakonga, *70*
balogal, *81*
Bamileke, *74, 75*
Bamum, *75, 76*
Bana, *76, 77, 82, 83*
bangles. *See* bracelets
Bantu, *102, 103*
baskets, Brazil, *238, 239*
bateba, *90*
Baule, 24, 39; *82, 83, 84, 85, 86, 87, 90*
bazuband, *117, 138, 139, 141*
beads: Africa, 36, 39; *dZi*, 109; *164, 165*; Himalayan, 109; Indonesia, 110. *See also* glass beads
Bedouin, *54, 60, 61, 112, 114, 115, 116, 117, 118*
belt buckles: Caucasus, *133*; China, *174, 175*; India, *141*; Indonesia, *191*; southwestern United States, *232*; *242*; Turkey, *120*; Uzbekistan, *128, 129*
belt ornaments: Philippines, *184, 187*; Tunisia, *54*
belt pendants: Angola, *100, 101*; Namibia, *100, 101*
belts, 18, 20; Admiralty Islands, 208; Cameroon, *75, 82, 83*; Central Asia, *120, 128, 129*; India, 105; *104, 105, 144, 145*; Papua New Guinea, *218, 219, 220, 221, 223*; Philippines, *184*; Solomon Islands, *224, 225*; Tibet, *164*; Turkoman, 105; Zaire, *70*
Bengal, 36
Benin, 36
Beni Yenni, *6, 7, 52, 53*
Berber, 41; *34, 35, 42, 43, 54*
bhiru, *160*
Bhutan, 108; Monpa, *163*
bilezik, *123, 130, 131*
bipaneu, *210, 211*
bissin, *186, 187*
Bobo, *66, 90, 91, 93*
Bochimans, *16, 17*
Bontoc, *182, 184, 185, 187*
Bororo, *238*
Bothia, *138, 139*
Bowdich, Thomas, 38
Boyer, Martha, *173*
bracelets, 18, 27, 30; Africa, 31; Algeria, *52*; Bhutan, *163*; Brazil, *236, 237*; Burkina Faso, *87, 90, 91, 97*; Burma, *182, 183*; Burundi, *66*; Cameroon, 30; *74, 75, 76, 77, 87*; Central Asia, 105; *123, 130, 131*; China, 109; *182, 183*; Dahomey, 35; Ethiopia, *47, 60, 61*; India, 27, 107; *104, 105, 134, 144, 145, 154, 155, 157*; Indonesia, 110; *190, 191, 192, 193, 194, 196, 197, 200, 202*; Ivory Coast, 24, 40; *82, 83, 84, 87*; Kenya, *64, 65*; Ladakh, *166, 167*; Laos, *182, 183*; Libya, *47*; Mali, *87, 92, 93, 96, 97, 98, 99*; Morocco, *47*; Nigeria, *80, 81, 92, 93*; North Africa, *47*; Oman, *118*; Pakistan, *134*; Papua New Guinea, *214, 215, 220, 221, 224, 225*;

Philippines, 111; Russia, *132, 133*; Saudi Arabia, *118*; Solomon Islands, 21; *224, 225*; South Africa, *100, 101*; southwestern United States, *241*; Sudan, 30; *47, 56, 57, 58, 59*; Thailand, *182, 183*; Tibet, *166, 167, 168, 169, 170*; Tunisia, *54*; Uganda, *64, 65*; Yemen, *118*; Zaire, *64, 65, 66. See also* wristbands

Brazil, *235*; Amazonia, *231, 236, 237, 238*; Bororo (Mato Grosso), *238*; Kamaiura (Upper Xingu), *238*; Katabi, *238, 239*; Kayapo (Amazonia), *231, 236, 237*; Mato Grosso, *235, 238, 239*; Mekragnoti (Xingu), *236, 237*; Rio Negro, *235*; Txicao (Amazonia), *237*; Xingu, *235, 236, 237*; Xingu River, *235*

breast ornaments: Central Asia, *122, 123, 124, 125*; Indonesia, *192. See also* breastplates; chest ornaments; pectorals

breastplates, Papua New Guinea, 207; *211*

bridal jewelry: Africa, 38; Angola, *100, 101*; Egypt, *8, 9*; India, *142, 148*; Indonesia, 110; *192, 198, 199, 202, 204, 205*; Japan, 111; Kazakstan, *130, 131*; Namibia, *100, 101*; Nepal, *160, 161*; Papua New Guinea, 208; Philippines, 110; Solomon Islands, *222*; Tunisia, *54, 55*; Turkoman, 105; *124, 125*; Yemen, *112, 113*

bronze, Africa, 24, 39–40

brooches: Japan, *179*; southwestern United States, 232; *243*

Bruyninx, E., Professor, *90*

buckles. *See* belt buckles

Bugis, *193, 202*

Bukhara, *31, 32–33, 128, 129, 130*

bukov, 122, 123

Burkina Faso, 18; *92, 93*; Bobo, *66, 90, 91, 93*; Bwa, *66, 67*; Gurunsi, *87, 88, 89*; Lobi, 35; *88, 90, 91, 93, 97*; Tusyan, *90, 91*

Burma, *182, 183*; Padaung, *16, 17*

Burundi, Tutsi, *66*

buttock shields: Africa, 35; Nigeria, *78, 79*; Zaire, *70*

buttons: China, 109; Golden Triangle, *180, 181*; southwestern United States, *243*

Bwa, *66, 67*

C

cabibi, 187

Cameroon, 24, 30, 40; *73, 74, 75, 82, 97*; Bamileke, *74, 75*; Bamum, *75, 76*; Bana, *76, 77, 82, 83*; Kirdi, 35; *76, 77, 87*; Tikar, *74, 75*

carnelian, Turkoman groups, 105, 108

Caucasus, *132, 133*

Central Asia: Bukhara, *31, 32–33, 128, 129, 130*; Kazakstan, *130, 131*; Uzbekistan, *128, 129, 130. See also* Turkoman groups

Chad, *56*; Kenga, *56*

Chambri (Tchambuli), 208

champakali necklaces, *147*

Chang, *152, 153*

charms. *See* talismans

cheikel, 126

chest ornaments, 18; Africa, 39; Central Asia, *130, 131*; Colombia, *232, 233*; India, *149, 157*; Indonesia, *26, 27*; Irian Jaya, *211*; Kenya, *64*; Niger, *50, 51*; Papua New Guinea, *214, 215, 216, 217, 221*; Philippines, 111; Solomon Islands, *225.*

See also breast ornaments; pectorals; pendants

chest pendants. *See* pendants

Chile, Mapuche, *234, 235*

China, 109; *174, 176, 177, 182, 183*; Kazak, *177*; Ming dynasty, *174, 175*; Qing dynasty, *174, 175, 176, 177*; Uighur, *177*

clasps, Turkoman, 105

cloak pins, Chile, *234, 235*

cloisonné, 40; *52*

Colombia: Quimbaya, *232*; Sinu, *232, 233*; Tairona, 231; *230, 231, 232, 233*

combs: India, 106; *141*; Indonesia, *194, 200*; Japan, 111; *179*; Vietnam, *182*; Zaire, *64, 65*

concha, 242

coral: Africa, *62, 63*; Himalayan, 108; Morocco, *42, 43, 44*; North Africa, 41; Saudi Arabia, *114, 115*

counterweights: China, *174, 176, 177*; Golden Triangle, *180, 181*; Niger, *50, 51*

cowrie shells: Africa, 35, 36–37; *74, 75, 84*; Oceania, 207–08; Solomon Islands, *216, 217*

crosses. *See* neck crosses

Cuanhama, *100, 101*

D

Dagestan, *132, 133*

daggers, Turkoman, 105

Dahomey, Somba, 35

Dan, 24, 40; *82, 83, 84*

dangles, China, 109

Dani, *210, 211*

Dayak, *188, 197*

deblej, 54

diadems, 40; Central Asia, *122, 123. See also* tiaras

Dinka, *56, 57*

djokelebale, 73

dobchu, 163

Dogon, 40, 246; *81, 92, 93, 97, 98, 99*

"Dogon Suns," *81*

Dorado, El, 231

douge, 97

duli, 187

dZi, 109; *164, 165*

E

ear ornaments, 20; Brazil, *236, 237*; Burkina Faso, *88, 89*; Colombia, *232*; India, 107; *140, 141, 152, 153, 157*; Indonesia, 110; Marquesas Islands, *228, 229*; Nepal, *160, 161*; New Zealand, 209; *226, 227*; Peru, 24, *25*; Tibet, *166, 167*; Zaire, *71. See also* ear plugs; earrings

ear plugs: Dahomey, 35; Golden Triangle, *180, 181*

earrings, 16; Americas, 231; Central Asia, *125, 128, 129, 130, 131*; Chile, *234, 235*; Golden Triangle, *180, 181*; India, *142, 148*; Indonesia, 110; *182, 183, 188, 191, 193, 195, 198, 199, 200, 201, 204, 205*; Mali, 37–38; *94*; Marquesas Islands, *229*; Mongolia, *173*; Morocco, *44*; Nepal, *160, 161*; Niger, *48, 49*; Oman, *119*; Philippines, *182, 183*; Saudi Arabia, *116, 117*; Solomon Islands, *222, 223*; South Africa, *100, 101*; southwestern United States,

240, 241; Sudan, *58, 59*; Tibet, *168, 169*

egme, 126, 127

Egypt, 36; *47, 60, 61*; Amun-Siwa Oasis, *8, 9*; Bedouin (Sinai), *60, 61*; Nubian Desert, *59*

ekalaitom, 61

enameling, India, 107

Ennamni, Mouschi, *54*

errap, 63

Ersari Turkoman, 105; *123, 126, 127*

Ethiopia, 35; *22, 23, 47, 60, 61, 97*; Sidamo, *61*; Sorma, *60, 61*

ettouben amulet boxes, *100, 101*

F

Fali, *80, 81*

Fang, *73*

feathers, Americas, 231–32; *237*

fibulas, 40; Algeria, *6, 7, 53*; Bhutan, *163*; Chile, *234, 235*; Morocco, *44, 45, 46, 47, 53*; North Africa, 41; Tibet, *168*; Tunisia, *54. See also* forehead ornaments

Fiji, *228, 229*

fikum, 187

finger rings, 18; Africa, 38–39, 40; Burkina Faso, *93*; Cameroon, *97*; Central Asia, *130, 131*; China, *174, 175*; Dahomey, 35; Ethiopia, *97*; Ghana, *93*; India, *168, 169*; Indonesia, *168, 169, 190, 191, 195*; Ivory Coast, *86, 87, 93*; Mali, *92, 93, 97*; Nepal, *159*; Niger, *97*; Nigeria, *40; 78, 79, 97*; southwestern United States, 232; *241*; Sudan, *56, 57*; Thailand, *182, 183*; Tibet, *168, 169, 170*; West Africa, 39

Foi, *214, 215*

forehead ornaments: Algeria, *6, 7*; Central Asia, *31, 32–33, 130*; Egypt, *60, 61*; Saudi Arabia, *114. See also* fibulas

Fulani, *96*

Fur, *56, 57*

G

Gabon, 39; Fang, *73*; Kota, *73*

Gaddang, *188*

gahu, 160, 161, 164

gelang, 184

Genghis Khan, 18

Ghana, 37; Akan, 38; *82, 84, 93*; Asante, 38; Ashanti, *82, 93*; Kasena, *88. See also* Gold Coast

Ghysels, Colette, 15–16

Ghysels, Jean-Pierre, 16

ginutu, 184

Giryama, *64, 65*

glass beads: Africa, 36; *75, 82*; India, *12, 13*; Philippines, 110

gokhru, 134

Goklan, *123*

gold: Africa, 37–38; Americas, 231; *232*; Ivory Coast, 24, 27

Gold Coast, 36, 38; *84. See also* Ghana

Golden Triangle: Akha, 109; *180, 181*; Hmong, *180, 181*; Lisu, 109; *180*; Mien, *180*

gonzuk, 124, 125

gungulu, 88

Gurung, *160, 161*

Gurunsi, *87, 88, 89*

gyenzen, 164

H

ha'akai, 228, 229
hairnets, Solomon Islands, 207
hair ornaments: Central Asia, 105; Mongolia, *170, 171*; Morocco, *42*; Tibet, *170*. *See also* combs; hairnets; hair pendants; hairpins; headbands; *under* headdresses
hair pendants, Tibet, *167*
hairpins: China, *176, 177*; Japan, 111; *178, 179*; Korea, *178*; Laos, *182*; Mongolia, *173*; South Africa, *101*; southwestern United States, *232*; *243*; Zaire, *68, 69*
halaq, 119
hansli, 134, 135, 138, 139
Haratine, *96*
Harijan, *138, 139*
hats, Philippines, *188*
Hausa, 40
Hawaii, 209; *228, 229*
headbands, 27; India, 107; Namibia, *16, 17*; Philippines, *187*; Solomon Islands, *222, 223*
headdresses, 16; *96*; Americas, 231; Asia, 27; Brazil, *237, 238*; India, 107; Indonesia, 110; Ladakh, *108*; Mali, *38*; Marquesas Islands, *229*; Mongolia, 18; *170, 171*; Morocco, *42, 43*; Nigeria, *19*; North Africa, 41; Oman, *118*; Papua New Guinea, *214, 215*; Peru, *237*; Philippines, 111; Saudi Arabia, *114*. *See also* diadems; tiaras
headdress ornaments: Algeria, *96*; Indonesia, *195, 197*; Mali, *96*; Morocco, *96*; Niger, *96*; Nigeria, *96*
headdress pendants: China, *177*; Mongolia, *172, 173*; Tunisia, *54*
head ornaments, Indonesia, *202, 203*. *See also* hair ornaments
"health necklace," 30
herz, 44, 112, 113, 119
hillal, 54
Himalayan peoples. *See* Bhutan; Ladakh; Nepal; Tibet
Himba, *100, 101*
hip ornaments, India, *12, 13*
Hmong, 109; *180, 181*. *See also* Meo

I

ibirezi, 66, 67
Ibo, *78, 79, 81*
ibzimen, 53
Ida Ounadif, *46, 47*
Idoma, *81*
ifa, 80, 81
Ifugao, *182, 183, 185*
igihete, 66, 67
igitembe, 66
ihelhalen, 52
ikhoko, 68, 69
ilagah pendants, *114*
India, 27, 36, 105–08; *134, 136, 138, 139, 141, 149, 168, 169*; Andhra Pradesh, *144, 145*; Angami (Nagaland), 107; *150, 151, 155*; Ao (Nagaland), 107; *152, 153, 156, 157*; Assam, *134*; Bothia (Uttar Pradesh), *138, 139*; Chang (Nagaland), *152, 153*; Deccan, *141*; Gujarat, *134, 140, 141*; Harijan (Gujarat), *138, 139*; Kabui (Nagaland), *157*; Karnataka, *1, 4, 134, 138,*

139, 140, 141, 142, 144; Kerala, *142, 143, 144, 145, 147*; Koli (Kutch), *136, 137*; Konyak (Nagaland), 107; *12, 13, 152, 154, 155, 157*; Kutch, 106; Lhota (Nagaland), 107; Madhya Pradesh, *134, 142*; Maharashtra, *134, 136*; Marwari (Rajasthan), *134, 135, 138, 139*; Naga (Assam), 24, 107; *150, 151*; Nagaland, *154, 157*; Orissa, *134*; Rabari (Kutch, Gujarat), *134, 135*; Rajasthan, 105; *136, 137, 138, 139, 142*; Sema (Nagaland), 107; Sri Lanka, *150*; Tamil Nadu, *104, 105, 142, 146, 147, 148*; Tangkhul (Nagaland), *157*; Toda (Tamil Nadu), *146, 147*; Tulu, *149*; Wancho (Nagaland), *157*
Indo-Javanese (Majapahit), *195*
Indonesia, 21, 109–10; Aceh (Sumatra), *188, 189, 192*; Alor, *204, 205*; Babar, *205*; Bali, *168, 169*; Borneo, *196, 197*; Bugis (Sulawesi), *202*; Bugis (Sumbawa), *193*; Dayak (Sarawak and Kalimantan), *188, 197*; East Sumba, *182, 183*; Enggano, *196, 197*; Flores, *197, 198, 199, 204, 205*; Java, *195*; Karo Batak (Sumatra), *191, 192*; Kisar, *205*; Minangkabau (Sumatra), *191, 193*; Moluccas, *194, 198, 199, 204, 205*; Nias, *188, 196, 197, 198, 199*; Sarawak, *188, 196, 197*; Sulawesi, *204, 205*; Sumatra, *188, 194*; Sumba, *198*; Sunda Islands, *194*; Tanimbar, *193, 200, 201*; Timor, *168, 169, 194, 200*; Toba Batak (Sumatra), *188, 190, 191, 194*; Toraja (Sulawesi), *202, 203*; West Sumba, *26, 27, 198*
Indonesian New Guinea. *See* Irian Jaya
intshegula, 100, 101
Iran, *117*; Yomud Turkoman, *126*
Irian Jaya: Asmat, 207, 209; *210, 211, 212*; Dani, *210, 211*
Islam, 38, 41; *97, 101*
Isneg, *26, 27, 186, 187*
ivory, 27
Ivory Coast, 24, 27; *82*; Baule, 24, 39; *82, 83, 84, 85, 86, 87, 90*; Dan, 24, 40; *82, 83, 84*; Senufo, *86, 87, 90, 93*

J

Jaba, *78, 79*
Japan, 111; *178, 179*
Jest, Corneille, *163*
Jewish smiths, 38, 40; *44, 94, 95, 112*
Jivaro, *237*
joclas, 242

K

Kabui, *157*
kaffat, 114
Kaiabi, *238, 239*
kalabubu, 196, 197
Kalinga, *182*
Kamaiura, *238*
kamar, 128, 129
kamba na njala, 70
kan-zashi, 178
kap-kaps, 208; *216, 217, 226, 227*
Karamayong, *63*
kara-ut, 221
Karo Batak, *191, 192*
Kasena, *88*
Kaiabi, *238, 239*
Kayapo, 231; *236, 237*

Kazaks, 18; *177*
Kazakstan, *130, 131*
Kenga, *56*
Kenya: Giryama, *64, 65*; Karamayong, *63*; Kikuyu, *63*; Maasai, *63, 64*; Turkana, *60, 61, 64, 65*
ketoh, 242
khelkhal, 48, 49, 54
khomissar, 49
Kichepo, *60, 61*
Kikuyu, *63*
kina, 214, 215
Kirdi, 35; *76, 77, 87*
kneebands, Papua New Guinea, *218, 219*
kogai, 179
Koli, *136, 137*
koma, 163
konda, 160, 161
kongas, 68, 69
Kongo, *68, 69*
Konyak, 107; *12, 13, 152, 154, 157*
Korea, *178*
Kota, *73*
Koutiala, *98*
Kru, 40; *87*
Kuba, *68, 69, 82*
kudagi zhuzik, 130, 131
kuru mahora, 226, 227
kuruwel, 94, 95
kushi, 179
kwoteneye kange earrings, *94*

L

labrets. *See* lip plugs
Ladakh, *108*; *160, 161, 162, 163, 166, 167*
Laos, *182, 183*; Meo, 109; *180, 181*
Lega, *64, 65*
leggings, South Africa, *102, 103*
leg ornaments: Nigeria, *79*; West Africa, *39–40*; Zaire, *68, 69*. *See also* anklets
lei, 229
Leopoldo, B., *8*
Lere, *92, 93, 98*
Lhasa, *166, 167*
Lhota, 107
Liberia, Kru, 40; *87*
Libya, *47, 54*
Limbu, *160, 161*
lip plugs, 16; Africa, 35; Americas, 231; Ethiopia, *60, 61*; Kenya, *60, 61*; Sudan, *60, 61*
Lisu, 109; *180*
Lobi, 35; *88, 89, 90, 91, 93, 97*
Lock, John, 38
Loeb, Pierre, Galerie, 15
loincloths, 18, 207; Admiralty Islands, *206, 207*; Cameroon, 35; *76, 77*; Dahomey, 35; Oceania, 208
lost-wax casting: Africa, *39–40*; *84, 87, 98*; America, *231, 232*; India, *154*
Lulua, *68, 69*

M

Maasai, *63, 64*
madaka, 198
Maghreb, *52*
makara heads, *104, 105*
Mali, *97*; Djenne, *87, 92, 93*; Dogon, 40, 246; *81, 92, 93, 97, 98, 99*; Koutiala, *98*; Lere, *92, 93, 98*; Malinke, *101*; Peul, *37–38*;

94, 95, 101; Sarakole, *96*; Tuareg, *96, 100, 101*
Malinke, *101*
mamuli, 110; *198*
Mandarin chains, China, *176, 177*
Mandaya, *184*
Mangbetu, 35; *68, 69*
Maori, 21, 207; *226, 227*
Maprik, 209
Mapuche, *234, 235*
marangga, 26, 27, 198
Margi, *80, 81*
Marquesas Islands, *228, 229*
marriage pendants, India, 148. *See also* bridal jewelry
Marwari, *134, 135, 138, 139*
mask pendants, Zaire, *68, 69*
masks, 28; Indonesia, *200, 201*
Mauritania, 36; *96*; Moors, *48, 49*
mbangba, 75
Mbole, *69*
me icags, 170
Mekragnoti, *236, 237*
Mendi, *214, 218, 219*
Meo, *182, 183. See also* Hmong
Meyer, P., *88*
Mien, *180*
Minangkabau, *191, 193*
Ming dynasty, *174, 175*
Moba, *81*
Moghul jewelry, 106, 107; *130, 138, 139*
Mongo, 35; *68, 69, 70*
Mongolia, 18; *173*; Gulchagan Honichin, *172, 173*; Khalkha, *170, 171*; Khalkha Darkhan Beile, *170, 171*
Monpa, *163*
"mooneater," *10, 11*
Moors, *48, 49*
Morocco, *49, 53*; Anti-Atlas, *42, 43, 44, 47*; Berber, *41; 42, 43*; Berber (Tiznit), *34, 35*; Fez, *47*; Haratine (Bani Oasis), *96*; Ida Ounadif, *46, 47*; Palmeraies du Bani, *44*; Rif, *46, 47*; Tiznit, *34, 35, 42, 44, 45, 47*
mouth ornaments, 16. *See also* lip plugs

N

Naga, 24, 107; *150, 151*
Namibia: Bochimans, *16, 17*; Cuanhama, *100, 101*; Himba, *100, 101*
Nauru, *222, 223*
Navajo, 232; *240, 241, 242, 243*
Ndengese, *66, 67*
ndome, 63
neck circlets, Central Asia, 105
neck crosses, Ethiopia, *22, 23*
necklaces, 20; Africa, 16, 18, 24; Algeria, *6, 7, 52*; Brazil, *235, 237, 238*; Cameroon, 24, 40; *74, 75*; Central Asia, *122, 123, 130*; China, *176, 177*; Egypt, *60, 61*; Fiji, *228, 229*; Golden Triangle, *180*; Hawaii, *229*; Himalayan, *109*; India, 106, 107–8; *138, 142, 143, 146, 147, 150, 151, 152, 153, 155, 156, 157*; Indonesia, *188, 189, 192, 193, 200, 201, 202, 203*; Irian Jaya, *210, 211*; Ivory Coast, *82, 84, 85*; Kenya, *64, 65*; Ladakh, *162, 163*; Mali, 38; *92, 93, 94, 95, 97, 98, 99, 100, 101*; Marquesas Islands, *229*; Morocco, *34, 35, 42, 43, 46, 47*; Namibia, *100, 101*; Nauru, *222, 223*; Nepal, 30; *158, 159, 160, 161*; Niger, *49*; North Africa, 41; Oman, *118, 119*; Papua New Guinea, *212, 214, 215, 216, 217, 218, 219*; Philippines, 111; *185, 186, 187*; Plains region of United States, *244, 245*; Saudi Arabia, *114, 115, 116, 117*; Senegal, *94, 95*; Siberia, *174*; Solomon Islands, *216, 217, 222*; Somalia, *62, 63*; South Africa, *103*; southwestern United States, *240, 241, 242*; Sri Lanka, *150, 151*; Tanzania, *64, 65*; Tibet, *164, 165, 168*; Tonga, *212*; Tunisia, *54, 55*; Yemen, *112, 113, 114, 115*; Zaire, *71*
neck ornaments, Hawaii, 209; *228, 229*
neck rings: Burkina Faso, *92, 93*; Burma, *16, 17*; China, 109; Egypt, *8, 9*; Golden Triangle, *180, 181*; India, 106, 107; *134, 135, 138, 139, 154*; Indonesia, 110; *196, 197*; Nigeria, *76, 77*; Pakistan, *134*; Swat, *134*; West Africa, 39; Zaire, *66, 69, 72, 73*
Nepal, 30, 108; *158, 160, 161*; Gurung, *160, 161*; Limbu, *160, 161*; Makalu, *160, 161*; Newar, 108; *158, 159, 160, 161*
netsuke, 174, 179
Newar, 108; *158, 159, 160, 161*
New Guinea. *See* Irian Jaya; Papua New Guinea
New Hebrides. *See* Vanuatu
New Ireland, 208; *216, 217*
New Zealand, 209; Maori, 21, 207; *226, 227*
Ngbaka, *66*
N'gombe, *69, 70*
niale, 220, 221
niello techniques, 40
Niger, *49, 97*; Hausa, 40; Tuareg, *48, 49, 50, 51, 96*; Wodaabe, 35
Nigeria, 36; *76, 77, 97*; Cross River, *79, 81, 92, 93*; Fali, *80, 81*; Fulani, *96*; Ibo, *78, 79, 81*; Idoma, *81*; Jaba, *78, 79*; Margi, *80, 81*; Tiv, 40; *78, 79*; Yoruba, *19*
niti, 200
North Africa, 30, 37, 38, 40–41; *47. See also specific country*
North America, Plains Indians, 24; *244, 245. See also* southwestern United States
nose ornaments: Americas, 231; Colombia, *232*; Dahomey, 35; India, *140, 141*; Irian Jaya, 209; *210, 211, 212*; Mali, 38; Oceania, 207; Papua New Guinea, *214, 215*; Santa Cruz Islands, 208; *214, 215, 220, 221. See also* nose rings
nose rings, 16; India, *138, 139*; Nepal, *160, 161*
Nuba, 30
Nubian Desert, *47, 58, 59*
Nuer, *56, 57*
nyambele, 90, 91
nyi-kar-yi, 86, 87
Nzakara, *71*

O

obi dome, 179
Oceania, 27, 207–09, 246. *See also specific country or island*
ogba, *78, 79*
Olam, *123*
omak, *211*
Oman, *118, 119*; Bedouin, *118*
onlua, 72, 73
ore, *218, 219*
ostrich eggshell: Africa, 27; Namibia, *16, 17*
otsj, 212

P

Padaung, *16, 17*
padung-padung, 110; 191
Pakistan, *134*; Swat, 106
pakol, 214
palangapang, 185
Palmeraies du Bani, *44*
pampadam, 148
pandieng, 191
Papua New Guinea, 207; *212, 214, 215, 216, 217, 218, 219, 220, 221, 223, 224, 225*; Abelam, *221*; Arapesh, 208; Chambri (Tchambuli), 208; Foi, *214, 215*; Humboldt Bay, 208; *212, 213*; Mendi, *214, 218, 219*; Mount Hagen, *211*; Sepik, 208, 209; *214, 215, 218. See also* Admiralty Islands; New Ireland
Park, Mungo, 37–38
pearl shells: Australia, 209; Papua New Guinea, 208
pectorals: Central Asia, 105; Fiji, *228, 229*; Indonesia, *205*; Irian Jaya, 207; *208*; Oceania, 207; Papua New Guinea, *212, 213*; Santa Cruz Islands, 208; Solomon Islands, *226, 227*; South Africa, *102, 103. See also* breast ornaments; chest ornaments
pendants: Americas, 231; Asia, 27; Brazil, *238, 239*; Burkina Faso, *66, 67, 88, 89, 90, 91*; Central Asia, *105; 2, 4, 124, 125, 126, 130*; Chile, *234, 235*; China, 109; Colombia, *230, 231*; Ethiopia, *61*; India, *1, 4, 138, 139, 144, 148, 154*; Indonesia, 110; *188, 189, 193, 198, 204, 205*; Iran, *126*; Ivory Coast, 24, 27, 39; *82, 83, 84, 85, 86, 87, 90*; Ladakh, *160, 161*; Mali, *81, 98*; Maprik, 209; Mongolia, *173*; Morocco, *44*; Namibia, *16, 17*; Nepal, *160, 161*; New Ireland, 208; *216, 217*; Niger, *49, 50*; North Africa, 41; Oceania, 207; Papua New Guinea, *214, 215, 221*; Philippines, *26, 27, 182, 183*; Russia, *133*; Rwanda, *66, 67*; Santa Cruz Islands, *226*; Saudi Arabia, *114*; Solomon Islands, 27; *216, 217*; Sudan, *59*; Tibet, *10, 11, 160, 161, 164, 166, 167*; Togo, *81*; Zaire, *66, 67, 68, 69, 71. See also* amulet-pendant; belt pendants; hair pendants; headdress pendants; marriage pendants; pubic pendants; temple pendants
Pende, *68, 69*
penile ornaments: Admiralty Islands, *216, 217. See also* pubic pendants
Peru, 231; Aguaruna, *24, 25*; Jivaro, *237*
Peul, 37–38; *94, 95, 101*
Philippines, 110–11; Bagobo, 110–11; *184*; Bontoc, *182, 184, 185, 187*; Gaddang, *188*; Ifugao, *182, 184, 185*; Isneg, *26, 27, 186, 187*; Kalinga, *182*; Mandaya, *184*
pins. *See* brooches; cloak pins; hairpins
pinyo, 178
Pitjantjara, *226, 227*
Plains Indians, 24; *244, 245*
plaques: Ivory Coast, *86, 87*; Turkoman, 105
Polo, Marco, 12, 14, 108
ponto karro karro tedong, 202
prayer boxes, Tibet, *164*
pubic pendants, Australia, 209; *226, 227*
purses, Tibet, *170*

Q

Qing dynasty, *174, 175, 176, 177*
quannouta, 54, 55
quartz, Africa, 36
Quimbaya, *232*

R

Rabari, *134, 135*
Rashaida, *47, 56*
redif, 44
rings: Africa, 24; Indonesia, 110; Ivory Coast, *86, 87;* Kazaks, *18;* Nigeria, 40. *See also* arm rings; earrings; finger rings; neck rings; nose rings; toe rings
Rodgers, Susan, *205*
rosary, Mongolia, *173*
Rublev, Andrei, 29
Russia, Dagestan, *132, 133*
Rwanda, Tutsi, *66, 67*

S

Safer, J. F., *184*
Sahara, *48, 49*
Samoa, *229*
sanggori, 202, 203
sangilot, 184
Santa Cruz Islands, 27, 208; *214, 215, 220, 221, 226*
Santo Domingo Pueblo, *242*
Saphrampolis, *120*
Sarakole, *96*
Saryk Turkoman, *126*
Saudi Arabia, 114–17, *118;* Bedouin (Najd), *114, 115, 116, 117*
Sema, 107
Senegal: Tukulor, *94, 95;* Wolof, *37*
Senufo, *86, 87, 90, 93*
Sepik, 208, *209; 214, 215, 218*
shab, 54, 55
shams u kmar bracelets, *47*
shells, Oceania, 207–09
Shi, *64, 65, 71*
shields, Kenya, *63. See also* buttock shields
Shilluk, *56, 57, 58, 59*
shoulder ornaments, Central Asia, 105
Siberia, *174*
Sidamo, *61*
siliop, 63
silver: North Africa, 41; southwestern United States, 232
simplah, 192
sipatal, 186, 187
skullcaps: Central Asia, *126, 127;* Kenya, *63*
Solomon Islands, 21, 207; *216, 217, 222, 223, 224, 225, 226, 227;* Choiseul, *224, 225. See also* Santa Cruz Islands
Somalia, *62, 63*
Somba, 35
Songhai, 38
Sorma, *60, 61*
soul disks, 39. *See also* chest ornaments
soul washer's badges, 39. *See also* chest ornaments
South Africa, 36; *102, 103;* Bantu, *102, 103;* Xhosa, *102, 103;* Zulu, 24; *100, 101, 102, 103*

southwestern United States: Navajo, *232; 240, 241, 242, 243;* Santo Domingo Pueblo, *242;* Zuni, 232; *241, 243*
Sri Lanka, *150*
stridhana, 142
Sudan: Dinka, *56, 57;* Fur, *56, 57;* Kichepo, *60, 61;* Nuba, 30; Nubian Desert, *58, 59;* Nuer, *56, 57;* Rashaida, *47, 56;* Shilluk, *56, 57, 58, 59;* Toposa, *59*
suklang, 188
Sukuma, *64, 65*
swar, 54
Swat, 106; *134*

T

Tabwa, *71*
tabzimt, 6, 7
tagemout, 44, 45
taiganja, 204, 205
taillo, 160
Tairona, 231; *230, 231, 232, 233*
taka, 193
talismans, North Africa, 30, 40. *See also* amulets
Tangkhul, *157*
tankil, 185
Tanzania, Sukuma, *64, 65*
ta'viz, 144
tavo, 160
tazlagt emm elherz, 52
Tchambuli (Chambri), 208
Teke, *72, 73*
Tekke Turkoman, 105; *2, 4, 123, 124, 125, 126, 127*
tema, 226
temple pendants: Central Asia, *120, 121;* Mongolia, *172, 173;* Uzbekistan, *128*
tenecir, 125
tepatu, 226
teraout, 50, 51
Thailand, *182, 183*
thali, 148
thungbubiel, 88, 89
tiaras, Central Asia, *126, 127. See also* diadems
Tibet, 108; *10, 11, 160, 161, 166, 167, 168, 169, 170;* Lhasa, *164, 165, 166, 167*
tikam, 187
Tikar, *74, 75*
tilla bargak, 31, 32–33
tinderboxes: Mongolia, *173;* Tibet, *170*
tingkhep, 163
Tiv, 40; *78, 79*
tizerzai, 44, 45, 46, 47
Toba Batak, *188, 190, 191, 194*
Toda, *146, 147*
toe rings: Africa, 38–39; India, 106
Togo, Moba, *81*
Tonga, *212, 229*
Toposa, *59*
Toraja, *202, 203*
tora tora, 202, 203
torcs. *See* neck rings
Tshokwe, *71*
Tuareg, *48, 49, 50, 51, 96, 100, 101*
Tukulor, *94, 95*

tumar, 125
Tunisia: Bedouin, *54;* Berber, *54;* Moknine, *54, 55*
Turkana, *60, 61, 64, 65*
Turkey, *120;* Saphrampolis, *120*
Turkoman groups, 105; Ersari, 105; *123, 126, 127;* Goklan, *123;* Olam, *123;* Saryk, *126;* Tekke, 105; *2, 4, 123, 124, 125, 126, 127;* Yomud, 105; *120, 121, 122, 123, 124, 125, 126*
turquoise: Himalayan, 108, (Tibet) 165–69; Saudi Arabia, *114;* southwestern United States, 241–243
Tusyan, *90, 91*
Tutsi, *66, 67*
Txicao, *237*

U

ubala abuyisse, 102, 103
Uganda, *64, 65*
Uighur, *177*
United States. *See* North America; southwestern United States
upud, 184
ushira, 76, 77
Uzbekistan, *31, 32–33, 128, 129, 130*

V

Vanuatu, *222, 223*
varloh, 134, 135
Vietnam, *182*

W

Wancho, *157*
wasekaseka, 228, 229
Wassing-Visser, R., *202*
wedding jewelry. *See* bridal jewelry
West Africa, 39–40; *84. See also specific country*
Wodaabe, 35
Wolof, *37*
wool, North Africa, 41
wristbands: Nepal, *158;* Papua New Guinea, 209; southwestern United States, *242. See also* bracelets

X

Xhosa, *102, 103*

Y

Yemen, *112, 114, 115, 118;* Bedouin, *112*
Yomud Turkoman, 105; *120, 121, 122, 123, 124, 125, 126*
yongjam, 178
Yoruba, *19*

Z

Zaire, 39; *66, 71;* Azande, *56, 68, 69;* Kongo, *68, 69;* Kuba, *68, 69, 82;* Lega, *64, 65;* Lulua, *68, 69;* Mangbetu, 35; *68, 69;* Mbole, *69;* Mongo, 35; *68, 69, 70;* Ndengese, *66, 67;* Ngbaka, *66;* N'gombe, *69, 70;* Nzakara, *71;* Pende, *68, 69;* Shi, *64, 65, 71;* Tabwa, *71;* Teke, *72, 73*
Zulu, 24; *100, 101, 102, 103*
Zuni, 232; *241, 243*

6731 S 11

256